\ Arapaho-Cheyenne Indians

CHEYENNE AND ARAPAHO ABORIGINAL OCCUPATION
Zachary Gussow

HISTORICAL DEVELOPMENT OF THE ARAPAHO-CHEYENNE LAND AREA
Leroy R. Hafen

CHEYENNE AND ARAPAHO INDIANS
Arthur A. Ekirch, Jr.

COMMISSION FINDINGS
Indian Claims Commission

Ⓖⓟ

Garland Publishing Inc., New York & London
1974

Library of Congress Cataloging in Publication Data

Gussow, Zachary, 1923-
    Cheyenne and Arapaho: aboriginal occupation.

    (American Indian ethnohistory: Plains Indians)
    At head of title: Arapaho-Cheyenne Indians.
    Z.Gussow's report: Indian Claims Commission docket
no. 329 and 348; L. R. Hafen's report: docket no. 329;
A. A. Ekirch, Jr.'s report: docket no. 329-A.
    Includes bibliography.
    1. Cheyenne Indians. 2. Arapahoe Indians.
3. Indians of North America--Great Plains--Claims.
I. Hafen, Le Roy Reuben, 1893-   Historical develop-
ment of the Arapaho-Cheyenne land area. 1974.
II. Ekirch, Arthur Alphonse, 1915-   Cheyenne and
Arapaho Indians. 1974. III. United States. Indian
Claims Commission. IV. Title. V. Title: Arapaho-
Cheyenne Indians. VI. Series.
E99.C53G88   970.4'8   74-8297
ISBN 0-8240-0732-8

A Garland Series

AMERICAN INDIAN ETHNOHISTORY

Plains Indians

compiled and edited by

DAVID AGEE HORR
Brandeis University

Contents

5

*Garland Publishing has repaginated this work (at outside center) to facilitate
scholarly use. However, original pagination has been retained for internal
reference.

Publisher's Preface

The Garland American Indian Ethnohistory series presents original documents on the history and anthropology of many American Indian tribes and groups who were involved in the Indian Claims actions of the 1950s and 1960s. These reports were written to be used as evidence in legal proceedings to determine the aboriginal rights of various Indian groups to certain geographical regions or areas within the United States. In each case, the Indian Claims Commission issued a set of findings which are an important historical outcome of the proceedings and of the reports.

The Garland volumes include, as background material, introductory sections on the Indian Claims actions and the gathering of the ethnohistorical materials by Ralph A. Barney, Chief of the Indian Claims Section of the Department of Justice since its inception in 1946, and Robert A. Manners, Professor of Anthropology at Brandeis University. Both were professionally involved in several cases and Dr. Manners has published on the Claims actions.

Each volume also contains a brief introductory historical sketch of the tribe or group which is representative of the kind of information available at the time of the Claims actions. Much of this material was summarized in a 1650-page document (House Report No. 2503), published in 1953 by order of the House of Representatives committee investigating the Bureau of Indian Affairs. In addition to summaries on history and population, the massive government report included maps which gave the 1950 location of the various American Indian groups, largely on reservations, as well as the estimated original range occupied by the group or tribe in question. This material appears in the Garland volumes in abridged form, since it gives a picture of the kind of information available to the United States government in the 1950s on which it might have based decisions concerning the

PREFACE

American Indians had the Indian Claims actions not taken place. In addition, these brief introductory sections will help orient the general reader to the groups covered by the ethnohistorical reports.

The reports in this series have been organized into logical groupings for maximum efficiency of use. Short reports have been bound together into single volumes by tribe or by geographical area when several tribes are represented by a single report, with Commission findings bound at the end of the pertinent volume. In those cases where many reports pertain to the same group or area they may comprise several volumes which are numbered consecutively. When several volumes deal with the same set of claims, the findings appear in the final volume of that set of interrelated reports. It should be noted that, since this series is intended to present these ethnohistorical materials as documents, the reports are reproduced *verbatim*, with no additions, deletions, or other editing by the compiler of the series or the original authors.

Within the body of the reports, reference is often made to exhibit numbers. These refer to other material accepted as evidence, often in the form of excerpts from existing publications or other documents pertaining to the tribes in question. This material is not included in the volumes themselves, although a bibliography of these items usually appears in the report. These exhibits are on file in the Indian Claims Commission offices in Washington, D.C., or in the National Archives.

General Nature and Content of the Series

The formal reports contained in this series represent only part of the evidence amassed in the 370-odd court actions assigned separate docket numbers by the Indian Claims Commission. Almost since the outset, those involved with the Indian Claims' activities have voiced the opinion that the specifically researched ethnohistorical studies should not simply be filed away in some federal depository though this did become the case with these reports. The present series is the result of careful searching through more than 600 unindexed file drawers in the Indian Claims Commission, the National Archives, and elsewhere, sometimes even in the papers of the originally participating scholars.

Each claims action was an adversary proceeding with a particular Indian tribe or group as plaintiff and the United States Government, represented by the Indian Claims Section of the Justice Department, as defendant. Each side collected evidence on the nature of aboriginal use and occupancy of particular areas in order to determine which Indian groups were entitled to compensation for lands taken by the United States, either by treaty or otherwise, and just what lands were in question. Once this phase of the action was settled, the proceedings moved on to the question of the value of the lands at the time they were taken from the Indians. It is with the title phase of the Claims proceedings that the present series is concerned. Therefore the numerous appraisals of economic value are omitted.

Claims to title were settled on the basis of several types of evidence presented during hearings before the Indian Claims Commission. The expert testimony submitted included verbal and written reports by anthropologists, archaeologists, and historians. During the early days of the Commission, virtually all such testimony was oral and is preserved only in the official court transcripts. Later on, the Government required its expert witnesses to submit formal written reports. The lawyers for the plaintiffs did not initially make this a requirement so that, for some cases, reports are available on the Government side but not for the Indians. Finally, the Commission did require all ethnohistorical reports to be submitted by both sides in written form. The title page of each individual report indicates whether it was submitted as an exhibit for the plaintiff (sometimes called claimant, petitioner or intervenor) or the defendant.

Since the formal reports were subject to examination by the Commissioners and by the opposing lawyers, they were carefully prepared. The specific nature of the reports did mean that some topics often included in an ethnography might be excluded. In the California cases, for example, some well-researched reports on pottery making and other craft industries were not used. On the other hand, data on political structure, kinship and property inheritance rights, and many other such topics, were often considered because they did bear upon how rights to property and power were determined within a group and the question of how the Indians originally used the land. Once the evidence was submitted and examined in the hearings, the Commissioners issued a set of Findings and Opinions, which, by themselves, are important historical documents.

The Garland series includes only the formal ethnohistorical reports and the title findings of the Commission since the entire documentation of the Claims actions is so voluminous. The lengthy hearing transcripts are uneconomic to reproduce without editing and our purpose is to present unedited documents as actually *used*. The transcript of the Kiowa-Comanche case is included because of its unique nature. The transcripts are all on file either in the Indian Claims Commission or the National Archives, and may be consulted there.

The content of this series was determined solely by those ethnohistorical reports submitted to the Commission. Therefore, American Indian tribes and groups not involved in Claims actions are not represented for various reasons. For example, the Indians of the northeastern and eastern United States had lost most of their lands prior to the establishment of the country in 1776. In other instances, the tribe no longer existed in 1946 or did not submit a claim. In some cases claims were submitted, but were denied before a report was commissioned for that tribe.

The reports for the various areas covered by the Claims Act have been approached in somewhat different ways. When possible, they deal with individual tribes or named groups. This does not mean that in such cases there were no overlapping claims; however, the overall tribal situation was not so complex as to prevent an initial identification of tribal groups with specific geographic areas. By contrast, in some areas such as the eastern and north central regions, reports tend to focus on Royce areas rather than individual tribes because the aboriginal claims situation often involved re-curring movement through the region by many different tribes over a relatively short time period. In these regions treaties ceding certain lands to the United States were often signed by several different tribes or perhaps only by certain parts of some of the tribes involved. Here the area reports *in toto* form an almost jigsaw-puzzle-like solution to the enormously complex tribal relationships. The Royce Area maps and designations were published in Bureau of American Ethnology, Annual Report, vol. 18, no. 2, 1896-7.

David Agee Horr

11

12

The Indian Claims Commission

Prior to the creation of the Indian Claims Commission by the Act of August 13, 1946 (60 Stat. 1049; 25 U.S.C. § 70 et seq.), no tribe of Indians could bring a suit against the United States without the special permission of Congress. This was a cumbersome and wholly unsatisfactory procedure. By the 1946 Act, Congress created a special judicial tribunal to "hear and determine" claims by Indian tribes in an effort to settle, once and for all, the claims of the Indians. The Act is unique in the true sense of the word. Never before has any government generally opened the doors of its courts to the claims of its aborigines. The Commission is authorized to consider claims by any "tribe, band or identifiable group of American Indians" that the United States in its previous dealings had not always carried out its treaty obligations, had imposed treaties upon them against their wishes, had failed to pay them adequately for their land, had failed to account properly for the expenditure of their tribal funds and, in many instances, had not been "fair and honorable" in their dealings with them.

The tribes had five years within which to file their claims and, after adjudication, they could have the Commission's decisions reviewed by the United States Court of Claims and by the Supreme Court of the United States. The Congress imposed one important limitation: the Commission could render only a money judgment in favor of the tribes. It could not return any land to them which might have been taken wrongfully, nor could it give them any land to supply a land base.

The present volumes deal with only one of the multifaceted aspects of Indian claims litigation: the area of land occupied by the tribes prior to the coming of the white man into the area in general, or the area occupied by a particular tribe for "a long time" prior to its acquisition by the United

States, or their dispossession by the whites.

The land problem was confounded by different concepts inherent in the nature of the disparate cultures. The culture of the Europeans who discovered and later settled this continent was basically legalistic, particularly where land was concerned. Land was the subject of "ownership" either by the monarch or his subjects, and "titles" were the capstone of such ownership. "Ownership" in the sense of a legal right was unknown to the Indian. As Justice Black said in *Shoshone Indians* v. *United States*, 324 U.S. 335, 357 (1945):

> ... Ownership meant no more to them than to roam the land as a great common, and to possess and enjoy it in the same way that they possessed and enjoyed sunlight and the west wind and the feel of spring in the air. Acquisitiveness, which develops a law of real property, is an accomplishment only of the "civilized."

When the Europeans "discovered" the North American continent they found it inhabited by the Indians and the question of their rights aroused a great moral debate. Charles V of Spain sought the advice of the theologian Franciscus de Victoria, primary professor of sacred theology in the University of Salamanca, who suggested that since the aborigines "were true owners, before the Spaniards came among them, both from the public and private point of view," they should be treated with to secure cessions of their lands. This view obviously could not prevail if the European monarchs owned the land and could parcel it out to their subjects.

The matter came to a head in 1823 when Chief Justice John Marshall decided the famous case of *Johnson* v. *McIntosh*, 21 U.S. (8 Wheat.) 453. In 1775 the Piankeshaw Indians had sold a tract of land to various individuals. However, in 1818, the United States sold and patented the same land to William McIntosh. Thus the contest was which deed was valid. From a long and detailed examination of the history of Indian relations in this country, Chief Justice Marshall concluded that the legal title was in the United

14

States Government and that the tribes had no right to sell and convey the land (at least, without governmental consent).

However, the Indians could not be ignored, particularly in the early days when they were numerically far stronger than the few settlers huddled along the coast. From this developed the theory that while the legal "title" was in the discovering nations and later in the United States, the Indians had a right of possession based on what was characterized as their "aboriginal title."

More than thirty years ago, long before the creation of the Indian Claims Commission, the Supreme Court had occasion to lay down the rule, which was later adopted by the Commission, as to what was necessary to establish Indian title. In *United States* v. *Santa Fe Pacific R. Co.*, 314 U. S. 339, 345 (1941), the Court said:

> Occupancy necessary to establish aboriginal possession is a question of fact to be determined as any other question of fact. If it were established as a fact that the lands in question were, or were included in, the ancestral home of the Walapais in the sense that they constituted a definable territory occupied exclusively by the Walapais (as distinguished from lands wandered over by many tribes), then the Walapais had "Indian title". . . .

The determination of the "question of fact" of the aboriginal or original Indian title is what the ethnographic studies in these volumes, and the findings and the opinions of the Commission are all about. The anthropologists have dug up the facts to the extent that they were able to do so. Based on these facts the Commission has made its determination of the areas of land occupied by the various tribes under their original title or their later occupancy, and it is on the basis of these determinations of the areas of aboriginal title that these cases then go forward to determine the amount of recovery by the several tribes.

Quite understandably much of the "evidence" consists of deductions made by the witnesses from the frequently

15

meager hard facts available and, of necessity, the determinations of the Commission are based on this type of evidence. While the boundaries of the areas exclusively and actually used and occupied may not always be correct, they represent in most instances a fair approximation of the areas occupied by the various tribes aboriginally or for "a long time" on the dates when the United States acquired the land or they were permanently dispossessed of it. All in all, it has been a difficult job well done.

I cannot close this brief introduction without expressing my admiration for the many scholars on both sides who so diligently sought out the facts to present to the Commission. They did a magnificent job for which all other scholars and interested laymen should be grateful. My personal acquaintance with them has been an outstanding experience.

I am also personally happy to see these ethnographic studies and the decisions of the Commission published instead of being buried in the National Archives. They will contribute greatly to our knowledge of the American Indian.

16

Ralph A. Barney

Introduction to the Ethnohistorical Reports on the Land Claims Cases

The research reports and the findings contained in this compilation may prove, in the long run, to have contributed little to resolving the massive economic and social problems which confront today's Native Americans. However, it is most unlikely that any of the diligent and often dedicated sponsors of the movement that led, in 1946, to the passage of the Indian Claims Commission Act ever had such lofty expectations. What is more likely is that the proponents of the legislation, as Ralph Barney observes in his introductory remarks, had simply hoped to "clean up the mess," to put an end to the stream of suits and claims against the federal government, each of which had required Congressional approval before it could be brought to trial. But the "mess" was not so easily resolved. Some cases have been settled. Others have been heard, adjudicated and appealed to higher courts. A few, like that of "the Indians of California," may be reopened.

But when, and if, all of the claims have been resolved in the courts, the government will not have succeeded in pacifying the claimants nor in satisfying their demands for decent compensation. In short, the Act has not fulfilled even the minimal goal of putting an end to Native American claims against the United States Government.

In light of the relatively meager benefits that have so far accrued to Native Americans as a consequence of the Act of 1946, it might seem almost callous to draw attention now to the richness of the by-product of that Act as represented in the 118 volumes in this series. For whatever one may feel about the intended benefits of the Act, it is clear that the

INTRODUCTION TO THE REPORTS

scholarly fallout is stunning indeed. The materials presented in these volumes include a concentrated body of ethno-historical research data and adversary findings unique in the record of cultural historiography and, so far as I know, in the annals of jurisprudence.

Literally hundreds of people were involved in the research and litigation that led to these reports and findings. Thousands of interviews were conducted. Extensive archaeological surveys were made. Large quantities of previously "unknown" or unexamined agency and other files, personal correspondence, photographs, diaries, and so on were uncovered and their contents incorporated in the reports. Regular archival and library resources were examined and reexamined with a thoroughness that would not have been possible without the support that both claimants and the defendant were able to provide. Then there were the adversary proceedings, which, though patently unpleasant to most of the experts, did provide an even more effective check on the quality of the research product than the customary scholarly scrutiny of one's colleagues. For where there is litigation, the experts on both sides have probably reviewed much, if not all, of the same data. Moreover, the litigous circumstances place a premium on revealing inaccuracies and/or slipshod research methods.[1]

Finally, I would like to emphasize that another apparent by-product of the Act and the research and hearings that followed its implementation may be detected in the effect that this research and its attendant litigation have had on the thinking of many Native Americans now pressing for improved economic, social and political conditions for *all* Indians in the United States. Thus, if the working-out of the Act has made only minor contributions to the welfare of a

[1] Some ethnohistorical and legal problems confronted by the plaintiffs' and defendant's experts and attorneys were explored at a 1954 symposium on the Claims Act (see *Ethnohistory* 2,4, pp. 287-375). The participants were Ralph A. Barney, Chief of the Indian Claims Section, Lands Division, Dept. of Justice; Donald C. Gormley of the law firm of Wilkinson, Boyden, Cragun & Barker; and anthropologists Verne Ray, Julian Steward, A. L. Kroeber, J. A. Jones and Nancy Oestreich Lurie.

handful of American Indians, it has apparently had a much more salutary effect on their thinking about the welfare of *all* Native Americans. For the "time immemorial" and the "exclusive occupancy" strictures of the Act resulted, in many ways, in pitting group against group to the detriment of all.[2] In most cases, the occupancy and/or use claims of one group conflicted, at least in part, with those of another or several other groups of Indians.[3] Where such joint use or occupancy was proved to the satisfaction of the Commission, none of the claimants benefitted, thus demonstrating (as I have been told by several Native Americans) the perils of division and intra-Indian competition and, by implication, the likely advantages of pan-Indian cooperation in future endeavors, political as well as legal.

This "unforeseen consequence" of the research and litigation, of the claims and counter-claims, has certainly been among the factors that have helped to persuade those Native Americans who were not already convinced of the pitfalls as well as the potential virtues of a revived "tribalism" of the need for a more unified, a pan-Indian approach to their problems. These volumes can only help to bolster the case for such unity and, thus, perhaps to enhance the political impact of Native Americans in the United States.

Robert A. Manners

19

[2] In this respect, the claim of "The Indians of California" is exceptional because an earlier case had laid the groundwork whereby a number of different groups (culturally and linguistically) were permitted to combine all of their separate land-use-and-occupation claims into one. If the Act had allowed *all* American Indian plaintiffs to combine their claims in this manner (and to share equally in the awards), and if they had been willing to do so, the resultant claims, litigation and decisions might have been, at the very least, quite interesting. . . . i.e., "The Indians of the United States vs. the United States Government for just compensation for the taking of all lands (less land held in existing reservations) between the Atlantic and the Pacific Oceans."

[3] A striking example, with which I am familiar, are the overlapping Navaho, Hopi, Walapai, Havasupai claims.

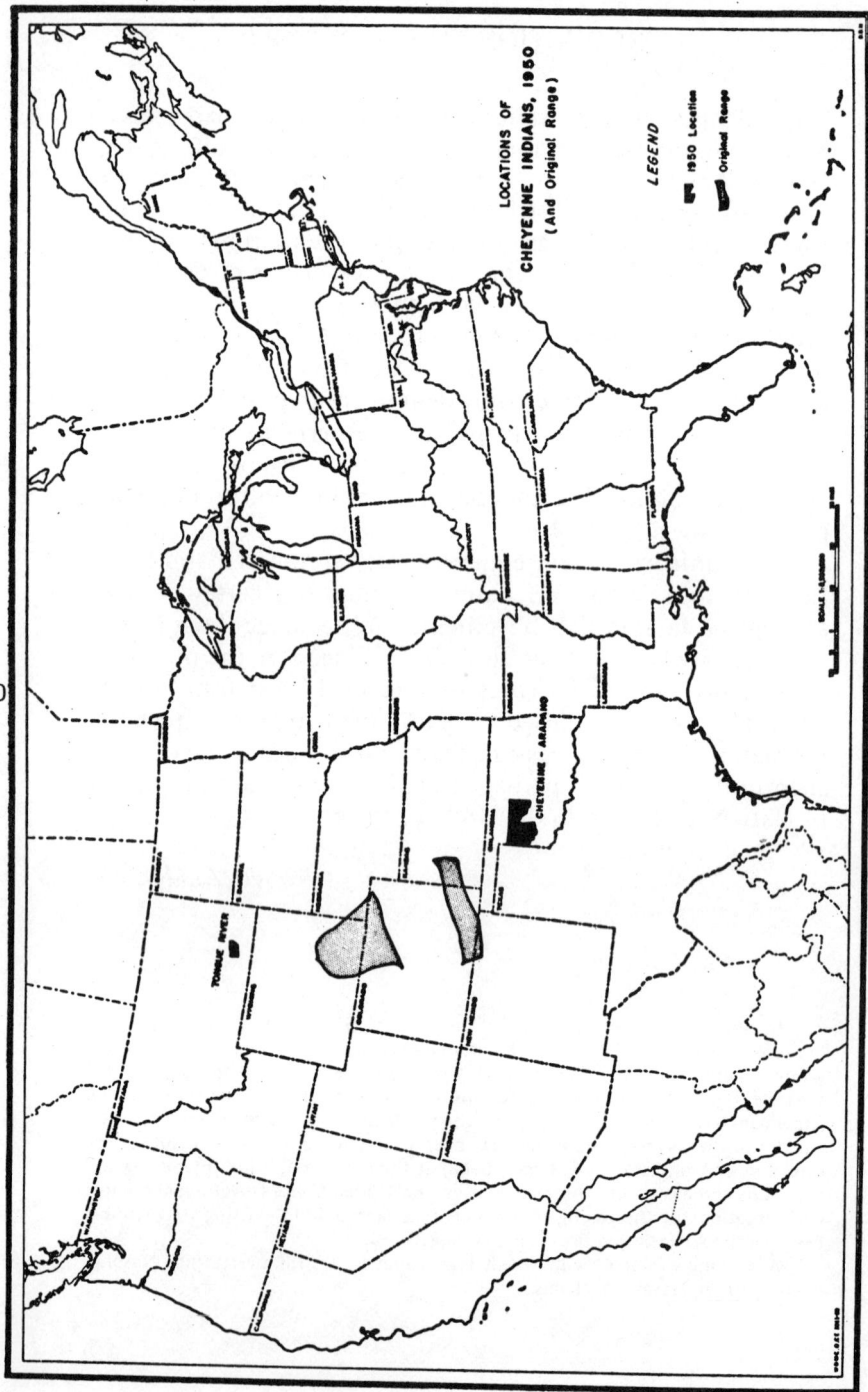

LOCATIONS OF
CHEYENNE INDIANS, 1950
(And Original Range)

LEGEND

1950 Location

Original Range

CHEYENNE - ARAPAHO

TONGUE RIVER

SCALE 1-11,000,000

20

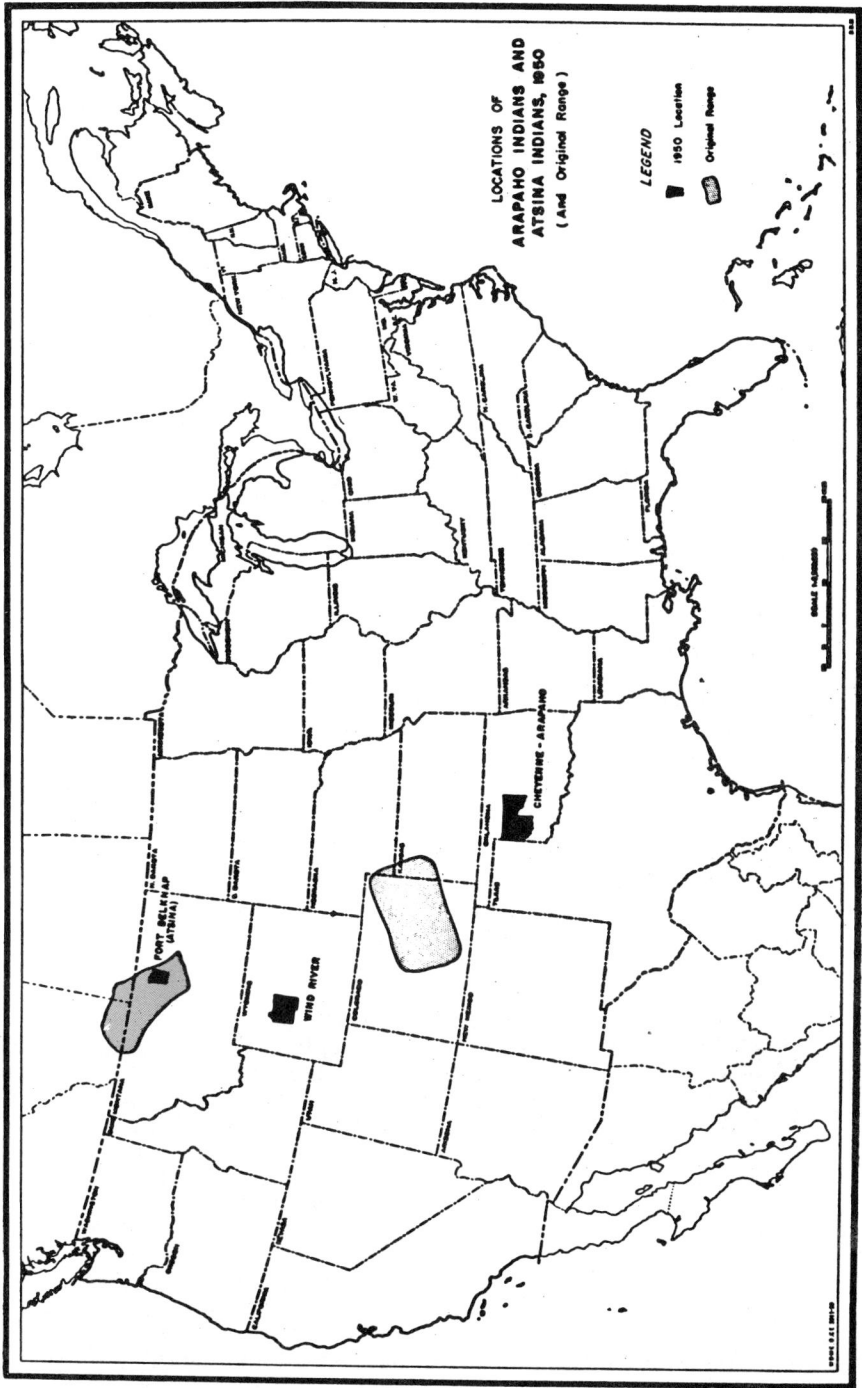

LOCATIONS OF
ARAPAHO INDIANS AND
ATSINA INDIANS, 1950
(And Original Range)

LEGEND

■ 1950 Location

▨ Original Range

FORT BELKNAP
(ATSINA)

WIND RIVER

CHEYENNE - ARAPAHO

SCALE 1:43,000,000

21

"The earliest authenticated habitat of the Cheyenne, before the year 1700, seems to have been that part of Minnesota bounded roughly by the Mississippi, Minnesota, and upper Red rs. The Sioux, living at that period more immediately on the Mississippi, to the e. and s. e., came in contact with the French as early as 1667, but the Cheyenne are first mentioned in 1680, under the name of Chaa, when a party of that tribe, described as living on the head of the great river, i. e., the Mississippi, visited La Salle's fort on Illinois r. to invite the French to come to their country, which they represented as abounding in beaver and other fur animals. The veteran Sioux missionary, Williamson, says that according to concurrent and reliable Sioux tradition the Cheyenne preceded the Sioux in the occupancy of the upper Mississippi region, and were found by them already established on the Minnesota. At a later period they moved over to the Cheyenne branch of Red r., N. Dak., which thus acquired its name, being known to the Sioux as 'the place where the Cheyenne plant,' showing that the latter were still an agricultural people (Williamson). This westward movement was due to pressure from the Sioux, who were themselves retiring before the Chippewa, then already in possession of guns from the E. Driven out by the Sioux, the Cheyenne moved w. toward Missouri r., where their further progress was opposed by the Sutaio—The Staitan of Lewis and Clark—a people speaking a closely cognate dialect, who had preceded them to the w. and were then apparently living between the river and the Black-hills. After a period of hostility the two tribes made an alliance, some time after which the Cheyenne crossed the Missouri below the entrance of the Cannonball, and later took refuge in the Black-hills about the heads of Cheyenne r. of South Dakota, where Lewis and Clark found them in 1804, since which time, their drift was constantly w. and s. until confined to reservations. Up to the time of Lewis and Clark they carried on desultory war with the Mandan and Hidatsa, who probably helped to drive them from Missouri r. They seem, however, to have kept on good terms with the Arikara. According to their own story, the Cheyenne, while living in Minnesota and on Missouri r., occupied fixed villages, practised agriculture, and made pottery, but lost these arts on being driven out into the plains to become roving buffalo hunters. On the Missouri, and perhaps also farther E., they occupied earth-covered log houses. Grinnell states that some Cheyenne had cultivated fields on Little Missouri r. as late as 1850. This was probably a recent settlement, as they are not mentioned in that locality by Lewis and Clark. At least one man among them still understands the art of making beads and figurines from pounded glass, as formerly practised by the Mandan. In a sacred tradition recited only by the priestly keeper, they still tell how they 'lost the corn' after leaving the eastern country. One of the starting points in this tradition is a great fall, apparently St. Anthony's falls on the Mississippi, and a stream known as the "river of turtles," which may be the Turtler.

22

tributary of Red r., or possibly the St. Croix, entering the Mississippi below the mouth of the Minnesota, and anciently known by a similar name. Consult for early habitat and migrations: Carver, Travels, 1796; Clark, Ind. Sign Lang., 1885; Comfort in Smithson. Rep. for 1871; La Salle in Margry, Decouvertes, II, 1877; Lewis and Clark, Travels, I, Ed. 1842; Mooney in 14th Rep. B. A. E., 1896; Williamson in Minn. Hist. Soc. Coll., I, 1872.

"Although the alliance between the Sutaio and the Cheyenne dates from the crossing of the Missouri r. by the latter, the actual incorporation of the Sutaio into the Cheyenne camp-circle probably occurred within the last hundred years, as the two tribes were regarded as distinct by Lewis and Clark. There is no good reason for supposing the Sutaio to have been a detached band of Siksika drifted down directly from the n., as has been suggested, as the Cheyenne expressly state that the Sutaio spoke 'a Cheyenne language,' i. e., a dialect fairly intelligible to the Cheyenne, and that they lived s. w. of the original Cheyenne country. The linguistic researches of Rev. Rudolph Petter, our best authority on the Cheyenne language, confirm the statement that the difference was only dialectic, which probably helps to account for the complete assimilation of the two tribes. The Cheyenne say also that they obtained the Sun dance and the Buffalo-head medicine from the Sutaio, but claim the Medicine-arrow ceremony as their own from the beginning. Up to 1835, and probably until reduced by the cholera of 1849, the Sutaio retained their distinctive dialect, dress, and ceremonies and camped apart from the Cheyenne. In 1851 they were still to some extent a distinct people, but exist now only as one of the component divisions of the (Southern) Cheyenne tribe, in no respect different from the others. Under the name Staitan (a contraction of *Sutai-hitan*, pl. *Sutai-hitanio*, 'Sutai men') they are mentioned by Lewis and Clark in 1804 as a small and savage tribe roving w. of the Black-hills. There is some doubt as to when or where the Cheyenne first met the Arapaho, with whom they have long been confederated; neither do they appear to have any clear idea as to the date of the alliance between the two tribes, which continues unbroken to the present day. Their connection with the Arapaho is a simple alliance, without assimilation, while the Sutaio have been incorporated bodily.

"Their modern history may be said to begin with the expedition of Lewis and Clark in 1804. Constantly pressed farther into the plains by the hostile Sioux in their rear they established themselves next on the upper branches of the Platte, driving the Kiowa in their turn farther to the s. They made their first treaty with the Government in 1825 at the mouth of Teton (Bad) r., on the Missouri, about the present Pierre, S. Dak. In consequence of the building of Bent's Fort on the upper Arkansas, in Colorado, in 1832, a large part of the tribe decided to move down and make permanent headquarters on the Arkansas, while the rest continued to rove about the headwaters of North Platte and Yellowstone rs. This separation was made permanent by the treaty of Ft. Laramie in 1851, the two sections being now

23

known respectively as Southern and Northern Cheyenne, but the distinction is purely geographic, although it has served to hasten the destruction of their former compact tribal organization. The Southern Cheyenne are known in the tribe as Sowania 'southerners,' while the Northern Cheyenne are commonly designated as 'O' mi'sis eaters,' from the division most numerously represented among them. Their advent upon the Arkansas brought them into constant collision with the Kiowa, who, with the Comanche, claimed the territory to the southward. The old men of both tribes tell of numerous encounters during the next few years, chief among these being a battle on an upper branch of Red r. in 1837, in which the Kiowa massacred an entire party of 48 Cheyenne warriors of the Bowstring society after a stout defense, and a notable battle in the following summer of 1838, in which the Cheyenne and Arapaho attacked the Kiowa and Comanche on Wolf cr., n. w. Okla., with considerable loss on both sides. About 1840 Cheyenne made peace with the Kiowa in the s., having already made peace with the Sioux in the n., since which time all these tribes together with the Arapaho, Kiowa, Kiowa Apache, and Comanche have usually acted as allies in the wars with other tribes and with the whites. For a long time the Cheyenne have mingled much with the western Sioux, from whom they have patterned in many details of dress and ceremony. They seem not to have suffered greatly from the smallpox of 1837–39, having been warned in time to escape to the mountains, but in common with other prairie tribes they suffered terribly from the cholera in 1849, several of their bands being nearly exterminated. Culbertson, writing a year later, states that they had lost about 200 lodges, estimated at 2,000 souls, or about two-thirds of their whole number before the epidemic. Their peace with the Kiowa enabled them to extend their incursions farther to the s., and in 1853 they made their first raid into Mexico, but with disastrous result, losing all but 3 men in a fight with Mexican lancers. From 1860 to 1878 they were prominent in border warfare, acting with the Sioux in the n. and with the Kiowa and Comanche in the s., and have probably lost more in conflict with the whites than any other tribe of the plains in proportion to their number. In 1864 the southern band suffered a severe blow by the notorious Chivington massacre in Colorado, and again in 1868 at the hands of Custer in the battle of the Washita. They took a leading part in the general outbreak of the southern tribes in 1874–75. The Northern Cheyenne joined with the Sioux in the Sitting Bull war in 1876 and were active participants in the Custer massacre. Later in the year they received such a severe blow from Mackenzie as to compel their surrender. In the winter of 1878–79 a band of Northern Cheyenne under Dull Knife, Wild Hog, and Little Wolf, who had been brought down as prisoners to Fort Reno to be colonized with the southern portion of the tribe in the present Oklahoma, made a desperate attempt at escape. Of an estimated 89 men and 146 women and children who broke away on the night of Sept. 9, about 75, including Dull Knife and most of the warriors, were killed in the pursuit which continued to the Dakota border, in the course of which about 50 whites lost their lives. Thirty-two of the Cheyenne slain were killed in a second break for liberty from Ft. Robinson, Nebr., where the captured fugitives had been confined. Little Wolf, with about 60 followers, got through in safety to the n. At a later period the Northern Cheyenne were assigned to the present reservation in Montana. The Southern Cheyenne were assigned to a reservation in w. Oklahoma by treaty of 1867, but refused to remain upon it until after the surrender of 1875, when a number of the most prominent hostiles were deported to Florida for a term of 3 years. In 1901–02 the lands of the Southern Cheyenne were allotted in severalty and the Indians are now American citizens. Those in the n. seem to hold their own in population, while those of the s. are steadily decreasing. They numbered in 1904—Southern Cheyenne, 1,903; Northern Cheyenne, 1,409, a total of 3,312."

Source: *Handbook of American Indians, Part 1*, pp. 251–253.
For history see also, E. S. Curtis. *The North American Indian.* Vol. 6. Historical Sketch, The Cheyenne pp. 87–102.

CHEYENNE POPULATION

"The Cheyenne have long been closely associated with their relatives, the Arapaho, although their habitat was generally north and west of that of the Arapaho. About 1835, the tribe divided, one portion remaining in Wyoming, and the other moving farther south and east. The southern Cheyenne are now located on the Arapaho and Cheyenne Reservation in Oklahoma, while the northern branch is concentrated on the Tongue River Reservation in Rosebud and Big Horn Counties in Montana. The number of the tribe enumerated in 1930 was 2,695, as compared with 3,055 in 1910. As in the case of the Arapaho, this decrease may be more apparent than actual. The number of Cheyenne in Montana showed a slight increase in 20 years, while the southern Cheyenne showed a decrease from 1,522 to 1,220."

Source: *The Indian Population of the United States and Alaska*, 1930, p. 37.

SELECTED REFERENCES ON THE CHEYENNE AS OF 1952

Arapahoe and Cheyenne Indians jurisdictional act. Hearings before the Committee on Indian affairs, House of representatives, Seventy-sixth Congress, first (-third) session, on H. R. 2775, a bill authorizing the Arapahoe and Cheyenne Indians to submit claims to the Court of claims, and for other purposes. Washington, U. S. Govt. Print. Off., 1939–40.
Arapahoe and Cheyenne Indians. Hearings before the Committee on Indian affairs, House of representatives, Seventieth Congress, first session, on H. R. 11359. March 1 and 15, 1928. Washington, U. S. Govt. Print. Off., 1928.
Cheyenne-Arapaho Ten Year Program Report Summary. 1944. 14 pp. (Bureau of Indian Affairs).
Grinnell, G. B. The Cheyenne Indians. 2 vols. New Haven, 1923.
Hobgood, Guy. Cheyenne-Arapaho Ten Year Program Report. 1944. 10 pp. (Bureau of Indian Affairs).
Jennings, Charles N. Tongue River Ten Year Program Report. 1944. 31 pp. (Bureau of Indian Affairs).

Krzywicki, Ludwik. Primitive Society and its Vital Statistics. London, 1934. pp. 451–2.

McCullough, H. D. Tongue River Ten Year Program Summary. 1944. 10 pp. (Bureau of Indian Affairs).

Murdock, Geo. P. Ethnographic Bibliography of North America. 1941. p. 72.

Social and Economic Survey of the Northern Cheyenne Reservation, Montana. Report No. 116, Feb. 28, 1951. 28 pp. (Billings Area Office, Bureau of Indian Affairs).

United States General Accounting Office. Report on the Arapaho and Cheyenne Claims Case K–103 forwarded to the Department of Justice Dec. 13, 1934. 3 vols, 1,820 pp. mss.

Wright, Muriel H. A Guide to the Indian Tribes of Oklahoma. Norman, 1951. Cheyenne pp. 76–84.

ARAPAHO POPULATION

"This tribe, which formerly ranged over a large area in the present States of Nebraska, Kansas, and Oklahoma, is now located on two reservations, one in Fremont County, Wyoming, and the other in Blaine and Canadian Counties in Oklahoma. The number enumerated in 1930 was 1,241, as compared with 1,419 in 1910. It is not at all certain, however, that there has been an actual decrease in numbers. The Arapaho in Wyoming increased from 703 to 863 in 20 years. The members of the tribe in Oklahoma are closely associated with the Cheyenne, with whom they share a reservation. The enumeration made by the Office of Indian Affairs on this reservation in 1932 shows a resident population of the two tribes combined of 2,417, as compared with the census figures of 1,580. The early reports of the Commissioner of Indian Affairs show a gradual decrease in the number of Arapaho from 3,229 in 1875 to 1,753 in 1910."

Source: *The Indian Population of the United States and Alaska*, 1930, p. 37.

SELECTED REFERENCES ON THE ARAPAHO AS OF 1952

Cheyenne-Arapaho Ten Year Program Report Summary. 1944. 14 pp. (Bureau of Indian Affairs.)

Hobgood, Guy. Cheyenne-Arapaho Ten Year Program Report. 1944. 50 pp. (Bureau of Indian Affairs.)

Kroeber, A. L. The Arapaho. Bulletin of the American Museum of Natural History, New York City, N. Y., Vol. XVIII, pp. 1–229, 279–454. 1902–1907.

Krzywicki, Ludwik. Primitive Society and its Vital Statistics. London, 1934. p. 448.

Linton, Ralph ed. Acculturation in Seven American Indian Tribes. N. Y., 1940. Section on the Northern Arapaho.

Mooney, J. Arapaho. Bulletin of the Bureau of American Ethnology, No. XXX, i, pp. 72–74. 1907.

Murdock, Geo. P. Ethnographic Bibliography of North America. 1941. p. 68.

Stone, Forrest E. Wind River Ten Year Program Report. 1944. 72 pp. (Bureau of Indian Affairs.)

United States General Accounting Office. Report on Arapaho and Cheyenne Claims Case K–103, forwarded to the Department of Justice Dec. 13, 1934. 3 vols., total pp. mss. 1,820.

Wind River Ten Year Program Report Summary. 1944. 15 pp. (Bureau of Indian Affairs.)

Wright, Muriel H. A. Guide to the Indian Tribes of Oklahoma. Norman, 1951. Arapaho, pp. 42–7.

An Ethnological Report on

CHEYENNE AND ARAPAHO: ABORIGINAL OCCUPATION

By Zachary Gussow, Ph. D. , Ethnologist

Re: CHEYENNE AND ARAPAHO TRIBES

v.

THE UNITED STATES Dockets 329 and 348

INDIAN CLAIMS COMMISSION

Zachary Gussow

June, 1954

28

TABLE OF CONTENTS

30

CHAPTER I.--INTRODUCTION

The determination of aboriginal land occupation among the Cheyenne and Arapaho Indians presents many complex problems of research and interpretation; some of which are unique to Plains Indians and are not encountered while dealing with sedentary or semi-sedentary people.

One of the first points that arises in regard to the Cheyenne and Arapaho is the question of historical, or time-levels. Within a period of approximately three hundred years the Cheyenne and Arapaho have experienced a number of radically different ways of life involving changes in economic and social organization. These changes have been accompanied by a series of migrations which have carried them from at least as far east as Minnesota to the foothills of the Rocky Mountains.

The nature of the traditional Cheyenne material makes it reasonable to assume that preceding their arrival in Minnesota they had a type of economy in which the hunting of small game was predominant. This was followed by a semi-horticultural period of earth-lodge dwelling which lasted until at least the third quarter of the 18th century at which time they were in the process of assuming their third type of existence based on equestrian buffalo-hunting on the Great Plains. The fourth and final phase of Cheyenne history involves the period following the establishment of Indian Reservations; a period which will not be of concern to us in the present study.

The early history of the Arapaho is much less well known. According to a few meager traditions the Arapaho are thought to have formerly lived in Minnesota where they raised corn. It is believed that they moved westward in the process of adopting an equestrian mode of life in the company of the Cheyenne who at that time were living on the Cheyenne fork of Red River, in Minnesota.

With the exception of some little archaeological material, in the case of the Cheyenne, some legendary and traditional data, and a few historical and cartographical references, again in the case of the Cheyenne, the bulk of our data concerning the Cheyenne and Arapaho, that is, knowledge concerning their economic and social practices, movements, trade relations, patterns of warfare, etc., all date essentially from a time after they had established themselves on the Great Plains as a fully developed, horse-using, buffalo-chasing, nomadic people. This period dates from the last quarter of the 18th century.

While we feel that some knowledge of the historical background of these people is essential to a proper understanding of their way of life no attempt will be made to include any territory occupied under earlier modes of existence and former places of residence in the final determination of aboriginal occupation. This is due to the fact that changes in territory were accompanied by significant changes in modes of existence. Once the Cheyenne and Arapaho had crossed the Missouri River in their westward movement they became firmly established as a buffalo-hunting, nomadic people. All former modes of existence

31

and places of residence were left behind. After embarking on a life on the Great Plains the Cheyenne and Arapaho never again, to our knowledge, recrossed the Missouri or returned to places occupied by them prior to their becoming a nomadic people. Nor do we have any knowledge of any attempts on their parts, to return to former modes of existence.

Therefore, in the determination of aboriginal land occupation we limit ourselves to that period in Cheyenne and Arapaho history at which time they appear on the scene as a fully developed, equestrian, buffalo-hunting, nomadic people. As we have said this period dates from approximately the third quarter of the 18th century, and concludes with the land occupation situation as of the middle of the 19th century, approximately at the time of the Treaty of Fort Laramie, 1851.

Another important point that arises in determining land occupation among the Cheyenne and Arapaho is the question of subsistence areas. The fact that the Cheyenne and Arapaho subsistence economy was oriented predominantly around the buffalo quest precludes the possibility of establishing primary, secondary or more areas of subsistence, based upon differences in subsistence items, as has been done in other land studies, notably among semi-sedentary peoples. For the Cheyenne and Arapaho we can delimit only one area of subsistence, namely, the area of buffalo hunting, as all other subsistence items, excluding those items obtained in trade or through raiding, were secured during the buffalo quest. While the Cheyenne and Arapaho had certain favorite areas where they gathered wild fruits and berries these areas usually fell within or were adjacent to areas frequented by the buffalo. In the same way favorite spots for the hunting

32 of animals other than the buffalo existed and were revisited, but in the main, these also fell within or were adjacent to the buffalo grounds.

In view of the fact that no system of land tenure can be discovered for most of the plains tribes (with the possible exclusion of the Blackfeet and Crow; reasons for which we need not examine here), plus the fact that a considerable body of land might serve as hunting grounds for a half a dozen or so tribes places difficulties in the way of delimiting tribal areas of occupancy and subsistence. Subsistence-wise the Cheyenne and Arapaho made little use of the land itself or of its immovable products. Their concern with the land was an indirect one in that they sought out certain animals who lived thereon. Though the range and seasonal movements of the buffalo were somewhat regularized they were not regularized enough to enable the Plains Indians to apportion out rights in hunting territory to any of the component social units of the tribe. Thus no bands or families had rights, reenforced by sanction and custom, to any sections or parts of the total hunting territory exclusive of other bands or families. A system of apportioned rights in land or to certain of its products, which may exist under sedentary as well as nomadic conditions, only develops where a regularized and stable yield is assured. Although the movements of the buffalo were to a degree regularized it was not always certain that large herds would be found in exactly the same places at all times. Thus under plains conditions it was not possible to apportion out rights in land to the various tribal sections. In contrast to a system of rights to specified tracts of land apportioned out to bands or family units for their own use the Cheyenne and Arapaho system recognized that all members of the group had the right to hunt or gather wild products from any part of the territory roamed over by them just as long as this right did not operate to the detriment of the tribe or band as a whole. Thus, unauthorized hunting acts, either on the part of single individuals or small parties of men, were prohibited where their actions would jeopardize the chances of a larger return when taken in an organized communal fashion.

Like the buffalo herds the Indians themselves wandered in a somewhat regularized fashion. This regularization followed from the needs of a people to know the terrain in which they were hunting. Unfamiliar country imposed hardships. Furthermore, familiar country allowed for the best possible protection against both natural as well as human enemies. Thus it came that, barring forced migrations, Plains Indians came to roam over a somewhat well defined territory, though making occasional as well as numerous forays into territories lying outside their usual range of movements. The extent of the territory covered seasonally by one Indian group, given their population size, made it impossible for them to control, by military means, the sharing of a territory with other groups whose movements may or may not have coincided with the movements of other nearby tribes. In this way the range of hunting territory seasonally covered by half a dozen or so Plains groups considerably overlapped. Yet to each group concerned the range of the territory habitually covered by them during any one year constituted their primary area of subsistence.[1]

While a vast range of territory might be hunted over during the course of a year not all parts of the area would be subjected to equal degrees of economic exploitation. The areas most intensively exploited might be called "areas of intense exploitation". Theoretically it might be possible to distinguish a number of areas of subsistence based on the relative degree of economic exploitation. However, in practice, given the nature of the data, I do not feel that this will be possible to do. The area of "intense exploitation" might be defined as the region in which the influence or the strength of the tribe was greatest, depending upon the extent to which reference has been made to their presence and economic use of the region. In other words, our method of analysis consists in defining the area which was the most frequented habitat of a tribe plus a penumbra of hunting territory. The penumbra of hunting territory might in some instances include "hostile", "neutral" or "debatable hunting grounds" (or which, regardless of claim, was exploited with relatively equal intensity by a number of tribes, and over which war might be part of every hunt), or less favorable areas of exploitation; areas not frequented by many tribes but secondary in terms of subsistence value.

In the face of the fluid aboriginal plains situation approximate methods are therefore the only ones that can profitably be employed in the determination of land occupation. What I have attempted to do in this study is first to delimit the Cheyenne and Arapaho habitat using historical sources. Then I have attempted to reconcile this area with land claims for tribes surrounding the Cheyenne and Arapaho, using ethnographical data. Following this general kind of approach and taking geographical conditions into consideration we can reasonably well define the territory which is not claimed by surrounding tribes and which therefore is assigneable to the Cheyenne and Arapaho. After territorial over-

33

---

[1] Exclusive of tribes like the Pawnee who were semi-sedentary, yet who came into contact with the Cheyenne and Arapaho on the east.

lappings are recorded what comes out in a core of occupied territory plus a
fringe of common hunting territory. I have made no attempt to check land claims
for tribes other than the Cheyenne and Arapaho with the historical sources. To
do something like this would be an altogether fearsome task and one, if done
properly, would require the assistance of a staff of trained experts.

Regarding aboriginal tribal boundaries present-day native informants
testify that in pre-Reservation times the Cheyenne and Arapaho had a well defined territory with marked boundaries which they and other tribes were cogni-
zant of and respected. These boundaries, some assert, were marked by medicine
wheels, that is, a wide and somewhat irregular circle of large stones. One
such arrangement of stones has been located in Medicine Mountain in the northwest corner of the Big Horn National Forest and has been described by Grinnell
(AA:24, no. 3, 1922) and Sims (AA:5, no. 1, 1903, ns). Grinnell notes that
similar stone arrangements are reported to have been at one time or another
located on the Big Horne River just below old Fort Smith in the Big Horn Can-
yon, and in northern Wyoming near the trial used by the Cheyennes of the Tongue
River Reservation when they visited the Shoshoni near Fort Washaki (Grinnell,
ibid, 310).

The suggestion that these stone monuments represented aboriginal tribal
boundary marks is, in the view of the writer, nothing more than a modernized
version of their original function, which was, most likely, ceremonial.

The division of the Cheyenne and Arapaho into northern and southern groups
requires some comment. Long before White westward movement resulted in the
settling of Indians on reservations, trading posts established throughout the
West gave some artificial direction to Plains Indian movements and to their
selection of preferable hunting areas. The trading posts supplied the Indians
with many articles of use in exchange for hides and furs which the Indians
found worth possessing. One of the consequences of this inter-relationship was
that there grew up a closer drawing together of certain tribes around the
vicinity of the posts or a shifting of tribes towards areas within reach of
one post or another. Trading posts established along the North Platte, for example, had in mind the very thing they accomplished, namely, the attraction of
some of the more northerly groups who found it difficult to reach the posts
along the Arkansas river. Further, the establishment of Bent's Fort on the
Arkansas resulted in the congregation around that post of the southern
Cheyenne and Arapaho. It is likely that the fur trade was decisive in dividing
the Cheyenne and Arapaho into northern and southern groups.

The division of the Cheyenne and Arapaho into northern and southern groups
became of real importance only after the establishment of Indian Reservations
at which time the southern groups were relocated to Oklahoma and the northern
ones to Wyoming and Montana. Prior to this the division of the Cheyenne and
Arapaho into northern and southern groups seems not to have been so pronounced.
In general, the southern Cheyenne and Arapaho occupied the more southerly ex-
tremes of their range while the northern groups occupied the more northerly
end, with a considerable amount of overlapping between the two. The presence
of trading posts along the Arkansas and the Platte served to direct the divisions
towards one region or the other. Yet on many occasions the divisions came
together, both for ceremonials as well as for communal hunts and warfare. In

this way the tribal organization remained intact, although the bands of one division may not have been in as close contact with the bands of the other division as they were prior to separation. Yet on the other hand, after the establishment of posts and with the cumulative effect of the fur trade on their economy it is further possible that while the divisions as a unit may have maintained a lesser amount of contact with one another, the bands within each division may have maintained closer contact. This appears to be truer of the southern bands than of the northern ones since ecological circumstances in the region between the Arkansas and the Platte seems to have permitted the bands to remain together for a longer period of time. This plus the trading posts around which many Indians settled may have resulted in the formation of a closer social unit among the southern groups. These points will be elobarated more fully in the cahpter on Social Organization.

Since the social organization of the different divisions of each tribe is so similar I will discuss these practices together in one chapter. In regard to subsistence resources and techniques of food procurement I will discuss both tribes, Cheyenne and Arapaho with their subdivisions, together, as there are no significant differences between any of them, at least not significant for our purposes. Where slight differences are relevant these, of course, will be noted. Separate chapters are devoted, however, to the question of tribal movements and subsistence areas.

Finally a note on the use of present-day native testimony. The use of present-day native testimony in the determination of aboriginal occupation among the Cheyenne and Arapaho is of little value in the estimate of the writer. 35 In fact, I feel, that very little information can be obtained today from Plains Indians regarding pre-Reservation times. This is so for a number of reasons. The cultural memory of the Cheyenne and Arapaho is extremely limited, particularly in regard to aboriginal movements and occupation. This is so since today they are residing, for the most part, in a region which was not occupied by them prior to the establishment of reservations. Secondly, with the exception of a few individuals most Indians have little concrete knowledge of their own past.

Because of the relatively inferior quality of information pertaining to aboriginal times presently obtainable this study will rely little on data obtained in the field. In addition, no data was forthcoming when the writer visited the Southern Cheyenne and Arapaho in Oklahoma as the tribal leaders refused to assist him. The writer did not press the point while he was among them as he was already convinced, from previous interviews with the Northern Cheyenne and Arapaho, that no really worth while information was any longer available from these sources.

Consequently, all of the data employed in this study comes from a variety of ethnographical, historical and archaeological sources.

CHAPTER II.--SUBSISTENCE RESOURCES, HUNTING PATTERNS AND TECHNIQUES OF THE CHEYENNE AND ARAPAHO

No complete study of the subsistence resources, patterns and techniques of procuring food and other necessities of life has been made of the Cheyenne and Arapaho while they were yet living a life of nomadic buffalo hunters on the Great Plains. In view of this our information concerning their subsistence activities comes to us from a variety of ethnographical and historical sources. In addition, some comparative data is introduced where the record is otherwise incomplete. Comparative data drawn from other Plains tribes is admissible since considerable uniformity in regard to many aspects of subsistence and technology existed among all the Plains people (Wissler, 1927).

From the latter part of the 18th and throughout much of the 19th centuries the Cheyenne and Arapaho were typical Plains Indian equestrian, nomadic buffalo hunters. As such the buffalo was the mainstay of their economy. Besides serving as their chief subsistence resource the buffalo provided them with materials from which they made many articles used by them in their daily lives. Almost every part of the animal was used. The hide was dressed with the hair left on to provide heavy winter robes; thinned and with the hair removed it was the material for shirts, leggings, mocassins, tent covers, bags and receptacles of all kinds. Cut into strips it furnished ropes and lines. Buffalo hair was used to stuff pillows and later, saddles, and to decorate garments, shields and quivers. The back sinews of the buffalo were used for thread and string and when attached with glue made from the hooves it served as a backing for wooden bows to give them greater strength and elasticity. The horns of the buffalo were softened by boiling and were shaped into spoons and ladles while the bones were fashioned into tools for dressing hides.

Following the buffalo, but clearly of secondary importance, were other large game animals, notably elk, antelope and deer. In addition, all kinds of smaller and less plentiful animals were hunted or trapped in order to vary the fare or else to stave off starvation. In this supplementary category the following animals are included: black bear, wolves, foxes, coyotes, young wildcats, panthers, mountain sheep, badgers, skunks and beaver. Dogs were also eaten, sometimes as a special delicacy, sometimes when no other food was available. Horses, especially the very old and useless, were also eaten on occasion (Grinnell, 1923, 247-311; Beals, 1935, 4; Elkin, 1940, 208).

In addition to animal food which formed the bulk of their diet the Cheyenne and Arapaho also collected a large variety of wild roots, berries, fruits, nuts and starchy-root-tubers, which were either eaten alone or when mixed with meat formed an important part of their supplementary diet. Included among the commonest plant foods gathered by Cheyenne and Arapaho women were service-berries, buffalo-berries, choke-cherries, prairie turnips, plums, currants, goose-berries, red-cherries, sand-cherries, acorns and pods from the knife-scabbard tree (Grinnell, 1923, 250; Beals, 1935, 4; Curtis, vol. 6, 1911, 159). There is no evidence that the Cheyenne and Arapaho ever gathered the camas plant which was utilized so extensively by the peoples of the Basin and Plateau areas.

According to Grinnell (1923, 308ff) the Cheyenne also fished on occasion. Beals (1935, 4) says that the Arapaho probably also did likewise, in distinction to the other Plains people who would not touch sea food. Turtles were also caught and eaten (Grinnell, 1923, 307).

Following their transition from a semi-horticultural to an equestrian nomadic life Grinnell's Cheyenne informants state that they continued to plant some vegetable food, along with tobacco, until as late as 1865 (Grinnell, 1923, 247-254). However, in view of our knowledge of plains life it is doubtful whether these practices contributed much to their subsistence resources. This view is supported by the reports of early western traders and travelers who testify as to the trading practices of the Cheyenne and Arapaho with the sedentary Upper Missouri River tribes (ie, Mandan, Hidatsa, Arikara) whereby the former obtained their agricultural products in exchange for horses, hides and other goods. For despite Perrin du Lac who in 1802 stated that the Cheyenne whom he met at the White River on the Missouri still planted some maize and tobacco although they were nomadic hunters during most of the year (Perrin du Lac, 1807, 63), we have the statement of Tabeau, covering the period 1803-1805, who informs us that the Cheyenne, far from planting, were trading products of the hunt with the Arikara for agricultural produce (Abel, 1939, 152). The importance of Perrin du Lac's statement when read alongside other accounts, such as the report of Trudeau who engaged directly in trade with the Cheyenne, that by 1794-95 they were a fully developed   37 nomadic people (Trudeau, 1914, 453ff) is the implication that some bands had made the transition from semi-horticulturists to nomadic hunters earlier than others.

In all the reports following the above mentioned ones the Cheyenne and Arapaho are always referred to as a fully developed nomadic people who, along with other western Plains tribes, engaged in trade relations for agricultural produce with the sedentary Missouri village tribes. While the Plains tribes visited the sedentary villages in most instances on occasion the procedure was reversed. Henry tells us that on the Hidatsa-Mandan expedition to the Cheyenne in 1806 the women were told to take along "plenty of corn and beans, to exchange with the Schians for dressed leather, robes and dried provisions" (Henry in Coues, 1897, 360). Tabeau (1803-1805) also tells us that the Arikara accompanied the Cheyenne to a rendezvous in the Black Hills where they traded corn and tobacco to "eight other friendly nations - The Caninanbiches (Arapaho), the Squihitanes (Snake?, Sisseton?), the Nimoussines (Sioux?), the Padaucas, the Catarkas (?), the Datamis (Kiowa?, Comanche?), the Tchiwak (?) and the Cayawa (Kiowa)" (Tabeau in Abel, 1939, 154).

The horse, the bow and arrow, the lance and, later the gun, along with certain ingenious contrivances, such as the pound and enclosure, were the principal means employed by the Cheyenne and Arapaho in pursuing the buffalo and in obtaining a livelihood.

When buffalo, which were found in great numbers on the open plains east of the Rocky Mountains, yet more or less migrating with the seasons, were plenty, small parties or single individuals were never permitted to chase the buffalo alone. During the months of late spring, summer and early fall when the herds were found in great numbers all hunting was of a communal nature. During these months the buffalo congregated in enormous herds, migrating along established routes to the richest pastures where they fattened themselves on the fresh grass, coming into prime condition from June to August. But in the late autumn and winter when feed was scarce and less nutritious they scattered more widely, forming smaller herds, and were compelled to shift more frequently from place to place. These considerations affected not only hunting methods but it also affected the distribution of the Indian population hunting them. While there was every advantage in the formation of large groups in late spring, summer and early fall for organized attacks on the herds, in winter there was need for the separation of the Indians into smaller groups scattered widely over the country.

As among other Plains people, the smaller Cheyenne and Arapaho units came together and formed tribal units only for that part of the year when abundant food and the opportunities for large-scale communal hunting favored concentration. For the rest of the year they were divided into a number of smaller groups which did not, however, lose their identity during the summer. These smaller groups or bands were fundamentally social and economic units; camp groups adapted to the requirements of the winter.

38   For the winter season each band or camp group retired to a traditional tract of territory in which it had one or more favored sites. Sheltered valleys and hollows at the foothills of the mountains and along streams, away from the open prairies, affording if possible wood, water and game, were sought out as protection against the cold winters and severe snows and winds. Group hunting played an important part of the winter food quest although the group formed was smaller than in summer and the buffalo were driven into pounds or enclosures large enough to hold a hundred head or more. Scouts from the camps reconnoitred the established trails in the neighborhood on the lookout for buffalo. When a herd was reported in the vicinity of the camp individual hunting was forbidden lest the animals be prematurely driven off by the relatively ineffective attacks of small parties preventing thereby a large meat supply from being obtained for the whole group.

Elkin tells us that at least among the Arapaho it was customary for the bands in winter to locate along streams about five to thirty miles from one another and so form an enclosed game-preserve between them. (Elkin, 1940, 210).

In hunting the buffalo the Cheyenne and Arapaho employed four distinct cooperative methods: driving over cliffs, impounding, grass firing and surrounding. Other methods, such as chasing the buffalo on snow shoes, on the ice, in the water, stalking, etc., were pursued by single individuals acting independently (Wissler, 1910, 47-48).

The pound or enclosure into which the buffalo were driven by large bodies of assembled hunters was principally employed in the winter when open prairie hunting was not practicable. In the days before the horse pounds were probably used throughout the year, but once they obtained the horse the large summer herds could be more easily surrounded than before. The sides of the pound were usually constructed of wood and brush with a gap on one side and a chute with diverging wings running far out on the prairie. Behind the diverging wings, hidden from the sight of the buffalo, awaited men, women and children. The strategy of the hunt was to entice the buffalo between these converging lines so that they could be driven into the pen. Once they were driven into the pen they were killed by an organized attack on them by all available persons (Grinnell, 1923, 265-268). Once horses became available herds were then brought to the pounds from several miles distance. By riding alongside a herd at a few hundred yards' distance it was possible for a small party of horsemen to guide the herd into the required direction. After the animals were slaughtered the entire camp moved to the scene where they flayed and cut up the animals, leaving nothing behind but a pile of surplus horn. Men, women, children and dogs were given loads to carry away. But before leaving nooses were frequently set at small openings in the fencing in order to catch the wolves, badgers and foxes which soon were attracted to the scene. Grinnell tells us that the remains of such piles of buffalo-horns were at one time visible at a point west of the Black Hills in the latter part of the last century but which have long since disappeared (Grinnell, 1923, 268).

The use of a cliff or cut-bank over which the buffalo fell into a pound below was also a popular hunting technique employed by the Cheyenne and Arapaho both before as well as after they had acquired the horse. The methods of driving the buffalo over the cliff were similar to those used by them in diverting them into the enclosure. Hornaday quotes T. R. Davis as stating that the Indians between the Platte and the Arkansas river were seen by him driving herds of buffalo over ledges (Hornaday, 1889, 483). The following extract from a letter written by Mr. Reese Kincaide confirms this practice. He writes:

> In talking to Washee, one of the Arapaho chiefs, about this matter, he said that he remembers seeing the Arapho hunters drive a herd of buffalo over a bluff in Colorado. The dead lay in a great pile and as the weather was very cold the bodies froze, so that the women worked for several weeks curing the meat and hides.
> George Bent, a Cheyenne, says that in the winter of 1872, he saw the Indians drive a bunch of buffalo over a bluff on the Cimarron River in Oklahoma and that many were killed. These likewise froze, so that the women could take their time insaving the meat and hides (cited in Wissler, 1910, 49).

The surround was effectively employed after the introduction of the horse. The surround on the open prairie was most effective in the summer when the buffalo formed large herds and moved eastward to the flatter, open country. Rich rewards resulted from successful hunting, but that success depended on the effective marshalling of large bodies of men. It was for the summer hunt that the various bands joined up into a few major groups and finally, at an appointed time, the whole tribe converged on the summer camp where for a number of weeks intensive hunting was followed by feasting, ceremonials and warfare.

The popular picture of a large party of mounted Indians circling continuously round a stampeding herd into which they shot their arrows represents the conditions of the late 18th and 19th centuries. When a herd had been reported by the scouts a plan of attack was quickly drawn up and the hunters divided themselves into a number of parties, which, by going by different routes surrounded the herd from all sides. To hem in the great herds more effectively the parched grass was sometimes fired, on the windward side. Later when guns became available large assemblages of hunters were no longer so necessary in order to bring down the herds. With the repeating rifle small hunting parties were capable of wounding or killing many buffalo. The camp followed in the wake of the hunters polishing off the wounded as they lay on the prairie. But long before this there had grown up a number of strict rules regulating communal hunting; rules which are to be found among every plains tribe.

Although the buffalo provided by far the greatest part of the food supply the Cheyenne and Arapho did not neglect other game. According to Grinnell the Cheyenne and Arapaho also captured elk by the enclosure or pit-below method (Grinnell, 1923, 276). Antelope were also captured by a method similar to the one used for buffalo, but for the antelope a pit, instead of a pound, was constructed. The pit was usually placed at the end of a high, angled fence made of brush and was concealed from the animals by a low transverse fence over which they were forced to leap. Men, women and children all armed with clubs and other weapons lay concealed in shallow trenches dug alongside the fence. Their job was to strike down the antelope as they fell into the pit below (Grinnell, 1923, 278; Grinnell, 1904, 60).

Deer were shot with arrows, something that was not difficult to do in former times when they were so numerous. The Cheyenne and Arapaho also hunted the wild sheep which in former times were found in abundance on the prairies near the bad lands and in the vicinity of all streams running through the northern plains country (Grinnell, 1923, 277).

Large grey wolves were captured in baited pitfalls dug so deep that the animals could not jump out. Foxes were trapped in deadfalls as were small wolves and coyotes (Grinnell, 1923, 297-299).

One important difference existed between the hunting of buffalo and the hunting and trapping of all other game. It was the wanderings of the buffalo herds which determined, to a large degree, the seasonal movements of the Cheyenne and Arapaho. It was largely during the winter when the buffalo was scarce that the Cheyenne and Arapaho seriously turned to the hunting of other game. Yet even at this time of year their movements, choice of camping sites and hunting trips were undertaken with an eye towards the buffalo. But unlike the buffalo for whom they went out and searched they expected that other game, by means of traps, pens, deadfalls, etc., would, more or less, come to them.

In other words, the hunting and trapping of game other than the buffalo was always carried on as a secondary pursuit while scouting for buffalo. In addition, game other than buffalo were to be found over the plains and wherever the Indians traveled in search of buffalo so that actually few major trips were undertaken into regions not frequented by the buffalo.

The gathering of wild plant foods also followed this pattern. Native informants testify to the fact that there were no favorite or special sites from which plant foods were gathered, but rather that these foods were to be found all over the plains wherever they moved in search of buffalo.

Horses: Horses, without which a fully developed plains life could not have been carried on, were obtained by the Cheyenne and Arapaho largely through raiding, though some were acquired in trade and through the capture of wild stock.

The stream of horses supplying the great majority of Plains tribes had its ultimate source in the Spanish settlements where the main raiding of stock from the rancherias was carried on by the Comanche, Kiowa and Apache (Mishkin, 1940, 11; Mooney, 1898, 165). Horses with Spanish brands eventually found their way up into Canada, passing from tribe to tribe. Bradbury tells us that he purchased such branded horses from the Arikara (Bradbury in Thwaites, vol. 5, 1906, 176-177).

The indirect source of supply was the Indian tribes themselves who raided one another. Although the Cheyenne did, on occasion, venture down into the Spanish southwest for horses (Bradbury, in Thwaites, vol. 5, 1906, 176 writes that the Arikara obtained their horses "... from the nations southwest of them, as the Cheyenne, Poncars, Ponies, etc., who make predatory excursions in Mexico, and steal horses from the Spaniards"), their chief source of supply came from raiding other tribes particularly the Pawnee, Comanche and Kiowa groups. In addition, the Cheyenne, prior to their separation in Northern and Southern groups, obtained many horses from the Arapaho in trade.

Trading was another important mechanism for the diffusion of the horse through the Plains. Teit and Haines both show how the Northern Plains tribes obtained horses from the tribes of the Plateau region (Teit, 1930; Haines, 1938). While this route was an important source of supply from the middle to the end of the 18th century it did not supply the Plains tribes with anywhere near the quantity they subsequently required. The subject of trade in horses between Plains tribes themselves is well described by James in his account of Long's Expedition. When, in July, 1820, while the party was in the vicinity of Denver, near Cherry Creek, a tributary of the South Platte, he wrote that:

> About four years previous (1816) to the time of our visit, there had been a large encampment of Indians and hunters on this creek. On that occasion, three nations of Indians, namely, the Kiowas, Arrapahoes, and Kaskaias, or Bad-hearts (?), had been assembled together with forty-five French hunters in the employ of Mr. Choteau and Mr.

- 11 -

Demun of St. Louis. They had assembled for the purpose
of holding a trading council with a band of Shiennes.
These last had been recently supplied with goods by the
British traders on the Missouri, and had come to exchange
them with the former for horses (James in Thwaites, vol.
15, 1906, 282).

James also implies that the meeting of nomadic tribes for trading purposes was a periodic affair when he states that the Arapaho, Kaskaias, Kiowa,
Comanche and Cheyenne "at distant periods, held a kind of fair on a tributary
of the Platte, near the mountains (hence called Grand Camp Creek), at which
they obtained British merchandise from the Shiennes of Shienne River (South
Dakota), who obtained the same at the Mandan village from the British traders..." (James in Thwaites, vol. 17, 1906, 156).

Although there were natural increases and wild horses were captured
whenever possible these sources of increment were insufficient in satisfying
the demand for horses. Capturing and breaking wild horses was a relatively
laborious and time-consuming process, whereas in trade and raiding there
was always the opportunity to exercise choice in acquiring animals already
broken for specialized tasks, such as war, hunting or transportation (Grinnell,
1923, 291-295; Mishkin, 1940, 6).

In addition, there are no indications in the literature that the Cheyenne
and Arapaho were acquainted with the techniques of domestication.

42

CHAPTER III. --SOCIAL ORGANIZATION

As was remarked previously, the distribution of the Cheyenne and Arapaho population was considerably affected by ecological circumstances. While there was every advantage in the formation of large groups in summer for organized attacks on the great herds of buffalo that congregated on the open plains at that season, in winter there was need for the separation of the people into smaller groups scattered over the country.[1]

The effective social and economic unit found among the Cheyenne and Arapaho was the "band", camp, or co-resident group, that is, the group which maintained daily face-to-face contact. The band was not composed exclusively of kindred nor was it exogamous.[2]

The feeling concerning descent was bilateral, or at best slightly patrilineal, but with matrilocal residence often leading to the identification of the children with the mother's band. But a change of band affiliation was possible and a family might return to the husband's band or join another one (Eggan, 1937, 37). The remnants of a camp group that has suffered misfortune, or a man who had quarrelled violently with his relatives might join another band and, since habitual residence and participation in band affairs was the only requisite of membership such newcomers soon became members and were eligible to rise to positions of leadership in the band. Grinnell offers up a case whereby a new Cheyenne band was temporarily established by the followers of an influential man who had been exiled from his own band (Grinnell, 1923, 98).

Thus, the bands of the Cheyenne and Arapaho were essentially camp groups of relatives, either in the male or female line, but often including connections by marriage and even members of different tribes. Each band had a name, usually referring to some pecularity and each functioned as a political, social and economic unit for much of the year under the leadership of its own leaders.

The bands had no formal chiefs, but rather informal, non-permanent leaders, who acquired general authority by virtue of their personal qualities. Skill on the hunt or in warfare, coupled with generosity and fairness in all dealings, were the qualities looked for in band leaders.

Both the Cheyenne and Arapaho were further divided into a series of "societies" which had military, social and ceremonial functions and which operated when all the bands united for communal activities in the summer. The "society" system of these tribes represents segmentary associations relatively independent of the band organization. The "societies" are primarily men's associations and are concerned with the important activities of protection and war, the tribal buffalo hunt and tribal ceremonies. Membership

43

---

[1] See end of chapter for discussion of population size.
[2] That is, marriages could take place between members of the same band providing they were not close relatives.

in the "societies" cross-cut band affiliation. In this way band autonomy was reduced under the tribal organization as the important military, economic and ceremonial activities of the summer were carried out by the "society" organization. Although we have said that the tribal organization operated as a unit only during the summer when all the bands came together there seems to be some evidence that in later times, perhaps already post-Reservation, perhaps after the southward movement of the Cheyenne and Arapaho to the region between the Platte and the Arkansas, the tribal organization continued functioning throughout the year. This evidence will be presented when we deal with the Cheyenne and Arapaho social organization in more detail.

Following the separation of the Cheyenne and Arapaho into northern and southern divisions (among the Cheyenne this separation took place about 1826; among the Arapaho probably much earlier) it is difficult to know with any degree of definiteness whether during the summer communal activities bands from both divisions came together or whether separate summer concentrations occured in each division. The implication of ethnographic writings is that all bands came together, though nowhere is this point made explicit. As we will see later, though the Cheyenne and Arapaho came to be separated into two divisions, the range of territory inhabited by each division overlapped to some extent. At no times does it appear that the northern and southern groups were actually very far from one another, thus making it probable that the two divisions came together at various intervals. From the number of lodges observed by Rufus Sage in 1842 in the vicinity of Fort Lancaster of Cheyenne, Arapaho and other tribes who came together for what seems to be a summer ceremonial, it appears extremely likely that at this concentration both northern and southern divisions were represented.

44

> Toward the last of August (1842) the Arapahos and Cheyennes held a grand convocation, in the vicinity of Fort Lancaster for the purpose of medicine-making: or in other words. paying their united devotion to the Great Spirit. The gathering might with propriety have been termed a "Protracted Meeting", as it continued for three successive days and nights, exclusive of the time occupied in preliminary arrangements. Besides the two tribes above named, a large number of Sioux, Comanche, Blackfeet and Riccarees, were present, swelling the concourse to nearly a Thousand lodges (Sage, 1860, 342).

Fort Lancaster was located on the South fork of the Platte, roughly half way between the range of the northern and southern divisions. Its selection as the site for the summer reunion signifies that it was within reach of both divisions. The selection of this site plus the numbers of lodges present implies that all bands were in attendance.

Finally a brief note on the question of confederation. On page 5 of the petition, no. 329, before the Indian Claims Commission the petitioners describe themselves "as a confederation of Cheyenne and Arapaho Tribes of Indians" and deem that they "owned or occupied...lands as described above for the common or joint use and enjoyment of all the member groups thereof". There is no evidence either in the historical or ethnographic literature that the Cheyenne and Arapaho ever actually effectuated a political alliance although the two tribes have long been in close association. Marriages between the two groups has long been a common practice. According to Executive Document, 1891-92, the Cheyenne and Arapaho are considered a confederated nation by sole virtue of intermarriage.

> The records of this office show that the Arapahoes and Cheyennes, to whom a tract of territory was assigned under the Fort Laramie treaty of 1851,...while speaking different languages, were a confederated nation by reason of intermarriages...(Executive Document: H.R. 1st sess. 52nd Congr. 1891-92, 50).

While the Cheyenne and Arapaho inhabited, in aboriginal times, a common territory and associated in numerous hunting and war parties and conducted summer ceremonials together we cannot show the details of political confederacy. There is no evidence bearing on the structure of their joint undertakings. We do know that when bands of the two tribes camped together, as they frequently did, one group camped slightly apart from the other. But in matters relating to joint hunts, war and ceremonial activities we have no way of knowing how the organization of one group was integrated with that of the other. Insofar as the ethnographic data is concerned the two groups are always treated separately and only in passing is reference made to the fact that they were in close association. That some kind of integration existed is an inescapable conclusion given the numerous instances in which they participated jointly and the fact that there is no recorded instance of warfare or enmity between them.

45

CHAPTER IV.--CHEYENNE SOCIAL ORGANIZATION

Historical Period

According to Grinnell there were among the Cheyenne, during aboriginal times, from ten to fourteen band or camp groups (Grinnell, 1902, 136; 1923, 88). Mooney speaks of ten such groups (Mooney, vol. 1, 1905, 411). During the greater part of the year the bands wandered from place to place, sometimes coalescing with other camp groups; occasionally losing families or individuals who went off to visit temporarily, or, perhaps, permanently, members of other bands. Occasionally two bands met, remained together for a period of time and then separated again to go off in different directions. These bands wandered about under their own leaders.

With the approach of spring and warm weather the bands left their favorite winter camping sites and began drifting down towards the plains in anticipation of renewing their attacks on the herds that soon would reappear. With the coming of summer the bands began to congregate together at prearranged places in order to carry on tribal hunts, ceremonials and warfare.

As a tribal unit the Cheyenne possessed a governmental organization with delegated functionaries of two orders: the tribal chiefs who made up the Council of Forty-Four and the military societies. The Council of Forty-Four formed the formal facade of government in the summer tribal organization and had real powers. The military societies were, theoretically, in a subordinate position.

In summer the bands camped together in a wide camp circle with all the lodges three and four deep. Although there is no unanimity as to the place occupied by each band in the camp circle it is fairly well agreed that the people camped according to their band affiliation. All of Grinnell's early informants agree that the I-vis-tsi-nih-pah band (orthography mine) pitched their lodges immediately to the south of the opening in the circle (Grinnell, 1923, 88-89).

When the bands came together band autonomy gave way to tribal rule. Each band, however, was represented in the Council of Forty-Four by four of their own band leaders. The Council of Forty-Four was composed of four principal chiefs and four leaders from each of the ten bands of the people. This account of the numerical composition of the Cheyenne council of chiefs, a point agreed upon by all ethnographers (Grinnell, 1923, 337; Llewellyn & Hoebel, 1941, 74; Mooney, 1905, 403) either represents an ideal description of the Cheyenne tribal council (since the number of bands in actual existence at any one time varied) or else, some bands were not fully represented. The number forty-four appears to remain constant regardless of the number of bands recorded.

We are told that the four principal chiefs of the council were equal in authority and were slightly more influential than the remaining forty whose real authority extended no further than over their own immediate following. However, their position, nevertheless, commanded general respect and led the people to listen to the advice which they forwarded. Tribal chiefs, we are

46

told, held office for ten years and could be chosen to serve a second term. Any one of the four principal chiefs of the tribe might, at the end of the ten year period, chose his own successor providing that his choice was acceptable to the people as a whole (Grinnell, 1923, 338-340). It does not appear that this prerogative extended equally to the band leaders.

At the meeting of the Council of Chiefs questions of interest to the tribe as a whole were considered. In regard to lesser matters one of the principal chiefs would express his opinion and, if supported by another principal chief, the Council would generally assent without further debate. Questions of great importance, however, such as the moving of camp when buffalo were scarce, of undertaking a tribal war or of seeking an alliance with other tribes for the purpose of proceeding to war against a third party, were discussed at great length; the deliberations perhaps extending over several meetings duration. In such debates the talking was done principally by the older men - those of greatest experience - yet, after the elders had stated their views the middle aged men expressed theirs and even younger men might speak, suggesting a different point of view or giving their reasons for or against a certain course of action or decision.

Llewellyn & Hoebel tell us that the authority of the Council Chiefs carried over into the winter band camps (Llewellyn & Hoebel, 1941, 74). While they do not illustrate this point in detail they seem to imply that something more is involved than simply the fact that the Council of Chiefs was composed of band leaders. The carrying over of tribal authority to the winter camps is seen in the Arapaho material. Elkin tells us that in the winter the bands would locate along streams five to thirty miles, one from the other, for the purpose of forming an enclosed game preserve between them. Members of the bands involved were forbidden to hunt or even to cross the preserve at will. But at given intervals the police (members of one of the military societies designated to supervise communal activities) rounded up a sizeable herd in a given area and one or more bands joined in a communal hunt (Elkin, 1940, 210, 222). Elkin's description of communal activity in the winter and Llewellyn & Hoebel's remark that the authority of the Council Chief's extended over into the winter band camps would seem to indicate that the winter bands, though camping separately, nevertheless remained fairly close to one another, close enough to carry on communal activity under communal supervision. It may well be that special ecological conditions in the region between the Platte and the Arkansas permitted larger population concentrations throughout the year than were to be found in the Northern Plains. If this is true of pre-Reservation times then, following the movement of the Cheyenne and Arapaho into the Southern Plains the population had no need for scattering so widely in the winter as was necessary in the north. Under these conditions there is less likelihood of a severe dichotomy existing between summer and winter organization thus strengthening the tribal structure as the year round social unit.

47

Another component of the tribal political structure among the Cheyenne was the military societies. Among the Cheyenne there were six such societies: Fox soldiers, Elk soldiers, Shield soldiers, Bowstring soldiers, Dog Men and Northern Crazy Dogs (Llewellyn & Hoebel, 1941, 99; Grinnell, vol. II, 1923, 49). Slightly different, but similar names, are given by Mooney (Mooney, 1905, 412-13); and Dorsey (Dorsey, 1905, vol. 9, no. 1, 16-26). Membership into these associations was voluntary. They were open to men of all ages and were of the ungraded type.

The military societies were a function of tribal government and operated as law-enforcement agencies when all the bands were under tribal rule. Llewellyn & Hoebel tell us that a chief of a military society was never permitted to be a tribal chief while holding the former office. When a chief of a military society was selected to fill the place of a deceased Council chief he was automatically retired from his position as leader of a military society and he gave up all affiliation with that organization. Their informants also state that they considered the appointment of a man to tribal chieftainship as a promotion to a position of responsibility to the entire tribe (Ibid, 1941, 102). This procedure served to keep intact the separation of tribal interests from the special interests of any one military society.

With the intensification of White-Indian wars, towards the middle of the 19th century, the balanced relationship between the tribal Council and the military societies changed with the military societies gaining in political strength. Llewellyn & Hoebel tell us that by 1850 the Dog Men military society was also a band within the tribe and camped as such in the tribal camp circle while the other military societies had their members scattered amongst all the other bands. This came about as all the members of the Flexed Leg band had joined the Dog soldier society so dominating it that the distinction between band and military society became lost. As a result of this the Dog society also became a band but an unusual one in that it was not governed by the usual band chiefs but by the military chiefs of the society (Llewellyn & Hoebel, 1941, 100).

48

In Wooden Leg's description of the post 1850 Cheyenne the military societies are clearly characterized as forming a cornerstone of the Cheyenne tribal government and rivalling in power the tribal Council. Wooden Leg tells us that the members of the warrior societies now selected the tribal Chiefs and that the Elk, Crazy Dog and Fox societies were the ruling agencies among the Northern Cheyenne. Although the Council of Forty-Four still functioned in a nominal way once a man was elected to a position on the tribal Council he was no longer compelled to give up his affiliation with the military societies, a situation quite distinct from previous times. (Marquis, 1931, 56-57).

The changes in social structure just described demanded as an essential precondition the continued functioning of the tribal organization throughout the year. This means that ecological conditions permitted such population arrangements. Llewellyn & Hoebel's remarks seem to indicate that this was the pattern prior to the establishment of reservations. If so then it is most likely that this pattern developed in the southern plains where the ecological conditions were more favorable and where population size, for both groups, was greatest.

The point of the above analysis is to show that, despite adequate ethnographic and historical data, the existence of a meaningful tribal organization among the Cheyenne and Arapaho is not fictional.

One of the main tasks which constantly confronted the tribal Council of Chiefs was to maintain a balanced relationship between the interests of the military societies and the rest of the people. By alternation the tribal chiefs delegated governmental powers to the various military societies. That is, one group or another of the military societies were called upon to serve as acting subordinate officials. In the camp circles, in the tribal movings, in the tribal hunts, in times of Great Medicine or other general ceremonial dances - in fact, at all times of important communal activity one or another of the military societies was authorized by the Council of Chiefs to take charge. Ordinarily delegated authority was rotated from one military society to another. A military society might be appointed to act for one day, for two or even longer. At any time their appointment might be revoked and another society named in their place.

During the periods when one of the military societies were delegated to supervise communal activities they were invested with strong coercive authority, almost bordering on the dictatorial. Any disputes arrising aὁ these times were settled by the warriors in charge (For materials relating to the Cheyenne military societies, see Llewellyn & Hoebel, 1941, 89-117; Marquis, 1931, 56-121; Grinnell, vol. II, 1923, 49-71).

49

CHAPTER V.--ARAPAHO SOCIAL ORGANIZATION
Historical Period

According to Kroeber's early informants the Arapaho were originally composed of five sub-tribes: Nawacinahaana, Haanaxawuunena, Hinanaeina, Baasawuunena and Hitounena (orthography mine). These groups ranged from south to north in the order given. Term 1 has some reference to the south, the windward direction. Term 2 is supposed to mean "rock-men". Term 3 were known by the sign for "father". Term 4 means "shelter-men" or "brush-hut-men" and term 5 were known by the gesture of a large or swelling belly. The traditional material indicates that these five divisions were separate, though allied, units. On occasion they came together. In later times most of them grew less in number and were finally absorbed by group three. Group five (Gros Ventres) however, maintain a separate existence (Kroeber, B-AMNH, vol. 18, 1902-07, 5-6).

It is further said that originally there were five band or camp groups in the tribe. Kroeber lists three of them as the "Ugly people", who, at the time when he obtained the material, were living in Cantonment, Oklahoma; the "ridiculous men" on the South Canadian river in Oklahoma and the "red willow men" in Wyoming (Kroeber, 1902-07, 8). Mooney lists five bands for the Arapaho. They are as follows: (1) Waquithi, "bad faces", the principal band, (2) Aqathinena, "pleasant men", (3) Gawuena or Gawunehana, "Blackfeet", so called because they are said to have had some Blackfoot blood, (4) Haqihana, "wolves", (5) Sasabaithi, "looking up" or "looking around", i.e., watchers or look-outs (Mooney, AR-BAE, vol. 14, pt. 2, 1893, 956-957) (Orthography mine). Elkin lists four bands among the Northern Arapaho. The "Quick Tempered", numbering about 800 in all was the largest and constituted the focal center in the tribal organization. Then came the Antelope with some 600 members and two smaller groups, the "Greasy Faced" with about 400 members and the "Middle People" with about 250 members (Elkin, 1940, 209). Present-day native informants told the writer that band names were always changing.

The band system of the Arapaho seems to have been organized along lines similar to that of the Cheyenne (Eggan, 1937, 37).

In addition to the band organization Arapaho society was further differentiated internally by a series of age-graded associations or societies. These groupings constituted a series covering the entire period from youth to old age. Each society was composed of a group of men, of approximately the same age, who, as a body, mounted the rungs in the series. Even children were members of well defined age-groupings. From the time a child left his mother's care to play in groups they were known as "Blackbirds". At about the age of ten they became "Wild Rose Bushes" or "thorny" and were given to much fighting and teasing. At puberty when they began to prepare themselves for the activities of manhood they became known as "Calves".

The system of men's societies and the approximate ages at which a man entered are as follows:

1. Kit Fox	17
2. Star	21
3. Tomahawk	25
4. Bitahenene	30
5. Crazy	35
6. Dog	45
7. Hinanahenene	60
8. Water-Sprinkling-Old-Men	70

The first men's society began when all the young men of the tribe of about seventeen years of age organized themselves into a Kit Fox society. Their first task was to get five or six of the bravest and best-liked members of the Tomahawk society to sponsor their activities. Henceforth the members of the Tomahawk society were known as "older brothers" to the Kit Foxes and controlled and regulated the activities of the new group.

The four societies, Tomahawk, Bitahenen, Crazy and Dog were very similar to one another in structure. They were differentiated from the two younger societies in that they were associated with particular "lodge-dance" ceremonies. To gain admittance to an advanced society they had to perform the "lodge-dance" ceremony connected with it.

The structure of the two oldest societies, the Hinanahenene and the Water-Sprinkling-Old-Men, differed from the younger groups in that they were not organized on the basis of age alone. The possession of supernatural power was an added requirement and participation therefore was restricted to a handful of old men.

Among the Arapaho the tribal government was a function of the age-society organization. Band leaders played only a small part in the tribal political structure, unlike among the Cheyenne. Individual members of the tribe were represented in the tribal political life not by the leaders of their band, but by the leaders of the age-organization to which they belonged. All formalized Arapaho political leadership was covered by various categories of chieftainship. Outstanding Kit-Fox and Star men were "little chiefs"; they had but meager authority but were expected to rise to higher ranks. The Tomahawk and Bitahenene became "brother chiefs", while others were "company chiefs". At the top of the chieftainship scale were four tribal chiefs who were formally inducted to office. When two of the four retired or died the remaining chiefs chose their successors from among the most capable of the Dog or Crazy society. There were also several "Chiefs' helpers".

When problems concerning communal activities arose, such as the need for devising plans for the protection of the camp, tribal movements, etc., the four tribal chiefs met first and discussed the matter. If they thought the matter should be discussed more broadly they they called a general meeting of all the societies. If, however, it came to pass that the matter required more thorough discussion or if there developed disagreement then the tribal chiefs asked that the matter first be discussed privately among the separate societies so that each society would arrive at a common decision before it was again discussed generally. If religious matters were involved then the two oldest societies decided. The Tomahawk and Bitahenene societies usually concerned themselves chiefly with matters concerning warfare. In most instances, however, both the older and younger societies awaited the decisions of the Crazy and Dog societies, there voices carrying most weight (Elkin, 1940, 221).

Beyond the formulation of general policy, the function of government included the enforcement of rules pertaining to a number of tribal activities: hunting, determination of the line of march, the breaking and formation of the camp circle and the maintenance of order within the camp.

Although the tribal chiefs were ultimately responsible for the enforcement of discipline they themselves did not directly perform these duties but assigned the responsibility for their execution to the first four military societies in the series, the Kit Foxes, Star, Tomahawk and Bitahenene. The tribal chiefs alternated responsibility from one society to another. In this matter they used their own judgement as which society should be at one time or another in command. While carrying out their orders the older members of the society involved had complete authority for the time being.

In the control of the tribal hunt the soldier-police showed the greatest extent of their power.

SOME POPULATION ESTIMATES OF THE CHEYENNE AND ARAPAHO

52   A few population estimates for the Cheyenne and Arapaho are available from the historical sources. The earliest known estimate for the Cheyenne is that given by Lewis and Clark, who noted it variously as 110, 130-150 and 300 lodges with 3 warriors or 11 persons per lodge (Lewis and Clark in Thwaites, Vol. 5, 1905, 356-57; Vol. 6, 1905, 100). These figures represent a minimum of 330 warriors or 1,100 persons and a maximum of 900 and 3,300 respectively. In The Report of the Sec'y of War, 1829, the Cheyenne population is given at 2,000 (Senate Executive Doc. # 72, 1829, 104). General Atkinson in 1835 reported the Cheyenne strength at 3,000 persons of whom 550-600 were listed as warriors (H. R. Doc. #117, 1826, 10). In 1837 Atkinson again listed the Cheyenne with 800 warriors (H. R. Doc. #276, 1837-38, 20). This figure comes close to the maximum estimate of Lewis and Clark. In 1835 Colonel Dodge reported the Cheyenne to consist of 220 lodges, 660 men and 2,640 souls in all (Dodge, 1861, 140). Culbertson in 1850 estimated the Cheyenne at 3,000 persons occupying 300 lodges (Culbertson, B-BAE #147, 1952, 137). James Mooney in his ethnological study of American Indian Population puts the Cheyenne population in the year 1780 at 3,500 and 3,351 in 1907 (Mooney, Smith. Misc. Coll. Vol. 80, No. 7, 1928, 12-13).

The above figures are fairly consistent in listing the number of persons per lodge. Lewis and Clark place it at 11, Culbertson at 10 and Dodge at 12.

The Report of the Sec'y of War, 1829, places the Arapaho population at 4,000 (Senate Executive Doc. #72, 1829, 104). In 1835 Dodge estimated there were 360 lodges, 1,080 men and a total of 3,600 Arapaho in all (Dodge, 1861, 140). Rufus Sage, 1841, gives the following breakdown: 575 lodges, 4,000 total population (Sage, 1860, 214). Mooney in his study of aboriginal population places them at

3,000 in 1780. Elkin more recently estimated that the aboriginal Northern Arapaho population was 2,000 in four bands: 800, 600, 400 and 250 respectively. (Elkin, 1940, 209). Dodge lists 10 persons per lodge; Sage 7. Currently, Eggan believes that in the 1860's the Arapaho had 380 lodges with a total population of 2,800 which averages out 7-8 persons per lodge. A household would normally have 2 or more lodges, according to Eggan (Eggan, 1937, 83). Eggan further believes that on the average the Cheyenne and Arapaho bands contained 300-350 members (Ibid, 84).

I am aware that the Rev. Morse has estimated the Arapaho population at 10,000 (in Hayden, 1862, 321). I consider this figure much too high and as can be seen it stands alone in comparison to all others. On the other hand his estimate of the Cheyenne population which he puts at 3,250 (in Hayden, 1862, 276) is completely acceptable.

The various epidemics which played havoc with so many American Indian tribes, particularly those of 1778, 1781-82, 1801, 1837-38 and 1849 do not seem to have appreciably affected the Cheyenne and Arapaho population as far as it can be determined. There is little mention of their being seriously afflicted in the historical literature although we know that on a few occasions they refused to come to the trading posts because of smallpox.

53

CHAPTER VI.--MOVEMENTS AND AREA OF OCCUPATION OF THE CHEYENNE

I

Early History

As has been previously noted, the Cheyenne have within a period of approximately three hundred years experienced four different modes of life involving three distinct trasitions.

In tracing the movements of the Cheyenne from the Northeast into the Great Plains documentary history, archaeology and native traditions have all been employed. The migration legends and traditions of the Cheyenne point to a Central Algonkian provenience, probably on the Canadian side of the Great Lakes (Mooney, 1905-07, 363; Grinnell, 1923, 4-6, 16). In addition, there are some Dakota legends to the effect that the Cheyennes were living in the Minnesota River valley area when they (ie Dakota) first arrived there (Hyde, 1937, 9; Williamson, 1872, 296).

The first historical reference to the Cheyenne appears to be on a map of Joliet and Franquelin which, according to Neill, was made prior to 1673 (Neill, 1883, 797). On this map they are called "Chaiena" and are listed together with seven other tribes on the east side of the Mississippi river some distance below the Wisconsin river. The "Siou" are also shown on the same side of the river below this group of tribal names. Thus in the third quarter of the seventeenth century the Cheyenne are placed in western Wisconsin just over the border of southeastern Minnesota.

According to Will, Franquelin's map of 1688 places the Cheyenne on the Minnesota river, while another one of his maps, approximately twelve years later in about 1700, locates them on the Sheyenne River in North Dakota (Will, 1914, 69). Although this is east of the point on the river where the only known Cheyenne horticultural site has been located and excavated (Strong, 1940, 370-376), it does tie in with the later historical references to that village which definitely places it on the Sheyenne river. Traditionally the Cheyenne are said to have lived in a village on the Minnesota river above the Otoes, while the Iowa were situated below the latter (Will, 1914, 69; Hyde, 1937, 9; Mooney, 1905-07, 364). When Le Seur, in October of 1700, founded his post at the mouth of Blue Earth river on his journey up the Minnesota he met "nine Scioux, who told him that the river belonged to the Scioux of the West, the Ayavois (Iowa), and Otoctatas (Oto), who lived a little further off,..." (Neill, 1883, 162). The fact that the Cheyenne are not mentioned in this connection, when taken together with the information provided by Franquelin's map of 1688, would seem to bear out the inference that they had, by this time, moved up the Minnesota to Big Stone Lake and Lake Traverse (Will, 1914, 68; Riggs, 1893, 194; Grinnell, 1923, 16-17), and thence up the Red river from which they branched off at the Sheyenne where Franquelin's map places them by 1700.

It is not until well over half a century later that we find the Cheyenne again mentioned in the historical literature, when they are referred to by Carver in 1766 as one of the eight bands of the Sioux of the Plains (Carver, 1778, 79-80). This point is of particular interest because the evidence indicates that just about this time the Cheyenne village site on the Sheyenne river was either still inhabited by members of the tribe who were engaged in horticultural activities, or that the settlement had only recently been destroyed. While it is not possible to accurately fix the date of occupancy of this site it seems safe to say, as others have suggested, that between 1700 and 1770 the Cheyenne were undergoing a process of change which eventuated in their becoming completely nomadic by the end of the 18th century (Strong, 1940, 359-376).

According to Will "while located on the Sheyenne river the Cheyenne entered upon their life on the real plains, and here their transition into a plains tribe began" (Will, 1914, 69-70). Grinnell conceives the process somewhat more dynamically when he says "it is probable that at the time when some of the villages were permanently situated at certain points, a part of the Cheyenne were still pushing westward, and that the tribe was partly migratory and partly sedentary, some established at one place and some moving about. It is possible that the permanent villages...in Minnesota and on the Sheyenne River..., and perhaps others, were occupied during the same period,...and that other groups may then have been wandering about on the plains after the buffalo" (Grinnell, 1923, 14-15).

There were also other Cheyenne horticultural village sites located along the Missouri and some of its western tributaries which also may have been settled either while the Sheyenne river site was still a going concern or shortly thereafter. None of these sites have been excavated, however (Will, 1914, 76; Lewis & Clark in Thwaites, vol. 1, 1904, 195; Grinnell, 1918, 367-377).

By 1795 some groups of the Cheyenne were already fully developed equestrian buffalo hunters. This was so noted by Trudeau when he was among the Arikara at that time (Trudeau, 1914, 543ff). This information supplied by Trudeau when taken in connection with Perrin du Lac's statement that the Cheyenne whom he met at White river on the Missouri still planted maize and tobacco, although they were nomadic hunters during most of the year (Perrin du Lac, 1807, 63) implies that some bands had become fully plainsized before others.

The undertaking of a fully nomadic plains existence was impossible without an adequate supply of horses. While it is not possible to ascertain exactly when the Cheyenne began obtaining horses in abundance it is safe to assume that some Cheyenne got horses between 1740 and 1770. The Verendryes first noted the appearance of horses among the Upper Missouri village tribes (Mandan, Hidatsa, Arikara) in 1738 (Verendrye, 1914, 351). In this connection we know that horses became common among the Sioux in Central Minnesota between 1766 and 1772. Haines says:

...Carver found a few horses at Prairie du Chien in 1766, but the Sioux whom he met in central Minnesota that same

55

year were using canoes rather than horses...Peter Pond, trading in the same area six years later, found horses in common use among the Sioux who, he says, are the same ones visited by Carver.

David Thompson, writing in 1796, reported that the Sioux were then using horses instead of canoes, indicating that they had made the change in comparatively recent times or it would not have been worth the emphasis he gave it (Haines, 1938, 434).

Also in this connection it is well to refer to an oftquoted Cheyenne tradition to the effect that some time after they had penetrated the Missouri river region and had moved on to the Black Hills the Sioux began coming in. "They (Cheyenne) declared that the first Sioux who came were very poor and had no horses, which the Cheyenne had already obtained...; that when the Sioux came, carrying their possessions on dog travois, the Cheyenne took pity on them and occasionally gave them a horse; that this generosity resulted in the coming of more and more Sioux to receive like presents,..." (Grinnell, 1915, 34).

If it is not possible to date exactly the process of change undergone by the Cheyenne from a semi-horticultural to a fully nomadic people, nevertheless, we have the evidence of Trudeau that by 1794-95 at least some groups of Cheyenne were fully plainsized. From this time on, with the exception of Perrin du Lac's statment to which reference has already been made, the Cheyenne are only referred to in the literature as a fully plainsized people.

56

As nomadic buffalo hunters the Cheyenne were, during the early years of the nineteenth century, contacted by a few western explorers, but chiefly by traders who met them at the Upper Missouri river villages where Europeans and Indians exchanged trade goods. In spite of some attempts on the part of the Cheyenne to lure traders to them instead of their seeking the traders out (Henry in Coues, 1897, 384) it was actually more profitable for both sides to meet at the villages of the Upper Missouri tribes. The reluctance of the trader to seek out the nomadic tribes in the area where they happened to be at this time was partly due to the fact that beaver was the main item sought by the Whites and in regards to beaver trapping the western Plains tribes had little interest. This resulted in a practice of the Cheyenne and other nomadic peoples to bring their buffalo robes and hides, for which there was a developing trade, to the Upper Missouri villages where they could at the same time trade for food staples and articles of European manufacture.

These conditions of contact have unfortunate consequences for any study of occupation for any of the western Plains tribes. This means that in the vast majority of instances the Cheyenne were contacted away from areas hunted over by them with the result that much of the early evidence regarding occupation rests upon testimony uncorroborated by direct observation. In addition, most of the early explorers who did venture westward in the early 19th century proceeded along the major river systems, particularly the Missouri and the Platte, thus observing little of the conditions of existence and tribal locations between the river systems.

Once the Cheyenne had abandoned village life and had crossed the Missouri river they made their way to the Black Hills via the tributaries of the Missouri. This process, as we have noticed, did not take place all at once, nor did all the Cheyenne bands undergo transformation simultaneously. This westward movement probably took place in the fashion outlined by Grinnell.

> In the (westward) movement...a camp or village followed its own ideas as to where it wished to go and did not usually consider the movements of other camps. It moved independently. There were no contemporaneous tribal migrations. The different camps did not unite in a forward movement. The trend of the tribal movement being westward, a group moved on, established itself at a point and remained there for a time - perhaps for many years, perhaps for a generation or two. Later, some village behind it moved forward, passed the first village and stopped somewhere beyond. The gradual westward progress consisted of a succession of such movements, the tail of the long procession often becoming the head, and the different camps or villages moving on successively and passing each other (Grinnell, 1918, 366).

II

The Nineteenth Century

It appears certain that with the opening up of the 19th century the Cheyenne were living west of the Missouri river and that some bands were living in the Black Hills of South Dakota and along the Cheyenne and White rivers. Lewis and Clark speak of the French as meeting with the Cheyenne in the Black Hills long before they themselves arrived there (Lewis & Clark in Thwaites, vol. 1, 1904, 176). Tabeau tells us that although a trader named Guenneville spent a winter (1804-05) with the Cheyenne in the Black Hills he was not the first trader among them (Tabeau in Abel, 1939, 87).

It further appears that the Cheyenne were not the first occupants of the Black Hills and that other tribes were already living there when the Cheyenne arrived. The Cheyenne say that both the Kiowa and Comanche were living in the Black Hills and along the Little Missouri, Powder and Tongue rivers when they got there (Grinnell, 1915, 33; Mooney, AR-BAE vol. 17, 1895-96, 157). This is acknowledged by the Kiowa themselves who relate that after making friends with the Crow they established themselves in the Black Hills until they were driven out by the invading Dakota and Cheyenne (Mooney, 1895-96, 155). The eventual expulsion of the Kiowa and Comanche by the Cheyenne also pushed the Crow further to the west (Grinnell, 1915, 34).

While making the Black Hills their home the Cheyenne, nevertheless, shared this area, along with the Cheyenne river region, with several other tribes for a number of years to come. Perrin du Lac, 1801-03, speaks of the Cheyenne as hunting buffalo on both sides of the Cheyenne river and as far south as the "immense savannahs near the Plate River" and sharing this area with other wandering hunters, the Cayowas (Kiowas), Tocaninambiches (Arapaho), Tokiouakos (?) and the Pitapahatos (?) (Perrin du Lac, 1807, 62-63).

Charles Le Raye who was among the Arikara in 1802 writes:

> Here we lfft the Missouri and proceeded a west course to
> the river Chien or Dog river...On the headwaters reside
> several tribes of Indians...The most powerful of these
> tribes are the Chien, or Dog Indians. There are also the
> Gensdi-rach or Kananawesh [Arapaho] , the Kites [Crow?]
> and Dotame (a small band allied with the Kiowa who re-
> side in the Black Hills), besides bands of the Mahas
> [Omaha] , Poncars [Poncas], and Kataka (Cataka, a small
> band of Kiowa-Apache, west of the Black Hills) (Le Raye,
> 1908, 159).

The original map sent back by Lewis and Clark in 1805 and published in Science, November 4, 1887, shows the Cheyenne, Ni-mou-sin (?), Do-ta-ine (Kiowa band), Ca-ta-ka (Kiowa-Apache) all scattered about the Black Hills. The Cheyenne are the largest of the four tribes having 110 lodges. The others have 15, 10 and 25 lodges respectively. This map which is considered remark-ably accurate is dotted with the names of many tribes, but north of the Platte river, excepting for the Poncars and Omahas between the Niobrara and the North Platte, no Sioux names appear west of the Missouri river although there are a number on that river. The Brule Sioux are on the Missouri between the mouths of the White river and the Teton or Bad river, and there are other Sioux groups just below the mouth of the Cheyenne river. On the tributaries of the North Platte, or at its head, are a group of Kites with 40 lodges, a group of Arapaho, 150 lodges and another camp of Kiowas just south of them with 40 lodges.

In other words, there were few Sioux west of the Missouri at this time, which is just what all of Grinnell's oldest Cheyenne informants tell us (Grinnell, 1923, 31).

At about this time many of the tribes which we noted shared, with the Cheyenne, the Black Hills and the forks of Cheyenne river, began, for a complex of reasons, to move south. Following Lewis and Clark we no longer note their presence in this region. The traditional explanation given for their southward migration has been that they were pushed out by the invading Cheyenne. To this explanation must be added the attraction of the southern plains as a source of supply of horses which were obtained through raids on the Spanish settlements.

Although the Cheyenne made the Black Hills their headquarters they did not confine themselves exclusively to this region. As early as 1806 Alexander Henry the younger informs us that the Cheyenne "generally pass the winter south of the Black Hills...Here, they say, is the source of two large rivers; one runs to the Northeast and the other to the South; the former falls into the Missourie...under the name of Riviere Platte; the other, of course, into the Gulf of Mexico. Near the source of these two rivers they make their annual hunt...in company with the Buffalo Indians, or, as some call them, the

Caveninavish tribe [Arapaho], a very numberous nation occupying that part of the country. They (Arapaho) consist of about 500 tents. The Schians, have made their winter's hunt, move northward" (Henry in Coues, vol. 1, 1897, 383-384).

In this statement Henry appears to be referring to the territory between the Platte and the Arkansas. However, in view of the fact that in 1802 Perrin du Lac pointed out that the Cheyenne also hunted in the vicinity of the Platte it is conceivable that Henry was jumping to conclusions about the latter river. It is barely possible that the two rivers may have been only the north and south branches of the Platte.

But by far the greatest significance of Henry's statement lies in the fact that other than the Cheyenne and Arapaho no other tribes are mentioned as occupying this region, thus lending some support to the belief that by this time the Comanche, Kiowa and Kiowa-Apache groups had already moved south of the Platte River.

There are occasional references in the literature to the effect that the westward-moving Teton Sioux bands while pushing to the Black Hills and beyond into the Big-horn country expelled the Cheyenne from their home in west-central and southwestern South Dakota. Various dates are assigned to this event. Thus Curtis writes:

> ...before this [1840 alliance between the Sioux and the Cheyenne] the Teton Sioux had spread over the prairies of western South Dakota to the Black Hills, forcing out the Cheyenne, who moved first westward and northward to the head-waters of Powder river and the foothills of the Big-horn mountains, where they conflicted with the Crow, and later southward to the heads of the North Platte where the previous occupants were the Kiowa. (Curtis, vol. VI, 89).

59

Ewers concurs with Curtis but assigns a much earlier date for the event. He writes:

> The Teton entered the Black Hills, favorite winter home of the buffalo, about 1765 and proceeded to dispossess the Cheyenne and Kiowa whom they found there. The final move-ment into Wyoming followed the defeat of the Crow in 1822-23 by the Teton and Cheyenne (Ewers, 1937, 4.)

With regards to the date assigned by Ewers, 1765 seems preposterously early for the Dakota to be pushing the Cheyenne out of the Black Hills. In the first place it is highly unlikely that the Cheyenne were occupying the Black Hills at this time in view of the fact that they only began to possess horses between 1740 and 1770. Furthermore, there is no corroborating evidence indicating that the Cheyenne left the Black Hills in company with the Kiowa. All evidence seems to point to the displacement of the Kiowa from the Black Hills by the Cheyenne long before the arrival of the Dakota.

While Ewers suggests that the Dakota were expelling the Cheyenne from the Black Hills in 1765, John Long, in 1791, locates the Dakota east of the Missouri. Long writes that

> They (Dakota) were bounded by a curved line extending east of North from Prairie du chien on the Mississippi, so as to include all the eastern tributaries of the Mississippi, to the first branch of Chippewa River; thence by a line running west of north to Spirit Lake; thence westwardly to Crow Wing River, Minnesota, and up that stream to Pembina; thence southwestwardly to the eastern bank of the Missouri near the Mandan villages; thence down the Missouri to a point probably not far from Soldiers River; thence east to Prairie du Chien (cited in Swanton, B-BAE #145, 1952, 281).

We have also noted that on Lewis and Clark's map, 1804-06, no Sioux names appear west of the Missouri although there are a number on that river. Hyde, in his history of the Oglala division of the Dakota writes that

> During the period 1800-1825 the Oglalas were hunting each summer in the plains immediately east of the Black Hills, in close connection with the Saones (another Dakota band) of Cheyenne River and the Cheyenne tribe. The latter people were sometimes on the head-branches of Cheyenne river and sometimes down on the North Platte where one of their favorite camping places was on Horse Creek just west of the present Nebraska-Wyoming line.

60

> During this period (1800-1825), the Oglalas had a regular beat, passing back and forth between the Black Hills and the mouth of Bad (Teton) River. At first they wintered on the Missouri, trading...with Loisel at Cedar Island below Bad River or with some other French traders from St. Louis; but soon after 1805 they began to spend their winters in the eastern edge of the Black Hills, usually near Bear Butte. In the spring they would go down Bad River, hunting as they went along, and on reaching the Missouri they joied the Saones and Brules (another Teton Dakota band) and took part in the pastime of stopping and robbing traders who were going up-river to the Arikara and Mandan (Hyde, 1937, 33-34).

On Catlin's map, 1832-1840, the only Sioux west of the Missouri are shown to be located along the south bank of the Teton (now known as Bad) River. In his book Catlin says that Fort Pierre which "is on the west bank of the Missouri, on a...plain near the mouth of the Teton river" is "in the heart of the Sioux country" (Catlin, vol. 1, 1876, 209). The Cheyenne "are a small tribe of about 3,000 in number, living neighbors to the Sioux, on the west of them..." (Catlin, vol. II, 1876, 2). In 1833 Hayden estimated there were 1,630 Dakota lodges residing on the Missouri and along its tributaries (Hayden, 1863, 371). All seven of the Dakota bands are included in this tabulation.

The foregoing data indicates that during the first quarter of the nineteenth century and possibly longer the Dakota Sioux, with the exception of raids
and forays, extended no further west than the eastern edge of the Black Hills
and that they shared parts of this territory with the Cheyenne who were living
on Cheyenne river.

It is not until about 1820 that we get our first reference to the effect
that a portion of the Cheyenne tribe had permanently left the region around the
forks of Cheyenne river and the Black Hills in order to take up residence in
the Southern Plains, although we know from previous sources that even while the
Cheyenne were more familiar with the more northerly region they did not always
confine themselves there. In 1820 while Long's party was in the vicinity of
Denver, near Cherry Creek, a tributary of the South Platte, they came upon a
camp of Kiowa, Kaskaia or Badhearts (?), Arapaho and Cheyenne, James wrote that
the last named group "who have united their destiny with [the Arapaho] are a
band of seceders from their own nation; and some time since, on the occurrence
of a serious dispute with their kindred on Shienne river of the Missouri, flew
their country, and placed themselves under the protection of the Bear Tooth
(the Arapaho chief)" (James in Thwaites, vol. XVI, 1906, 211).

Additional support of the fact that some distinction had already begun to
exist at this time between the Cheyenne of the Missouri and those in the south
is implied in Fowler's description of a trade encampment held on the Arkansas
river in November and December, 1821. At this camp were gathered over 700
lodges of Kiowa, Arapaho, Ietans (Comanche), Snake and Cheyenne. Fowler writes
(I have revised his original orthorgaphy somewhat):   61

> We are afraid we will not be able to obtain horses from the
> Arapaho since they have few in comparison with the others
> owing to their having last summer traded them to the Cheyennes
> of the Missouri River...(Fowler in Coues, 1898, 65).

Rev. Morse in his report to the Secretary of War in 1820 also remarks to
the effect of a northern and southern division. He writes:

> A small band of this tribe (Cheyenne)reside near the
> head of Chien river. Sometime since they left their own
> nation and attached themselves to the Arrapahuys. (Morse,
> 1822, 254).

That the group of Cheyenne encountered by Fowler were the same who were
met by Long in the preceding year seems to be indicated by their connection
with the Arapaho.

When Fowler in 1821 visited the trade encampment on the Arkansas river
(mentioned above) he stated that there were "about 200 lodges " of Cheyenne
present (Fowler in Coues, 1898, 65). Morse, while writing of the Cheyenne who
had attached themselves to the Arapaho, speaks of there being only about 200
members of the Cheyenne tribe still residing near the head of Cheyenne river
in the Northern Plains (Morse, 1822, 254). These two statements when taken
together would seem to indicate that as early as 1820 the majority of the

Cheyenne had already abandoned the northern region in favor of the area to the south. James, on the other hand, gives no indication that the southern Cheyenne population was, at this time, anywhere near as large as the two previous writers suggest. In fact, he speaks of them only as "a band of seceders from their own nation, ... [of] kindred on Shienne river of the Missouri...(James in Thwaites, vol. XVI, 1906, 211).

In view of the fact that subsequent writings up until about 1830 speak of the Cheyenne as principally occupying the area around the Black Hills and the Cheyenne river region, it is doubtful whether any large-scale movement took place as early as 1820. It would seem that James was right and that the Cheyenne found by him and Fowler along the Arkansas in company with the Arapaho were only a small band while the remainder, and largest part of the tribe, still lived in the north.

We know that in 1825 according to General Atkinson's report on the Treaty of 1825 that the Cheyenne were still inhabiting the northern country. He writes:

> [The Cheyenne]... now inhabit the country on the Cheyenne river, from near its mouth, back to the Black Hills...They are estimated at 3,000 souls...Their principal rendezvous is towards the Black Hills, and their trading ground at the mouth of Cherry river, a branch of the Cheyenne, 40 miles above its mouth (Atkinson, 1826, 10).

62

Thomas Fitzpatrick, the first Indian Agent of the Upper Platte and Arkansas rivers, wrote as follows in his report of 1847.

> The Chyennes...claim [the Arkansas River] and on it about fifty miles above this place (Bent's Fort), have already selected a place for their settlement. But if the right of preemption stands good, the Aripahoes have much the best right, as they occupied this country long before the Chyennes ever saw it. Twenty years ago (1827) the Aripahoes were in possession of this country, and north to the South Fork of Platte and beyond, without any tribe to dispute their claim. The Chyennes at that time were living on the south side of Missouri river, between the Chyenne and White rivers, and along the Black Hills (Hafen, 1932, 134).

This places the Cheyenne in the same vicinity as Atkinson did in 1825.

In 1826, or thereabouts, we were told by Porcupine Bull that the Cheyenne and Arapaho "began making raids on the Kiowa and Comanches, who lived south of the Arkansas" (Grinnell, 1923a, 31). In view of the fact that both Fowler and James writing around 1820 indicated that the Arapaho were on friendly terms with the Kiowa and Comanche, Porcupine Bull's statement indicates that a change in the relationship must have taken place a few years later. The antagonistic relationship which developed between the two sets of tribes, the Cheyenne and Arapaho on the one hand, and the Kiowa and Comanche on the other was probably caused by the increased presence of Cheyenne in the region south of the Platte. Together with the Arapaho they began to dominate the area between the Platte and the Arkansas driving the Kiowa and Comanche before them. It is at this time that the Southern Cheyenne begin to be distinguished from their northern kinsmen, and not in 1820. Fitzpatrick states that it was pressure from the Sioux which forced the Cheyenne below the Platte around 1827 or later (Hafen, 1832, 134) thus agreeing substantially with Grinnell's information. Doane Robinson, Secretary of the State Historical Society of South Dakota says that the division of the Cheyenne occurred in about 1830 "...on account of a wish on the part of a portion of the tribe to follow the fur traders. One division migrated to the valleys of the Platte and Arkansas rivers and became known as the Southern Cheyenne. That portion that remained in their old possessions were designated the Northern Cheyenne..." (Robinson, 1902, editorial note no. 85, 147). The traders referred to were the Bent brothers and Ceran St. Vrain. According to Grinnell it was probably in 1828 that the Cheyenne met them on the Arkansas river in southeastern Colorado.

> The Bents were encamped at the mouth of the Purgatoire, or had a stockade there, and to this place came a party of Cheyenne who had been south (ie. below the Arkansas) catching wild horses and were returning north to their camp. Porcupine Bull stated that the leaders of this party were Yellow Wolf, Little Wolf and Wolf Chief, and that it was at this meeting that Yellow Wolf made friends with the Bents and gave them names. The question of trade was also discussed, and Yellow Wolf told the Bents that a post on the Arkansas near the mountains was too far from the buffalo range for the Indians to frequent. He suggested that the Bents and St. Vrain build a post near the mouth of the Purgatoire, and said that if they would do this he would bring his band and others there to trade. It is said that Charles Bent at once accepted the chief's proposal and that this was how Bent's Fort came to be built.

63

> The Bent brothers and Ceran St. Vrain began this fort in 1828, but it was not completed until 1832...(Grinnell, 1923a, 31).

Further distinguishing not only between the Northern and Southern Cheyenne, but also between similar divisions of the Arapaho, Grinnel states that Fort St. Vrain, built by the same traders on the South Platte, a short distance below St. Vrain's Fork, was "intended for the trade of the northern Indians; that is, for the Sioux and the northern bands of Cheyennes and Arapahoes, who seldom got down south as far as the Arkansas river and so did not often come to Bent's Fort, and indeed did much of their trading at Fort Laramie, on the Platte" (Grinnell, 1923a, 41-42).

Mooney tells us that a part of the Cheyenne tribe, as a consequence of having met William Bent as a trader at the mouth of the Yellowstone, decided to move down to the Arkansas river when in 1828 the Bent brothers and St.

Vrain established a small trading post at the present Pueblo, Colorado. The Cheyenne, at that time, "camped chiefly in the western Black Hills, Wyoming, but frequently raided to the southward against the Kiowa and others" (Mooney, vol. 1, 1905, 376). The Hevhaitaneo band led the van of the migration, but was obliged to turn back on account of an outbreak of smallpox at that post. A few years later, however, Bent's Fort was built on the Arkansas river, in south-eastern Colorado, and this time, on the invitation of William Bent himself, the main body of Cheyenne removed permanently to the upper Arkansas, arriving in the fall of 1833. "The rest of the tribe continued to rove about the head-waters of the North Platte and Yellowstone" (Mooney, vol. 1, 1905, 376-377).

It would be hard to assign a single cause for the Cheyenne decision to move south in the period described. It is likely that it resulted from a com-plex of events: increasing pressures of tribes from the north, including the numerous west-ward moving Dakotas; increasing competition among the tribes of the Northern Plains for the commerce of the trading posts which were springing up along the Missiour and Yellowstone rivers; an opportunity to withdraw from the northern situation by taking advantage of the relatively exclusive facili-ties offered by Bent's Fort; opportunity of obtaining an increased number of horses direct from the southern plains via raids on the Spanish and other settlements.

At different periods in history Cheyenne relations with the various Dakota Sioux bands were alternately hostile and friendly. During the first quarter of the nineteenth century, or while the Cheyenne were visiting the Upper Missouri River village trading centers the Cheyenne and Sioux were rare-ly on friendly terms. Jablow in his study of Plains Indian trade relations tells us that, " in their [Dakota Sioux] attempt to monopolize the production of the Arikara, the Teton Sioux came into opposition with the nomadic tribes west of the Missouri, especially the Cheyenne" (Jablow, 1951, 56). Trudeau, while among the Arikara, mentions trying to "maintain peace with the Cheyennes and the village of the Sioux settle here, who are at variance with one another" (Trudeau, 1914, 470). Le Raye who arrived at the mouth of the Cheyenne River in 1802, wrote that "... on the headwaters reside several tribes of Indians, with which the Sioux are at war, the most powerful of these tribes are the Chien, or Dog Indians" (Le Raye in Cutler, 1812, 171).

Tabeau stated that the Cheyenne and Sioux "live in mutual fear of treachery and always, potentially, in a state of war" (Tabeau in Abel, 1939, 152). Lewis and Clark write that the Cheyenne "...confess to be at war with no nation except the Sieoux..." (Lewis and Clark in Thwaites, Vol. 5, 1914, 357).

Freed from competition for the production of the settled Upper Missouri Villages and for the trade goods that found its way there, Cheyenne-Sioux antagonisms diminished somewhat. Although it has been stated that it was pres-sure from the westward moving Sioux which forced the Cheyenne west and then south, an inference which would indicate that hostile relations between the two tribes continued, yet according to Hyde and Ewers the Teton and Cheyenne combined on an attack against the Crow in the early 1820's, thus indicating that at times they acted in concert. Furthermore, acc.rding to Hyde various Oglala bands, during the first quarter of the nineteenth century, were encamped in the Black Hills in friendly association with the Cheyenne. In addition, I have indicated above that the presence of the Sioux was not the single cause for the southward drift of the Cheyenne.

There is no doubt but that following the 1830's, so slightly earlier, some Sioux bands were to be found as far south as the Platte river and west to the Rockies, sharing this country with the Cheyenne and Arapaho and often acting in close association with them. Evidence to this effect will be brought out subsequently.

Following the separation of the Cheyenne into Northern and Southern division, the available data refers only to the Southern Cheyenne. The Northern Cheyenne appear to retain, along with some bands of the Sioux, a share in the territory extending from the forks of Cheyenne river and the Black Hills west to the Yellowstone and southward to the North Platte on the eastern side of the Rocky Mountains.

According to Grinnell's old Southern Cheyenne informants much is heard about the wars with the Kiowa and Comanche "but all this fighting seems to have taken place in the southern country, where about 1835 the Arkansas River separated the range of the Cheyenne and Arapahoes from that of the allied Kiowas, Comanches and Prairie Apaches, who roamed in the country south of that river and toward Texas" (Grinnell, 1915, 34). "During the early thirties", Grinnell continues, "none of these tribes appear to have considered the valley of the Arkansas its home. The river and its valley was a danger zone constantly being crossed by war parties. At that period the Southern Cheyennes were newcomers in the southern country which lay between the South Platte and the Arkansas, and they did not often move their camps down to the Arkansas until after the completion of Bent's Fort" (Grinnell, 1923a, 68-69).

65

On Catlin's map, 1832-1840, the region between the Arkansas and the Platte is called "Hostile Ground", thus agreeing substantially with Grinnell's information (Catlin, Vol. 1, 1876, frontspiece).

The establishment of Bent's Fort on the Arkansas in the early part of the 1830's led to the congregation around that Fort of large numbers of Cheyenne and Arapaho, many of the former tribe having only recently migrated to the southern plains. The pressure of increased numbers on Cheyenne and Arapaho in the southern region soon led to the expulsion of the Kiowa, Comanche and Kiowa-Apache groups south of the Arkansas. Farnham states that Bent's Fort was erected"...for purposes of trade with the Spaniards of Santa Fe and Taos, and the Eutaw, Cheyenne and Cumanche Indians" (Farnham in Thwaites, Vol. 28, 1906, 161). As regards trade with the Comanche with the Bents, we are told by Grinnell that "Adobe Fort was built on the South Canadian (south of the Arkansas), at the request of the chiefs of the Kiowas, Comanches and Apaches. Before peace was made between these tribes and the Cheyenne and Arapahoes, in 1840, the three tribes that lived south of the Arkansas were usually afraid to visit Bent's Fort to trade, lest they should there meet a large camp of their enemies" (Grinnell, 1923a, 42). From this statement it seems clear that the Kiowa, Comanche and Apache were pretty effectively contained below the Arkansas river after the arrival of the Cheyenne in the southern plains.

Following 1835 or thereabouts, even though the Kiowa, Comanche and Apache bands were pretty effectively contained south of the Arkansas we should not fall heir to the mistaken notion that the entire area between the South Platte and the Arkansas on the north-south axis and the region between the Rockies and the forks of the Platte on the east-west axis was occupied exclusively by the Cheyenne and Arapaho. The description of this territory provided by Colonel Henry Dodge, who, in 1835 conducted a party of Dragoons to the Rocky Mountains should prove instructive in dispelling this notion. I am including a rather lengthy quotation from his report at this time, for besides telling us much of the Indian occupation of this region he also provides us with an excellent description of its geography. On July 6, 1835, while proceeding southwest from the forks of the Platte, Colonel Dodge wrote:

> The country...began to assume a differnt character. We had heretofore been marching through a level and fertile valley, terminated by hills alternating from high to low, with a sufficient quantity of wood for fuel. The elements of the scene now were of an unbounded prairie, a broad river, with innumerable herds of buffalo grazing upon its banks, and occasionally a solitary tree... Saw, also, great numbers of antelopes and some deer. The soil was of coarse, dry sand or gravel. The grass short, thick and dry. No timber...This section of country is what is called the neutral ground. It extends from the forks of the Platte almost to the foot of the Mountains [Rocky] . It will not admit the permanent residence of any Indians, and is only frequented by the war parties of different nations. The Arapahoes and Cheyennes sometimes move into this country for a short time during the summer to hunt buffalo.

> ...visited the Fontaine que Bouille...a mineral spring near the foot of Pike's Peak...Rio Salard, a large valley in the mountains, where the Arapahoes frequently pitch their lodges and remain encamped for a considerable length of time during the summer.

> The whole route from the Platte to the Arkansas is frequented by large parties of the Blackfeet, Crows, Snakes, and sometimes the Eutaus, who live upon the waters of the Rio del Norte, but frequently come over through the mountain passes to steal horsed from the Arapahoes and Cheyennes.

> ...left the valley of the Fontaine que Bouille and crossed the dividing ridge between that and the Arkansas. Encamped on the Arkansas. Shortly...we were visited by three Arapahoes; they informed us that there were 50 lodges on the opposite side of the river; that the remainder of the nation, with a large number of Cheyennes, were hunting buffalo about two day's ride from there, between the Platte and the Arkansas.

66

> The Cheyennes formerly lived on the Missouri river...
> They left that country shortly after [1825] and came to
> the south fork of the Platte, and have since been living
> with the Arapahoes...There is now about 220 lodges, 660
> men or 2,640 souls in all. They range between the Platte
> and the Arkansas near the mountain.
>
> Of the Arapahoes there are about 360 lodges, 1,080
> men or 3,600 souls in all. They range with the Cheyennes
> the Platte and the Arkansas.
>
> The Gros Ventres of Fort du Prairie, now living
> with the Arapahoes, are a band Blackfeet. There are about
> 350 of them living with the Arapahoes. 700 lodges came to
> the Arkansas in the summer of 1824 and returned in 1832,
> and are expected again on the Platte and Arkansas in
> September 1835. There is also a small band of the Black-
> feet proper, consisting of about 50, who live with the
> Cheyennes and Arapahoes. A band of Kiowa, called the
> Upper band, consisting of 1,800 or 2,000, and another
> who are called Appaches of the plains, consisting of
> about 1,200, also frequent the Arkansas and the Platte,
> near the mountains for the purpose of killing buffalo...
> (Dodge, 1835, 139-141).

As shown by Dodge's quote, although the region between the Platte and th[e] Arkansas was frequented by many tribes, it does, however, appear that these
tribes only made partial use of it insofar as only segments of the total trib[e]
frequented the area. As far as the Cheyenne and Arapaho are concerned population statistics indicate that the bulk of the population of these two
tribes was concentrated in this region. Other tribes, although sharing in the
area, nevertheless, had additional ranges or other subsistence areas also
located elsewhere. This is particularly true of the Utes, Blackfeet and Gros
Ventres whose main habitat existed to the west and north of this region.

In the years 1841-42 Rufas Sage visisted the Platte river and wrote:

> It [Fort Platte] is situated in the immediate vicinity
> of the Oglallia and Brule divisions of the Sioux nation,
> and but little remote from the Cheyennes and Arapaho
> tribes (Sage, 1860, 96).

Fort Platte was situated next to Fort Hall which occupied the left bank
of the North fork of the Platte about three-fourths of a mile above the mouth
of the Laramie river. If our inference is correct that the Platte river was
the dividing line between the northern and southern divisions of the Cheyenne
and Arapaho, then Sage was referring to the Northern Cheyenne and Arapaho who
shared their country, or parts of it, with some Sioux bands. Some bands of
the Sioux were also found in company with the Southern Cheyenne and Arapaho.
Along Beaver creek, an affluent of the South Platte in Colorado, Sage came

67

across "six or seven hundred lodges of Arapahoes, Cheyennes, and Sioux, encamped in a large valley...This village, being prepared to move, in a few
moments succeeding our arrival, was enroute for the Platte river" (Sage, 1860,
338).

The increased number of Sioux found in company with the Southern Cheyenne
and Arapaho followed the General Cheyenne-Sioux alliance of 1840. Fremont,
1842-1844, also noted the presence of large bodies of Sioux associated with
the Cheyenne and Arapaho.

> On the 1st of July (1844) we arrived at Bent's Fort. On
> the 5th we resumed our journey down the Arkansas...and
> encamped about 20 miles below the fort. On the way we
> met a large village of Sioux and Cheyenne Indians, who,
> with the Arapahoes were returning from the crossing of
> the Arkansas, where they had been to meet the Kioway
> and Comanche Indians (Fremont, 1854, 422).

Nor did the Cheyenne and Arapaho always confine themselves to the region
between the Platte and the Arkansas. In connection with the Sioux, or others,
they frequently crossed the Rockies in order to attack and carry out raids
upon the Indians living on the other side of the mountains. Fremont in 1841
wrote:

> ...the Gros Ventre Indians had united with the Oglallalas
> and Cheyennes, and taken the field in great force...,to
> the amount of eight hundred lodges. Their object was to
> make an attack on a camp of Snake and Crow Indians, and a
> body of about one hundred whites, who had made a rendez-
> vous somewhere in the Green river valley, or on the
> Sweet Water. After spending some time in buffalo hunting
> in the neighborhood of the Medicine Bow mountain, they
> were to cross over to the Green river waters, and return
> to Laramie by way of the South Pass and the Sweet Water
> valley (Fremont, 1854, 57).

In another place Fremont describes how the conditions of the natural
environment determined their movements and their choice of hunting areas.

> We continued our way, and four miles beyond the ford
> Indians were discovered again;...In a short time
> they returned, accompanied by a number of Indians of
> the Oglallah band of Sioux...They had formed part of
> the great village, which they informed us had broken
> up, and was on its way home. The greater part of the
> village, including the Arapahoes, Cheyennes, and
> Oglallahs, had crossed the Platte eight or ten miles
> below the mouth of the Sweet Water, and were now
> behind the mountains to the south of us, intending
> to regain the Platte by way of Deer Creek. They had
> taken this unusual route in search of grass and game.
> They gave us a very discouraging picture of the

68

country. The great drought, and the plague of grasshop-
pers, had swept it so that scarce a blade of grass was to
be seen, and there was not a buffalo to be found in the
whole region (Fremont, 1854, 76).

The "parks" within the mountains were well supplied with buffalo and other
game and were frequented by the Cheyenne and Arapaho as well as by tribes from
the other side of the mountains. These "parks" constituted a well-known war-
ground between tribes from both sides. Fremont writes:

The country...called Old Park, in which is formed Grand
River, one of the principal branches of the Colorado of
California. We are now moving with some caution, as from
the trail, we found the Arapahoe village had also passed
this way; as we were coming out of their enemy's country,
and this was a war-ground.
    Our scouts...made from a butte this morning the sig-
nal of Indians and we rode up in time to meet a party of
about 30 Arapahoes. They were men and women going into
the hills - the men for game, the women for roots - and
informed us that the village was encamped a few miles
above, on the main fork of Grand river;...Knowing that we
had trouble to expect, I descended immediately to the
bottoms of Grand River...We had scarcely made our few
preparations, when about 200 of them appeared...armed
for war. About 20 Sioux were with them (Fremont, 1854,
414-15).

And again,

[June 20, 1844] We saw today the returning trail of an
Arapaho party which had been sent from the village
[described above] to look for Utahs in the Bayou Salade
[South Park] (Fremont, 1854, 416).

On the east the Southern Cheyenne and Arapaho ranged indefinitely towards
the region between the forks of the Platte river and the Arkansas. During the
1800's the range of the great bison herds was in the short-grass plains
generally west of the 100 meridian (Wedel, 1953, 501-02). The eastward range
of the Cheyenne and Arapaho merged imperceptibly into the western range of the
Pawnee (Wedel, 1936, 4).

Although the Cheyenne on occasion raided into country claimed by the Pawnee
on the east (see Grinnell's account of warfare between these two tribes in about
the late 1830's at which time the Pawnee are alleged to have captured the
Cheyenne medicine arrows, Grinnell, AA:12, no. 4, 1910, 550-561), we have seen
that on most occasions they kept closer to the Rock Mountains, the region
further to the east not being suitable for permanent occupation.

69

CHAPTER VII--MOVEMENTS AND AREA OF OCCUPATION
OF THE ARAPAHO

Very little is known of the early history of the Arapaho prior to the beginning of the 19th century. According to a few meager traditions the Arapaho are believed to have once lived in Minnesota where they raised corn. From this country it is believed that they moved westward perhaps in the company of the Cheyenne who, at that time, are alleged to have been living on the Cheyenne fork of Red River (Mooney, 1892-93, 954; Clark, W.P., 1885, 39-40). Outside of these legends a northeasterly point of origin is assumed for the Arapaho based on the fact that they speak an Algonkian dialect. Additionally, their close association with the Cheyenne while on the great plains during the 19th century raises the possibility of earlier historical connections. These points, however, regarding the early home and subsequent migrations of the Arapaho cannot be verified historically or archaeologically as no Arapaho archaeology has as yet been turned up and in the scant early historical references to the Cheyenne east of the Missouri river there exists no mention of the Arapaho whatsoever.

The absence of any early reference to the Arapaho in the early historical literature may be due either to the fact that they migrated westward well in advance of the Cheyenne, or else that in their westward movement they took a more northerly route and hence escaped detection. The latter of these two assumptions receives some additional support when once the relationship between the Arapaho and the Atsina or Gros Ventres of the Prairie is examined. It is held that at one time the Gros Ventres, also known variously as Atsina, Paunche, Big Belly, Fall or Rapid Indians and whose home, during the 19th century, bordered about the Red and Sasketchewan rivers of Canada, were once part of the Arapaho tribe from whom they became detached at an early date, possibly while moving westward (Curtis, Vol. 6, 1911, 137; Tyrell, 1916, 304; Gallatin, Vol. II, 1836, 132). Curtis believes that the Gros Ventres were originally one of the northern bands of the Arapaho who, after that tribe crossed the Missouri, pushed northwestward beyond the South Sasketchewan while the remainder of the tribe moved in a generally southward direction (Curtis, Vol. 6, 1911, 138).

If the assumption is correct that the Atsina were historically a part of the Arapaho tribe and moved westward with them, then the Arapaho must have been west of the Missouri river prior to the beginning of the 19th century. Mackenzie, 1789-1793, writes that "Next to [the Blackfeet], and [extending] to the confluence of the South and North branches [of the Sasketchewan] are the Fall, or Big-bellied Indians [Atsina], who may amount to about 600 warriors" (Mackenzie, 1802, 87). Umfreville, 1790, speaks of them as follows:

> This nation [Atsina] is thus named by us, and by the Nehethawa Indians from their inhabiting a country on the Southern branch of the river [Sasketchewan], where the rapids are frequent.

In this people another instance occurs of the impropriety with which the Canadian-French name the Indians. They call them gros ventres, or big-bellies,...(Umfreville, 1790, 197).

By 1796 the Arapaho (called Tokaninambick in this instance) are located by Collot on the south branch of Cheyenne River, the Pitapahabe Nation (?) are on the north branch while the Chaguine (Cheyenne) are at the forks of the river (Collot's map, reprinted in Wedel's Introduction to Pawnee Archaeology (Wedel, 1936, map 6).

Alexander Henry, 1799-1814, distinguishes between the Gros Ventres of the Prairie, or Atsina, whom he calls "Rapid Indians" or "Big Bellies"[1], and of whom he says "are now stationed South of the Slaves, between the South Branch [of the Sasketchewan] and the Missourie", and, who "formerly inhabited the point of land between the North and South branches of the Sasketchewan to the junction of these two streams..." (Henry in Coues, Vol. 1, 1897, 530), and the "Buffalo Indians", or, as some call them, the Caveninavish tribe [Arapaho]", who, in the company of the Cheyenne "make their annual hunts of bear and beaver...near the source of...two rivers [North Platte and either the Rio Grande or the South Platte]"[2]. The Arapaho, Henry continues, "consist of about 500 tents" (Henry in Coues, Vol. 1, 1897, 384). Thus, by 1796 the Arapaho are known to have been residing on the South fork of the Cheyenne river and by 1799 hunting as far south as the Platte.

Although the Atsina principally made their home, during the 18th and 19th centuries, along the Red river of Canada and between the branches of the Sasketchewan and extending as far south as the Upper Missouri, Milk and Yellowstone rivers (Hayden, 1862, 321; Hewes, 1948, 5; Henry in Coues, Vol. 1, 1897, 530), they periodically traveled south to the Platte and Arkansas rivers where they spent a number of years in the company of the Arapaho, only, in time, to return to their own country in the north. Colonel Henry Dodge, 1835, tells us that "The Gros Ventres of Fort du Prairie Atsina, now living with the Arapaho, are a band of Blackfeet.[3] There are now about 350 of them living with the Arapahos. 700 lodges came to the Arkansas in the summer of 1824 and returned in 1832, and are expected again on the Platte and Arkansas in September 1835" (Dodge, 1835, 140-141). Dodge also speaks of the Blackfeet proper, thus distinguishing between them and the Gros Ventre.

---

[1] Not to be confused with the Hidatsa who are variously referred to as Gros Ventres, Big Belly or Minnetaree, etc. See ed. note #43, p. 322 and ed. note #6, p. 530, Henry in Coues, Vol. 1, 1897. Mooney says that Gros Ventres signify "belly-people" and that the Arapaho division of that name are the Gros Ventre of the Prairie", while the Hidatsa or Minnitaree with whom Lewis and Clark wintered are sometimes called "Gros Ventre of the Missouri". (Mooney, 1892-93, 955).

[2] See page 52 of previous chapter for a reinterpretation of the second of the two rivers mentioned by Henry.

[3] The Atsina were often thought of as being Blackfeet since they shared a common territory and were frequently found camping and hunting in close proximity.

The scant treatment afforded the Arapaho in the historical literature covering the period of the first, and the early part of the second decades of the 19th century, makes for considerable difficulty in determing their area of habitation at this time. At best, information concerning the movements and area of occupation of the Arapaho at this period can be found only by following up data on the Cheyenne who, at this time, were competing with the Sioux for the Upper Missouri village trade. Active trade relations between the Cheyenne and the Upper Missouri village tribes goes, at least, as far back as 1793-94. Jablow in his excellent study of Cheyenne trade relations writes that "Even before the arrival of Trudeau among the Arikara (1795), in whose vicinity he met and traded with the Cheyenne, there had been White traders who mention only the Cheyenne in connection with the Upper Missouri villages. One of them had spent the entire winter of 1793-94 among them and said they were situated below the Pawnee Hoca (Arikara?) on the Missouri" (Jablow, 1952, 42). The importance of the Cheyenne as an instrument for establishing trade relations with the other western nomadic tribes, implying a priority for the Cheyenne in Upper Missouri tribal relations, was recognized by Trudeau himself when he wrote that

> On the Southwest and to the West, on the branches of a
> large river (which I name the river of the Cheyennes) which
> empties into the Missouri about three miles above the
> second Ricara village (of the two Arikara villages near
> the Grand River) are situated several nations called the
> Cayoguas (Kiowas), the Caminabiches (Arapahos), the Pita-
> pahotas (Noisy Pawnees?), etc., all of different speech.
> The Cheyennes wander over the country along the river, a
> little below those first named...The vast country, not far
> from here, over which these different nations roam, abounds
> in beaver and otter, since they have never hunted these
> animals, not having had any intercourse with the White men.
> It would be easy by means of the Cheyennes, who are their
> friends, to extend our commerce with these nations and ob-
> tain from them fine furs (Trudeau in Jablow, 1952, 43).

72

According to Trudeau in 1795 bands of Arapaho, Kiowa and Pawnee (?) were located along the branches of the Cheyenne river a little above the Cheyenne tribe. The Cheyenne, but not the Arapaho, were engaged in trade relations with the Upper Missouri villages at this time. According to Tabeau it is not until 1803-1805 that the Arapaho begin to take part in the Upper Missouri village tribe.

> ...the Cheyenne nation has only a half-knowledge of the
> value of merchandise and prides itself, none the less, on
> being ignorant in this respect. This vain-glory has been
> conducive to my detriment in the slight trade of the
> Caninanbiches [Arapaho] and others who obstinately defer to
> its judgement. However it may be, it is certain that, if it
> had not been for the interference of the Cheyennes, I should
> have made better use of the nations who accompanied them
> this year for the first time in their visit to the Ricaras
> (Tabeau in Abel, 1939, 153. Emphasis added).

Although the testimony of Trudeau and Le Raye (1802) who writes that "On the headwaters [of the Cheyenne river] reside several tribes of Indians...The most powerful [of which] are the Chien, or Dog Indians. There are also the Gensdi-rach, or Kananawesh [Arapaho], the Kites [Crow?], and Dotame [a small band allied with the Kiowa], besides bands of the Mahas [Omaha], Poncars [Ponca], and Kataka [Kiowa-Apache]" (Le Raye, 1908, 159), locates the Arapaho and others along the Cheyenne river in the early years of the first decade of the 19th century, the information provided by Perrin du Lac (1801-03), Lewis and Clark (1806) and Henry (1799-1814) tells us that the Arapaho were not confined to this region and that they roamed as far south as the Platte river. The testimony of Henry has already been referred to. Perrin du Lac who visited the Cheyenne during the years 1801-02 writes:

> The Chaguyennes...[wander] on both... banks[of the Cheyenne river] in pursuit of buffalo... Not content with hunting on the banks of this river, they pass onto the[immense savannahs near the Plate River...Many other wandering nations that are allied to the Chaguyennes, hunt in the same country. They are the Cayowas [Kiowa], the Tocaninambiches [Arapaho], the Tokiouskos (?), the Pitapahatos [Pawnee?] (Perrin du Lac, 1807, 62-63).

In their Journals, Lewis and Clark make reference to the Arapaho by two different terms: Ca-ne-na-vich and Sta-e-tan. In the printed Statistical View data for these two groups are given separately: 150 lodges, 400 warriors, and 1,500 people are assigned to the Canenavish branch; and 40 lodges, 100 warriors, and 400 people to the Staetan; otherwise there is no additional information (Lewis and Clark in Thwaites, Vol. 6, 1905, editorial note #1, 101). On the same page in their Journals Lewis and Clark tell us that these two tribes are known among the Canadian traders as Kite Indians. The water courses on which they are supposed to be found is given as the head of the River Loup, otherwise known as Wolf River, a northwest branch of the Platte running to the southwest of the Black Hills. Lewis and Clark further remark that "no limits can be described for any of the Nations and tribes in this quarter as war with their neighbors frequently happen which force one party to remove a considerable distance from the others, untill peace is restored, at which period all lands are Generally in common, yet it is not common for two tribes to camp to gether for any long time or hunt in the Same place" (Lewis and Clark in Thwaites, Vol. 6, 1905, 101).

Although the Arapaho began to participate in the Upper Missouri village trade between 1803 and 1805 there is no evidence to indicate that they ever participated in it on a large scale. The few references which mention the Arapaho in this connection indicate, that at best, only a small number traveled to the Arikara village for trading purposes and then always in the company of the Cheyenne. Alexander Henry, while he was at the Arikara village in 1806, noted a camp of 120 lodges of western nomadic Indians nearby waiting to trade. This camp, he writes, "was composed of both of these nations [Cheyenne and Sioux], and a few Buffalo Indians [Arapaho]" (Henry in Coues, Vol. 1, 1897, 377).

The relative lateness with which the Arapaho make their appearance at the Upper Missouri village trading centers; the fact that most accounts fail to mention the Arapaho and then only to record that a few were present accompanied by many Cheyenne; plus the fact that Perrin du Lac, Lewis and Clark and Alexander Henry refer to the Arapaho as hunting as far south as the Platte may indicate that a small portion of the Arapaho tribe moved north especially to take advantage of the Upper Missouri village trade where articles of European manufacture could be obtained. It is possible that the Cheyenne encouraged them to do so in order that their presence might strengthen the Cheyenne hand in their competition with the Sioux. Since these trade sessions were generally carried out at the beginning of August (Tabeau in Abel, 1939, 153), it is possible that small parties of Arapaho came north during the summer months in order to hunt and trade only to return south once the summer was over. The other possibility, of course, is that during the first and early part of the second decades of the 19th century a small part of the Arapaho tribe lived along the South fork of Cheyenne river and beyond to the Black Hills sharing this area with other tribes; another, and larger section, lived and roamed further to the south in the vicinity of the Platte river.

As has been already pointed out during the first two decades of the 19th century there exists scant reference to the Arapaho in the historical literature. Thwaites in an editorial note to Bradbury (1809-1811) states that

> The Arapaho occupied the central mountainous region, roaming through Wyoming and Southern Idaho. They traded with the Spaniards, and supplied their kindred the Cheyenne with Spanish horses (ed. note 120. Bradbury in Thwaites, Vol. 5, 1904, 225).

The reference to the Arapaho in Wyoming and Southern Idaho at this early date is difficult to deal with. It is entirely possible that the Arapaho here are confused with another group as there is no corroborating evidence that the Arapaho ever ranged that far west. Further, during this early period when the Arapaho and some of the other western tribes were not too well known sometimes the same term might erroneously be used for a number of different tribes or one particular group of people might be variously known by a number of different names. In this connection we might point out that in the Report from the Sec'y, 1829, six tribes are mentioned as occupying "the country east of the Rocky Mountains, on the heads of the Yellowstone, Platte, Arkansas, and Rio de Norte". The six tribes mentioned in this report are: "Arripahas", "Kaninahoieh", "Kaskaias", "Kawas", "Staitans or Kite Indians", and "Padoucas, proper" (Senate Executive Doc., no. 72, 1829, 104). In this report the term "Kaninahoich", which is a variant of one of the popular early terms for the Arapaho is reserved for a group other than the Arapaho. That this group might be the Atsina is adduced from the date of the report, as we know from previous sources that the Atsina were camping with the Arapaho in the southern plains at about this time. A more obvious instance in which the Atsina are erroneously referred to as Arapaho is provided by Indian Agent Graham. In 1824 Graham writes that the "Arrepahas, who inhabit the country south of the Yellowstone [are] a tribe of the Blackfeet Indians; making their range...along the base of the Rocky Mountains from the Rio del Norte to the Saska-tehewine" (Graham, 1834, 451). We know from other sources that it was the Atsina and not the Arapaho who were

in alliance with the Blackfeet. We might suggest here that wherever, in the
early part of the 19th century, reference is made to the effect that the
Arapaho occupied the region on the western side of the Rocky Mountains in
central Wyoming, Idaho, Montana or northward the citation should be read as
probably referring to the Atsina.

It is not until 1816 that we get out next reference to the Arapaho at
which time they appear to have been ranging along the eastern slopes of the
Rocky Mountains near the sources of the Platte, Arkansas and Red [Candian]
rivers; an area they shared with a number of other tribes. In 1820 James wrote
that

> These nations [Kiawas, Badhearts, Shiennes and Arrapahoes]
> have been for the past three years wandering on the head-
> waters and tributaries of Red river, having returned to the
> Arkansa only the day which preceded our first interview
> with them, on their way to the mountains at the sources of
> the Platte river. They have no permanent town, but con-
> stantly rove, as necessity urges them...in the vicinity of
> the sources of the Platte, Arkansas, and Red rivers (James
> in Thwaites, Vol. 16, 1905, 211).

From about 1816 until the arrival of the Cheyenne in the southern plains
in great numbers the Arapaho appear to have been on friendly terms with the
Kiowa and Badhearts [Comanche?] with whom they shared this southern region.
According to James these southern tribes met on the South Platte in order to
trade with the Cheyenne who brought down goods obtained on the Missouri in
exchange for horses. When in July, 1820, Long's party was in the vicinity of
Denver, near Cherry Creek, a tributary of the South Platte, James wrote that

> About four years previous (circa 1816) to the time of our
> visit, there had been a large encampment of Indians and
> hunters on this creek. On that occasion, three nations of
> Indians, namely, the Kiowas, Arrapahoes, and Kaskaias, or
> Badhearts (?), had been assembled together, with forty-
> five French hunters in the employ of Mr. Choteau and Mr.
> Demun of St. Louis. They had assembled for the purpose of
> holding a trading council with a band of Shiennes. These
> last had been recently supplied with goods by the British
> traders on the Missouri, and had come to exchange them with
> the former for horses. The Kiawas, Arrapahoes, etc., who
> wander in the fertile plains of the Arkansas and Red river,
> have always great numbers of horses, which they rear with
> much less difficulty than the Shiennes, whose country is
> cold and barren (James in Thwaites, Vol. 15, 1906, 282).

James also implies that the meetings of the southern nomadic tribes for
trading purposes were periodic affairs when he states that the Arapaho,
Kaskaias, Kiowa, Comanche and Cheyenne "at distant periods, held a kind of
fair on a tributary of the Platte, near the mountains (hence called Grand Camp
Creek), at which time they obtained British merchandise from the Shiennes of
Shienne River, who obtained the same at the Mandan village from the British
traders..." (James in Thwaites, Vol. 17, 1906, 156).

Following the arrival of the Cheyenne in the southern plains and the building of the Bent's Fort friendly relations between the Arapaho on the one hand and the Kiowa, Comanche and Apache groups on the other gave way to enmity as the two sets of tribes competed for the Bent's Fort trade. In this struggle the Cheyenne and Arapaho were victorious and the Kiowa, Comanche and Apache groups were driven south divided from the former tribes and Bent's Fort by the Upper Arkansas river. Accordingly Grinnell writes:

> At the time of the building of Bent's Fort (completed in 1832), the upper Arkansas river was not only the boundary between the United States and Mexico, but was also the dividing line between two hostile groups of plains tribes. To the south of the river lived the Kiowas, Comanches and Prairie Apaches; to the north were the Southern Cheyennes and Arapahoes; and for many years these two groups were actively at war with each other (Grinnell, 1923a, 68)

Although the Cheyenne and Arapaho dominated the Bent's Fort trade, Grinnell goes on to say, however, that:

> William Bent and the traders were naturally especially anxious that there should be no collisions near the Fort. Each tribe would expect the trader to take its parts, and this could not be done without incurring the enmity of the other tribes. The trader wished to be on good terms with all, and this William Bent accomplished with singular discretion. Although he had a Cheyenne wife, he was on excellent terms, and always remained so, with the enemies of the Cheyennes (Grinnell, 1923a, 42).

Nevertheless, according to Jablow, "although the Bent's succeeded in maintaining the friendship of both sides, in actual practice it was the Cheyenne who were in possession, so to speak, whereas the Kiowa or Comanche might pay fleeting visits to the fort in small parties when the Cheyenne were not around. Large scale Indian trading at the fort took place chiefly with the Cheyenne and Arapaho" (Jablow, 1951, 66).

Until peace was made between the Cheyenne and Arapaho and the tribes south of the Arkansas in 1840 the Arkansas river and its valley in the vicinity of Bent's Fort and the mountains was a danger zone constantly being crossed by war parties from both sides. During this period, according to Grinnell, "The Southern Arapahoes ranged more or less with the Cheyennes, but seem to have kept nearer the mountains..." (Grinnell, 1923a, 69).

The region between the Platte and the Arkansas was visted by Colonel Dodge in 1835 while leading a party of Dragoons to the Rocky Mountains. We have previously quoted extensively from Dodge in an effort to show that this region far from being occupied by the Cheyenne and Arapaho alone, was fequented by other tribes as well. However, there remains a few points observed by Dodge which are germaine to this study and which have not been previously mentioned. On Dodge's map of this region (Dodge, 1861, 130) he locates the Comanche and Kiowa groups south of the Arkansas. Between the Arkansas and the South Platte Dodge places the Cheyenne and the Gros Ventre of the Prairie; the latter appearing just north of the Cheyenne. It is obvious from the discussion which follows that the Gros Ventres of the Prairie are the Arapaho as the latter term appears in the text while the former appears on the map. This is important as we have previously pointed out that the two terms were often used interchangeably. Further in the discussion Dodge distinguishes between the Arapaho and the "Gros Ventres of Fort du Prairie", a band of Blackfeet temporarily living with the Arapaho. These are the Atsina whom we have referred to before (Dodge, 1861, 140-141).

Although population estimates must be accepted judiciously, especially in regard to the Plains Indians, if Dodge's figures of the Cheyenne and Arapaho population is anywhere near accurate, then it must be inferred, in the light of other population figures, that, during the 1830's the bulk of the Cheyenne and Arapaho were inhabiting the region between the Platte and the Arkansas. Of the Cheyenne, Dodge says "There is not about 220 lodges, 660 men or 2,640 in all". Of the Arapaho, he tells us that "there are about 360 lodges, 1,080 men, or 3,600 souls in all" (Dodge, 1861, 140). These estimates agree substantially with the figures provided by Lewis and Clark and Culbertson. Lewis and Clark estimated that each lodge contained 11 persons of whom 3 could be reckoned as warriors. Culbertson placed the figure at about 10 persons per lodge.

This inference that the bulk of the Cheyenne and Arapaho were, during the 1830's, living between the South Platte and the Arkansas with a few remaining camps north of the South Platte, more particularly between the North and South Platte is supported by Hyde's interpretation of tribal occupation at this time. Hyde writes:

77

> The lands along the Upper [North] Platte which the Oglalas had occupied (the Oglalas in 1834 were suddenly uprooted and taken from their old home in the Black Hills country to a new land on the North Platte - due to the establishment of a trading post there by Kiplin and Sabille of the Rocky Mt. Company) were claimed by the Cheyennes and Arapahoes. Many of the bands of these two tribes had gone down to the Arkansas to live; but there were still several of their camps in the Platte country, and even as late as 1865 the district between the forks of the Platte was known as Cheyenne and Arapaho territory though the Oglalas had long been in full possession (Hyde, 1937, 46).

According to Dodge, the Cheyenne and Arapaho, during the summer, hunted in the region called "nuetral ground", that is, the area which "extends from the forks of the Platte almost to the foot of the mountains" on the east-west axis and between the Platte and the Arkansas on the north-south axis (Dodge, 1861, 138). This region was also inhabited by other tribes as well. Dodge writes:

> The Gros Ventres of Fort du Prairie [Atsina], now living with the Arapahos, are a band of Blackfeet. There are now about 350 of them living with the Arapahos. 700 lodges came to the Arkansas in the summer of 1824 and returned in 1832, and are expected again on the Platte and Arkansas in September 1835. There is also a small band of the

Blackfeet proper, consisting of about 50, who live with the
Cheyenne and Arapahoes. A band of Kiowa, called the Upper
band, consisting of 1,800 or 2,000, and another who are
called Appaches of the plains, consisting of about 1,200,
also frequent this portion of the country. All of these
Indians frequent the Arkansas and the Platte, near the
mountains for the purpose of killing buffalo... (Dodge,
1861, 140-141).

Another favorite summer hunting and camping area of the Arapaho, according
to Dodge, was in the valley of "the Fontaine que Bouille...a mineral spring
near the foot of Pike's Peak" and the "Rio Salard, a large valley in the mountains, where the Arapahas frequently pitch their lodges and remain encamped for
a considerable length of time during the summer" (Dodge, 1861, 139). This area
is known today as "South Park" at the headwaters of the South Platte. Also
known in the literature as "Bayou Salade". Dodge informs us that the Arapaho
were not the only people who frequented these mountains without, however, spec-
ifying who the other tribes were.

> The valley of the Fontaine que Bouille is very much fre-
> quented by the Indians, especially the Arepahas, who come up
> here in the fall to gather the wild fruit that grows in abun-
> dance near the base of the mountains (Dodge, 1861, 140).

Rufus Sage who visited with the Cheyenne in the 1840's tells us that Fort
Platte which "occupies the left bank of the North Fork of Platte river, 3/4 of
a mile above the mouth of Laramie" in eastern Wyoming "...is situated in the
immediate vicinity of the Oglallia and Brule divisions of the Sioux nations,
and but little remote from the Cheyenne and Arapaho tribes" (Sage, 1860, 96).
Sage is undoubtedly referring to the Northern Cheyenne and Arapaho who ranged
between the forks of the Platte along with some of the Sioux. This confirms
Grinnell's statement that the forts built among the Northern Platte, ie., Fort
Platte, Fort Hall, Fort St. Vrain, etc., "were intended for the trade of the
northern Indians; that is, for the Sioux and the northern bands of Cheyenne
and Arapaho, who seldom got down as far as the Arkansas river and so did...much
of their trading...on the [North] Platte" (Grinnell, 1923a, 31).

Further along we learn from Sage that the Medicine Bow range was the western boundary of the Sioux, Cheyenne and Arapaho bands living in the Northern
Plains.

> Continuing up the right bank of the creek (which I have
> named Medicine Bow...) and travelling by easy stages four
> successive days, we arrived at its head, - a distance of
> more than 50 miles above its junction with the Platte.
> On the right lay a broad expanse of undulating prai-
> rie...and in front, the lofty peaks of Medicine Bow...
> This section of country, being the great war-ground be-
> tween the Sioux and Cheyennes on the one side, and the
> Snakes and Crows on the other, is considered dangerous,
> particularly from May till November of each year (Sage,
> 1860, 169).

The fact that the Arapaho are not mentioned in this connection may be due
to an oversight on the part of Sage for they are so mentioned by Fremont in
August, 1841 when he wrote that:

> ...the Gros Ventre Indians [Arapaho] had united with the
> Oglallahas and Cheyennes, and taken the field in great
> force - so far as I could ascertain, to the amount of
> eight hundred lodges. Their object was to make an attack
> on a camp of Snake and Crow Indians, and a body of about
> one hundred whites, who had made a rendezvous somewhere in
> the Green river valley, or on the Sweet Water. After spend-
> ing some time in buffalo hunting in the neighborhood of the
> Medicine Bow mountain, they were to cross over to the Green
> river waters, and return to Laramie by way of the South Pass
> and the Sweet Water valley (Fremont, 1854, 57).

In view of the size of the raiding force estimated by Fremont - eight
hundred lodges - one of two conclusions are in order. Either the force was
predominantly composed of Sioux, or else they were joined by southern bands,
for from what we know of the distribution of the Cheyenne and Arapaho population it is doubtful whether there were that many Cheyenne and Arapaho living
to the north of the Platte. Further along Fremont again records an instance
where a party of Cheyenne and Arapaho cross over the mountains in order to
raid in the Green river country, only this time the party is much smaller. In
1843 Fremont writes:

79

> ...we traveled towards the North fork of the Platte, we had
> expected to meet some difficulty in crossing the river, but
> happened to strike it where there was a very excellent
> ford...two hundred miles from St. Vrain's fort...[While in
> this vicinity]...the camp was thrown into a sudden tumult,
> by a charge of about 70 mounted Indians...They proved to
> be a war party of Arapaho and Cheyenne Indians...They were
> returning from an expedition against the Shoshone Indians,
> one of whose villages they had surprised at Bridger's fort,
> on Ham's fork of Green river...(Fremont, 1854, 156-159).

The Southern Cheyenne and Arapaho also found the mountains on their west
to be their western boundary, beyond which they were clearly in enemy territory, a fact, however, which did not prevent them from crossing over. The
"parks" within the mountains were traversed and exploited by Indians from both
sides. In an entry of June 17, 1844 Fremont remarks as follows:

> The country...called Old Park, in which is formed Grand
> River, one of the principal branches of the Colorado of the
> California. We are now moving with some caution, as from
> the trail, we found the Arapaho village had also passed
> this way; as we were coming out of their enemy's country,
> and this was a war-ground,...(Fremont, 1854, 414).

And again, June 20, 1844:

> We saw today the returning trail of an Arapaho party which
> had been sent from the village [mentioned above] to look for
> Utahs in the Bayou Salade [South Park] (Fremont, 1854,
> 416).

On the south Fremont noted the Arkansas river acted as a natural barrier
between tribes north and south of the river.

> On the 1st of July (1844) we arrived at Bent's fort. On the
> 5th we resumed our journey down the Arkansas...and encamped
> about 30 miles below the fort. On the way we met a large
> village of Sioux and Cheyenne, who, with the Araphaoes were
> returning from the crossing of the Arkansas, where they had
> been to meet the Kioway and Comanche Indians (Fremont,
> 1854, 422).

On the east the Arapaho ranged rather indefinitely. The eastward extension
of the Arapaho range was coterminous with that of the Cheyenne referred to
previously.

Between Fremont and the Treaty of Fort Laramie, 1851, there does not
appear to have been any changes on the part of the Cheyenne or Arapaho insofar
as area of occupation goes. The scattered references dealing with the following
seven years are too meager, furthermore, to bear citing. At best they only
80 make reference to the location of camping grounds, all of which fall within the
areas previously mentioned.

CHAPTER VIII.--CONCLUSIONS

From the period of the third quarter of the eighteenth to the middle of the nineteenth century the Cheyenne and Arapaho were buffalo hunting nomadic Indians living in close association with one another and residing on the Great Plains. The conditions of buffalo hunting precluded permanent settlements and permitted tribal assemblages to take place only under favorable ecological and seasonal conditions. As a result of their conditions of existence the Cheyenne and Arapaho were constantly on the move; the length of time spent at any one camping site varied with the time of year and the availability of resources. Depending upon the size and movements of the buffalo these Indians wandered seasonally over a fairly wide range of territory. To the extent that the movements of the buffalo was regularized, so were the movements of these nomadic Indians. In winter when buffalo was scarce and the weather inclement camp movements were held down to a minimum as bands holed up in favorable hollows and valleys subsisting in part on what they had saved up from previous hunts. In fairer weather they emerged on the open plains, ranging far and wide. In addition to hunting within the confines of a broad and familiar country, raids and forays, large and small, were carried out in all directions against both White and Indian groups situated beyond the confines of their regular hunting territory.

We have seen that the Cheyenne and Arapaho were not the exclusive occupants of the expanse of country ranged over by them seasonally. Other tribes and bands shared in this territory, some to a greater, some to a lesser extent. In some instances, as among the Ogalala Sioux, friendly relations were maintained as these groups hunted and fought alongside the Cheyenne and Arapaho. In other instances relations were hostile to the extreme and war might be part of every encounter.

In the Introduction I spoke of the possibility of distinguishing "areas of intense economic exploitation", defined as the region in which the influence or strength of the tribe was greatest, depending upon the extent to which reference has been made to their presence and economic use of the region. This area would be their most frequented habitat. The remaining regions would constitute a penumbra of hunting territory; areas exploited by a number of tribes, areas of secondary economic value or just regions less intensively exploited. As desirable as this kind of classification might be, the nature of our data permits us to make such a distinction only in the most general sense. Again, even so far as "areas of intense economic exploitation" are concerned, the Cheyenne and Arapaho did not always occupy these regions exclusively.

There was no system of land tenure among the Cheyenne and Arapaho if we mean by land tenure a system whereby rights in land or rights to certain products of the land are maintained in specific families or kinship units, reenforced by tribal sanction and custom. As a consequence of the absence of any system of land tenure, there existed no tribal boundaries in any formal sense. Although there were no fixed tribal boundaries, and I might add here that I do not believe the Plains Indians ever thought in terms of tribal boundaries or conceptualized their claims in land until such ideas were introduced to them by Government Agents intent upon concluding land treaties, it is nevertheless possible to define their range of hunting and occupation area by relating this territory to similar areas for surrounding peoples. Although the Cheyenne and Arapaho did not conceptualize their holdings in land nor develop mechanisms for maintaining their rights, I believe we can assume that at any time they knew fairly well the pattern of movements and probable location of all surrounding peoples and kept away from them as far as this was desirable or possible. It is, therefore, only in the sense that over periods of time tribal movements were to a degree regularized that we can speak of a Cheyenne territory, Arapaho territory, and so forth. In the main, however, large-scale natural features, such as mountains, river-systems, "bad lands", etc., helped to maintain distances between tribes and preserve territorial integrity. That this integrity was not always respected we have ample evidence.

It was pointed out earlier that the determination of Cheyenne and Arapaho aboriginal rights in land, insofar as this study is concerned, would rest with the utilization of two procedures. The first method was to delimit the Cheyenne and Arapaho areas of habitation and subsistence, prior to 1851, on the basis of historical materials. The second method was to collate this area with land claims of surrounding tribes based upon the ethnographic evidence. It was reasoned, that following this general kind of approach, we could reasonably well define a territory not claimed by surrounding tribes which therefore would be assigneable to the Cheyenne and Arapaho. The area claimed by tribes surrounding the Cheyenne and Arapaho which comes to us from ethnographies devoted to these people, plus in some cases, statements from early historians can be found in the Appendix to this report.

The map accompanying this report is a composite of the two methods outlined above. This map suffers from a deficiency common to all maps; the difficulty of conceptualizing time on a two dimension plane surface. The main features of the map are as follows:

The area outlined in solid red on three sides represents the area of hunting and occupation of the Cheyenne and Arapaho prior to 1851. This region runs from the forks of the Platte northwestward to where the North Platte meets the northern edge of the Laramie Mountains; thence down the eastern edge of the Rockies to the Arkansas river, then eastward along the Arkansas river to about the border between Colorado and Kansas. I have made no attempt to define the eastern boundary as between the eastern boundary of the Cheyenne and Arapaho range and the western boundary of the Pawnee range there existed a tract of communal hunting territory, referred to in the historical literature as "hostile ground", "neutral ground", etc. The heavy red hatchure lines within the confines of the Cheyenne and Arapaho range represents an attempt at defining "areas of intense economic exploitation". In general these areas were to be found along the sources of the Arkansas and Platte rivers along the eastern edge of the mountains and in the valleys of these rivers. As far as the region between the rivers and away from the mountains are concerned our data is too sketchy to permit any generalizations. However, it may be assumed that this interior region while good buffalo hunting country was too remote from wood, water and protection to enable it to be utilized extensively for purposes of habitation. In general, the region outlined in red was occupied by the Cheyenne together with other tribes from about the beginning of the second quarter of the 19th century onward. The available evidence would indicate that the Arapaho roamed over this region from a much earlier time, coming to share it with the Cheyenne and others after the latter tribe moved southward.

I have made no attempt to indicate on the map which portions of this total territory can be considered Northern Cheyenne and Arapaho territory and which portions can be considered Southern country. It would be very difficult to draw such lines, but in general we might say that the region between the forks of the Platte and extending westward to the Rockies might be considered the range of the Northern divisions, while the remaining area belonged to the Southern sections. However, in practice the range of the two divisions probably overlapped considerably. The available data is too deficient in detail to permit much certainty in regard to this question.*

The region outlined in double, broken red lines interspersed with circles, extending from the northern end of the North Platte northeastwards to the Black Hills and beyond and including the forks of Cheyenne river was occupied and inhabited by the Cheyenne probably from the last quarter of the 18th century up to about the second quarter of the 19th century, at which time they moved southward.

The rest of the map is, I believe, self explanatory. However, at no time, as the text indicates, did the Cheyenne and Arapaho occupy these regions exclusively, though the region outlined in solid red, was, during the 19th century, more frequented by them than by any other groups of people.

83

Due to the nomadic way of life of the Cheyenne and Arapaho Indians and the paucity of detail available to us a more refined and detailed mapping of their territory is, in the opinion of the writer, not possible to achieve.

* Unfortunately, the map to which Dr. Gussow refers has become separated from the report and cannot be found.

APPENDIX

Area of Occupation of Tribes Surrounding Cheyenne and Arapaho
as defined by Ethnographers and Early Historians

Bands of the Dakota Sioux

The following data is from Hayden, Curtis and Bradley. The data from Hayden is particularly good for our purposes as his material was gathered from repeated visits to the Missouri Valley between 1850 and 1860.

Brule: on headwaters of White and Niobrara rivers, extending down these rivers about half their length. Teton (Bad) river formed their northern limit. 500 lodges.

Oglala: from Fort Laramie on Platte, extending northeast, including Black Hills, the sources of Teton (Bad) river, and reaching as low down as the forks of the Cheyenne. They sometimes ranged as far west as the head of Grand river. 300 lodges.

Miniconjon: usually found from Cherry Creek on Cheyenne river to Slender Butte on Grand river. 260 lodges.

Two Kettle: confined themselves to the Cheyenne and Moreau rivers seldom going higher on the former than the mouth of Cherry Creek, but passing up and down Cheyenne, Moreau and Grand rivers. 350 lodges.

Hunkpapa: occupy nearly the same district, and are so often encamped
Blackfoot: near each other and otherwise so connected in their
Sans Arc: operations, as scarcely to admit being treated separately. Their country lies along the Moreau, Cannonball, Heart and Grand rivers, seldom extending very high up the Grand river, but of late years reaching to the Little Missouri. 220 lodges.

Source: Hayden, F.V., 1863, 372-374

Curtis writes: "...within the...recent historical period they [seven Dakota bands] have held as their homeland the region west of the Missouri river and north of the Platte, extending permanently as far west as the Black Hills, and on the upper Missouri sending occasional parties as far west as central Montana, where the country of the Blackfeet was met. Along the northern line of Wyoming they attempted to take up their abode even beyond the Big horn. This, however, was the land claimed and held by the...Crow, who, notwithstanding their inferior numbers, more than held their own and forced the Dakota to the east of Powder river (Curtis, Vol. 3, 1908, 3).

Bradley, in his History of the Sioux, writes: "The Santees dwelt formerly about the Rum and lower Minnesota Rivers. The Yanktons, to the west of the Santees and north of the Minnesota river, stretching southwestward across the plains of Dakota to James River and even to the Missouri; while the Tetons, though now and then extending their range north of the Missouri, roamed generally over the prairie country on its south side in southwestern Dakota and northern Nebraska" (Bradley, 1923, 49).

Crow

In regard to the area occupied by the Crow, Hayden writes:

"The country usually inhabited by the Crows, is in and near the Rocky Mountains, along the sources of Powder, Wind, and Big-horn Rivers, on the southside of the Yellowstone, as far as Laramie Fork on the River Platte. They are also found on the west and north side of that river, as far as the source of the Mussel-shell, and as low down as the mouth of the Yellowstone" (Hayden, 1863, 392).

Curtis writes: "The Crow pushed westward until further progress was impeded by the main range of the Rocky Mountains, and from that time until they submitted to the restraint of reservation boundaries they roamed at will through the valleys of the Yellowstone and its tributaries, the Big-horn, Wind, Tongue and Powder rivers, and north of the Yellowstone along the Musselshell as far as its junction with the Missouri. Southward they hunted as far as the Black Hills on the east and the headwaters of Wind river and the Platte on the west..." (Curtis, Vol. 4, 1909, 39-40).

Hodge writes: "Since their separation from the Hidatsa (Hayden says this event occurred in 1776; Mathews states that it occurred within the last 200 years) they [Crow] migrated to the vicinity of the Rocky Mountains...At the time of the Lewis and Clark expedition (1804-1806) they dwelt chiefly on Big horn river. In 1817 they were located on the Yellowstone and the east side of the Rocky Mountains. Drake (1834) [located them] on the south branch of the Yellowstone, in latitude 46; longitude 105 (Hodge, B-BAE, Vol. 30, 1907, 367-368).

Lowie, in his volume Crow, writes: "As hunters of buffalo and other game they roamed over the Yellowstone and Big horn country, extending towards the sources of the Cheyenne River and the Rocky Mountains" (Lowie, 1935, xiv).

Assiniboin

In regard to the area inhabited by the Assiniboin, Denig, who, was married to an Assiniboin woman and for 21 years resided among them and with some surrounding groups, writes:

"Their [Assiniboin] migration has been referred to and the extent of land they occupied in the British territory of the Sasketchewan, etc., was very large, but at present [circa 1854]...the Northern Assiniboin, 250-300 lodges, rove the country from the west banks of the Sasketchewan, Assiniboin and Red Rivers in a westward direction to the Woody Mountains north and west

85

among small spurs of the Rocky Mountains east of the Missouri, and among chains of small lakes through this immense area. Occasionally making peace with some of the northern bands of Blackfeet enables them to come a little farther west and deal with these Indians, but, these "peaces" being of short duration, they are for the most part limited to the prairies east and north of the Blackfeet range.

The rest of the Assiniboin, say 500-520 lodges, [known as Southern Assiniboin], occupy the following district, viz, commencing at the mouth of White Earth River on the east, extending up that river to its head, thence northwest along the Coteau de Prairie or divide, as far as the Cyprus Mountains on the north Fork of the Milk River, thence down Milk river to its junction with the Missouri River, thence down the Missouri to the mouth of White Earth River, or the starting point. Formerly they inhabited a portion of country on the north side of the Missouri River along the Yellowstone River, but of late years, having met with great losses by Blackfeet, Sioux and Crow war parties, they have...abandoned this region and now they never go there (Denig, AR-BAE, Vol. 46, 1930, 396-397).

Lowie, on the Assiniboin, writes: "De Smet's 'Assiniboin of the Forest' are even said to have roamed about the sources of the Sasketchewan and the Athabaska and to have been seldom seen on the plains.

The younger Henry defines the Assiniboin country as beginning at the Hair Hills, near Red River, running west along the Assiniboin, from there to the junction of the northern and southern branches of the Sasketchewan, up the former branch to Fort Vermilion, then extending due south to Battle River, and southeast to the Missouri, down the Missouri almost as far as the Mandan village, and ultimately back to the Hair Hills again. (Lowie, 1909, 7).

Gros Ventres (Atsina)

Regarding the habitat of the Gros Ventre, Kroeber, writes: "Historically the Gros Ventre are known to have formed an independent tribe closely associated with the Blackfeet during the 19th century. The Arapaho regard the Gros Ventre as the northermost one of a group of five closely affiliated or related tribes of which they themselves form the largest. There is no very great amount of intercourse between them and the Arapaho at present, nor does there appear to have been any unusual amount of communication during the greater part of the 19th century, but on both sides there is a mutual recognition as of separated relatives.

According to Hayden, the Gros Ventre, about 1860, were south of the Sasketchewan; about 1820 they united with the Arapaho for a few years, and then, following a quarrel, journeyed north, had a disastrous encounter with the Crow, and became neighbors and allies of the Blackfeet" (Kroeber, AP-AMNH, Vol. 1, pt. 4, 1907, 145-146).

Kiowa

Regarding the Kiowa, Mooney writes: "The heading facts in the traditional history of the Kiowa are those of their early residence at the extreme head

of the Missouri and their subsequent removal to the east and alliance with the
Crow - this probably before 1700.

After making friends with the Crow, they established themselves in the
Black Hills until driven out by the invading Dakota and Cheyenne, and now for
more than 70 years they have had their main headquarters in the Wichita
Mountains.

The Northern Arapaho...have distinct recollection of this former northern
residence of the Kiowa...They say...that the Kiowa moved down from the mountains
and eastward along the Yellowstone in company with the Crow, and then turned
southeastward to about...Fort Robinson, Nebraska, where they parted with the
Crows and continued southward. 'Plenty-poles', then nearly 90 years old, first
met the Kiowa when he was a small boy on the head of the North Platte west of
present town of Cheyenne, Wyoming.

The friendship between the Kiowa and the Crows...continued after the Kiowa
had entirely removed from the north and established themselves on the Arkansas.
They made common cause against the invading Dakota and the Cheyenne from the
east by whom they were finally dispossessed

The northern Cheyenne informed Grinnell that on first coming into their
present country they found the region between the Yellowstone and Cheyenne
rivers, including the Black Hills, in possession of the Kiowa and Comanche (?),
whom they drove out and forced to the south. When the author (Mooney) was
among the Dakota some years ago, they informed him that they had first known   87
the Kiowa in the Black Hills, and had driven them out from that region. This
is admitted by the Kiowa...

They (ie Dakota) first reached the Black Hills in 1775...so that the final
expulsion of the Kiowa must have occurred between that date and 1805, when Lewis
and Clark found the Cheyenne in possession of the same region..." (Mooney, 17th
AR-BAE, 1895-96, 155-57).

Kiowa-Apache

Regarding the Kiowa-Apache, Hodge writes: "...associated with the Kiowa
from the earliest traditional period and forming a component part of the Kiowa
tribal circle...

The Kiowa-Apache did not emigrate from the Southwest into the plains
country, but came with the Kiowa from the Northwest plains region...

In 1815 Lewis and Clark described the Kiowa-Apache as living between the
heads of the two forks of Cheyenne river in the Black Hills region of North-
eastern Wyoming, and numbering 300 in 25 tipis. The Kiowa then lived on the
North Platte...In 1853 they are mentioned as...ranging the waters of the
Canadian river in the same great plains occupied by the Comanche. (Hodge,
B-BAE, Vol. 30, 1907, 701-02).

Comanche

Richardson says of the Comanche: "In his map of Texas in the 18th century,
Bolton shows the Indian situation in the western half of Texas as follows: The

Apaches occupy the region northwest of the Camino Real, which ran from the Presidio del Rio Grande to Bexar, with the Lipan-Apache extending as a kind or protruding finger eastward to the country around the present Mason; north of the Apaches are the Comanche tribes and east of these, divided by about the 98th meridian, were the Wichitas. It would not do violence to the facts to state that the West Texas Indian situation remained thus until the Indians were displaced by white settlers" (Richardson, 1929, 60).

Richardson, in 1933, in a longer account writes: "The Penatekas or Honey-eaters inhabited Texas during the later Spanish and the Anglo-American periods, and much of the Comanche history pertains to them. They were the southernmost of the various divisions and had, according to their tradition, wandered off a great distance from the other bands so that communications between them was discontinued for a long time. Finally the northern warriors, on their way to the Mexican frontier, rediscovered these Comanches of the south.

The extreme northern part of the Comanche country was occupied by the Yamparikas, or Root-eaters. According to their own accounts they came from the Rocky mountain country, north of the headwaters of the Arkansas river, to the valley of that stream in what is now eastern Colorado and western Kansas, about 1700. In 1786 Governor Don Juan Bantista de Anza of New Mexico stated that their country was approximately what is now Colorado north of the Arkansas river.

It has already been stated that the Comanche came from the Wyoming country, and that when white men first learned of them early in the 18th century, they were living in what is now Colorado and western Kansas. They continued their southward migration until about 1840, at which time their country might have been described as a blunt irregular wedge, point downward, the broad end extending from the vicinity of the great bend of the Arkansas river to the mouth of the Purgatory, the point extending almost to Austin.

The range of the Comanche is an entirely different matter from their homeland proper. As late as 1802 bands of these people occasionally roamed as far north as the upper stretches of the Missouri, and during the first half of the 19th century they harried Mexican settlements almost or quite as far south as Durango.

On the northwest border along the upper Arkansas river were the Cheyennes and Arapahoes, who appeared in great numbers at about 1830. War frequently prevailed between the Comanche and these tribes until 1840, when a lasting peace was made with them.

To the east and northeast of the Comanche country were the Osages... (Richardson, 1933, 18-19, 47-50).

In a footnote on page 19 Richardson writes the following: "It is my opinion that the Comanche moved into the South Plains in order to secure a more abundant supply of horses. Furthermore, there was no country in America better suited for nomadic, mounted Indians than the South Plains. I do not think the Comanches were driven into this country. On the contrary, it seems but they visited it, found that it was well suited to their mode of existence, and proceeded to fight for it and take it")

Pawnee

The range of the Pawnee comes from Wedel's "Introduction to Pawnee Archaeology". Wedel writes: "The territory claimed by the Pawnne was bounded on the north by the Niobrara River, on the south by the Arkansas or possibly the Canadian, on the east by the Missouri, and on the west extended rather indefinitely toward the Rockies. Actually, however, it was much more limited. On the west the Padouca (Comanche) were firmly established in the forks of the Dismal River, on the shores of some of the lakes in the sandhill region of the present Cherry County, Nebraska, and on the upper reaches of the Smokey Hill River in the present northern Kansas. Between Pawnee and Padouca there was incessant warfare, and it is unlikely that the former at any time ventured far beyond the forks of the Platte, save on occasional war or hunting trips. Early in the nineteenth century the Padouca were pushed southward by the Cheyenne, Arapaho, and Teton Dakota, who formed an equally effective check against westward movements by the Pawnee" (Wedel, 1936, 3-4. See also map no. 1).

89

90

BIBLIOGRAPHY

Many volumes have been consulted in the preparation
of this report. However, only those cited in the
text appear below.

Abel, A. H., editor, Tabeau's Narrative of Loisel's Expedition to the Upper
Missouri. Norman, Oklahoma, 1939.

Atkinson, General H., "Movements of the Expedition which Lately Ascended the
Missouri River, etc." 19th Congr., 1st Session, Doc. 117, House of Representatives, War Department. Washington, 1826.

_____, Correspondence with A. G. Harrison of the House of Representatives.
Quoted in U. S. House of Representatives, Doc. 276, 25th Congr., 2nd
Session. Washington, 1837-38.

Beals, R., Ethnology of Rocky Mountain National Park: The Ute and Arapaho.
U. S. Dep't. Interior. National Park Service, Berkeley, California, 1935.

Bradbury, J., "Travels In the Interior of American in the Years 1809, 1810,
1811." Reprinted in Thwaites, Vol. 5, 1906.

Bradley, J. H., History of the Sioux. Historical Society of Montana, Vol. 9,
1923.

Carver, J., Travels through the Interior Parts of North America in the Years
1766, 1767, 1768. London, 1778.

Catlin, G., Illustrations of the Manners, Customs and Condition of the North
American Indians, 2 Vols. London, 1876.

Clark, W. P., The Indian Sign Language. Philadelphia, 1885.

Collot, Map, 1776. From a Journey in North America, Vol. 1. Reprinted in
Wedel, 1936.

Coues, E., editor, New Light on the Early History of the Greater Northwest:
The Manuscript Journals of Alexander Henry and of David Thompson, 1799-
1814, 3 Vols. New York, 1897.

Culbertson, T., Journal of an Expedition to the Mauvaises Terres and the Upper
Missouri in 1850. Bureau American Ethnology, Bulletin, 147. Washington,
1952.

Curtis, E. S., The North American Indians, Vols. III, IV, VI. Cambridge, 1908;
Cambridge, 1909; Norwood, 1911.

91

Denig, E. T., Indian Tribes of the Upper Missouri, ed., J. N. B. Hewitt. 46th Annual Report, Bureau American Ethnology. Washington, 1930.

Dodge, Colonel H., Report on the Expedition of Dragoons, under Col. Henry Dodge, to the Rocky Mountains in 1835. American State Papers, Military Affairs, Vol. 6, 1861.

Dorsey, G. A., The Cheyenne. Field (Columbian) Museum (of Natural History) Anthropological Series, Vol. 9, 1905.

Eggan, F., "The Cheyenne and Arapaho Kinship System." In Social Anthropology of North American Tribes, ed., Eggan, F., Chicago, 1937.

Elkin, H., The Northern Arapaho of Wyoming. In Acculturation in Seven American Indian Tribes, ed., Linton, R., New York, 1940.

Ewers, J. C., Teton Dakota: History and Ethnology. U. S. Dep't. of Interior. National Park Service, Berkeley, California, 1937.

Executive Document: House of Representatives, 1st Session, 52nd Congr., 1891-92.

Farnham, T. J., "Travels in the Great Western Prairies, the Anahuac and Rocky Mountains, and In the Oregon Country." Reprinted in Thwaites, Vols. 28 & 29, 1906.

Fowler, J., "The Journal of Jacob Fowler, 1821-22." Vol. 1 American Explorers Series. Elliott Coues, ed., Francis P. Harper.

Fremont, Colonel J. C., The Exploring Expedition to the Rocky Mountains. Buffalo, 1854.

Gallatin, A., A Synopsis of the Indian Tribes of North America. Transactions and Collections of the American Antiquarian Society, Archaeologia Americana, Vol. II, Cambridge, 1836.

Graham, American State Papers, Indian Affairs, II, 1834.

Grinnell, G. B., Social Organization of the Cheyenne. Proceedings of the International Congress of Americanists, Vol. 13, 1902.

—————, "The Great Mysteries of the Cheyenne." American Anthropologist, Vol. 12, No. 4, 1910.

—————, The Fighting Cheyennes. New York, 1915.

—————, "Early Cheyenne Villages." American Anthropologist, Vol. 20, No. 4, 1918.

—————, "Cheyenne Medicine Wheels." American Anthropologist, Vol. 24, No. 3, 1922.

92

Grinnell, G. B., "Bent's Old Fort and Its Builders." Collections pf the Kansas State Historical Society, Vol. 15, 1923a.

_____, The Cheyenne Indians, their History and Ways of Life. 2 Vols. New Haven, 1923.

Hafen, L. R., "A Report from the First Indian Agent of the Upper Platte and Arkansas." New Spain and the Anglo-American West, Historical Contributions. Presented to Herbert Eugene Bolton. Charles W. Hackett, editor, 1932.

Haines, F., "The Northward Spread of Horses Among the Plains Indians." American Anthropologist, Vol. 40, 1938.

Hayden, F. V., "On the Ethnography and Philology of the Indian Tribes of the Missouri Valley." Transactions of the American Philosophical Society, Vol. 12, Philadelphia, 1863.

Hewes, G., "Early Tribal Migrations in the Northern Great Plains." Plains Archaeological Conference News Letter, Vol. 1, No. 4, July 15, 1948.

Hodge, F. W., editor, Handbook of American Indians North of Mexico. Smithsonian Institute, Bureau of American Ethnology, Bulletin, 30, 1907. 2 Vols.

Hyde, G. E., Red Cloud's Folk: A History of the Oglala Sioux Indians. Norman, Oklahoma, 1937.

Jablow, J., The Cheyenne in Plains Indian Trade Relations 1795-1840. Monographs of the American Ethnological Society, Vol. 19, 1951.

James, E., "Account of an Expedition from Pittsburgh to the Rocky Mountains, performed in the Years 1819, 1820...under the Command of Maj. S. H. Long." Reprinted in Thwaites, Vols. 14, 15, 16, 17, 1906 under the title "James' Account of S. H. Long's expedition, 1819-1820."

Kroeber, A. L., The Arapaho. American Museum of Natural History, Bulletin, Vol. 18, 1902-07.

Le Ray, C., The Journal of Charles Le Raye. South Dakota Historical Collections, Vol. 4, 1908.

Llewellyn, K. N., and Hoebel, E. A., The Cheyenne Way. University Oklahoma Press, 1941.

Lowie, R. H., The Assiniboin. Anthropological Papers, American Museum of Natural History, Vol. 4, Part I, New York, 1909.

_____, The Crow. New York, 1935.

Mackenzie, Sir A., Voyages from Montreal to the Frozen and Pacific Oceans in the Years 1789 and 1793, Vol. 1, London, 1802.

93

Marquis, T. B., A Warrior Who Fought Custer: Interpreted by Thomas B. Marquis; Narrated by Wooden Leg. The Midwest Co., Minneapolis, 1931.

Mishkin, B., Rank and Warfare Among the Plains Indians. Monographs of the American Ethnological Society, Vol. III, New York, 1940.

Mooney, J., The Ghost Dance Religion. 14th Annual Report, Bureau of American Ethnology, Part. II, 1893.

_____, Calendar History of the Kiowa Indians. 17th Annual Report, Bureau of American Ethnology, Part I, 1895-96. Washington, 1898.

_____, The Cheyenne Indians. Memoirs of the American Anthropological Association, Vol. I, Part 6, 1905-07.

_____, Arapaho. Bureau of American Ethnology, Bulletin, 30, 1907.

Morse, Rev. J., A Report to the Secretary of War, On Indian Affairs, Comprising a Narrative of a Tour Performed In the Summer of 1820...New Haven, 1822.

Neill, Rev. E. D., The History of Minnesota: From the Earliest French Explorations to the Present Time. 5th ed., Minneapolis, 1883.

Perrin du Lac, M., "Travels through the Two Louisanas and Among the Savage Nations of the Missouri...In 1801, 1802, and 1803. London, 1807.

Report from the Secretary of War: In Senate Executive Document, No. 72, 20th Congr., 2nd Session, 1829.

Richardson, R. N., "The Culture of the Comanche Indians." Texas Archaeological and Paleontological Society, Bulletin, Vol. 1, 1929.

_____, The Comanche Barrier to South Plains Settlement. California, 1933.

Riggs, S. R., Dakota Grammar, Texts and Ethnography. Contributions to North American Ethnology, Vol. 9, Dep't of the Interior, U. S. Geographical and Geological Survey of the Rocky Mountain Region, 1893.

Robinson, D., "A History of the Dakota or Sioux Indians." South Dakota Historical Collections, Vol. II, 1904.

Science Magazine, Original Map of Lewis and Clark. November 4, 1887.

Scott, H. L., "The Early History of the Arapaho." American Anthropologist, Vol. 9, 1907.

Simms, S. C., "A Wheel-shaped Stone Monument." American Anthropologist, Vol. 5, n. s., 1903.

Strong, W. D., An Introduction to Nebraska Archaeology. Smithsonian Institute Miscellaneous Collections, Vol. 93. No. 10, 1935.

94

Swanton, J. R., The Indian Tribes of North America. Bureau of American Ethnology, Bulletin, 145. Washington, 1952.

Sage, R., Rocky Mountain Life..., Boston, 1860.

Teit, J. A., The Salishan Tribes of the Western Plateaus. 45th Annual Report, Bureau of American Ethnology. Washington, 1930.

Trudeau, J. B., Trudeau's Journal. South Dakota Historical Collections, Vol. 7, 1914.

Tyrrell, J. B., editor, David Thompson's Narrative of his Explorations in Western America, 1784-1812. The Champlain Society, Toronto, 1916.

Thwaites, R. G., editor, Original Journals of The Lewis and Clark Expedition 1804-1806. 7 Vols. New York, 1904.

Umfreville, E., The Present State of Hudson's Bay. London, 1790.

Verendrye, The Chevalier Verendrye's Journal 1742-43. South Dakota Historical Collections, Vol. 7, 1914.

Wedel, W. R., An Introduction to Pawnee Archaeology. Smithsonian Institution, Bureau of American Ethnology, Bulletin, No. 112. Washington, 1936.

_____, "Human Ecology in the Central Plains." American Anthropologist, Vol. 55, No. 4, 1953.

Will, G. F., "The Cheyenne Indians of North Dakota." Proceedings of the Mississippi Valley Historical Associations, Vol. 7, 1913-14.

Williamson, Rev. T. S., "Who Were The First Men?" Minnesota Historical Society Collections, Vol. 1, 1872.

Wissler, C., Material Culture of the Blackfoot Indians. Anthropological Papers, American Museum of Natural History, Vol. 5, 1910.

_____, North American Indians of the Plains. Handbook Series, No. 1. American Museum of Natural History, New York, 1922.

Cutler, J., A Topographical Description of the State of Ohio, Indiana Territory, and Louisiana...To which is added An Interesting Journal of Mr. Chas. Le Raye...Boston, 1812.

Kroeber, A. L., Gros Ventre. Anthropological Papers, American Museum of Natural History, Vol. 1, Part 4, New York, 1907.

Mooney, J., The Aboriginal Population of America North of Mexico. Smithsonian Miscellaneous Collections, Vol. 80, No. 7, 1928.

95

HISTORICAL BACKGROUND AND DEVELOPMENT
OF THE ARAPAHO-CHEYENNE LAND AREA

LEROY R. HAFEN

State Historian of Colorado, Emeritus

Professor of History, Brigham Young University

Docket 329

TABLE OF CONTENTS

CONTENTS (Cont'd)

100

CONTENTS (Cont'd)

INTRODUCTION

In determining the value of the Arapaho-Cheyenne Land Tract, a large area near the center of the United States, it is well to examine the historical background that explains the importance of this land.

After looking at national policy regarding disposal of the public domain, we shall trace the general economic history of the United States, to get the setting for our area. Of immediate interest is the history of the Arapaho-Cheyenne land--its early exploration, the white occupancy and exploitation of the land, and relations between the whites and the Indians. Lastly, we may examine more closely the economic development of the region and appraise its status and prospects in October, 1865.

I. THE PUBLIC DOMAIN AND POLICY REGARDING IT

A. EARLY NATIONAL CLAIMS AND TITLES

Following the discovery of America, the nations of Europe engaged in the exploitation of the New World. Spain, most alert to the immediate opportunities, began at once the conquest and settlement of the West Indies. From that base she quickly expanded to the continents of North and South America.

England, late in beginning actual settlement, occupied the narrow tidewater strip along the Atlantic seaboard, and after sinking roots deep in that fertile soil, began the push westward to and across the Appalachians.

France, contemporaneously with England, entered by way of the St. Lawrence and penetrated to the Great Lakes. Concentrating especially on the fur trade, she expanded to the Mississippi River and was soon exploiting the fur resources and claiming the land of the entire Mississippi Valley.

These three major colonizing nations were soon involved in an international struggle for possession of North America. The series of four principal colonial wars culminated in the great French and Indian War. At its termination in 1763, France was eliminated from North America, and Britain and Spain glared at each other across the Mississippi River as a boundary line.

B. CREATION OF THE PUBLIC DOMAIN

When the English colonies revolted from their mother country and won independence, they obtained control of the English land extending from the Atlantic Coast to the Mississippi. During the Revolutionary War and the "Critical Period" that followed, many divisive forces and rivalries pulled the thirteen states apart. One of the problems that prevented unanimity was the question of ownership of the Western lands. Some states had excellent claims, others had none.

Maryland, one of the landless states, insisted that the Western territory had been won through joint efforts in the war, and that it should therefore be considered as the common property of all the states. She refused to sign the Articles of Confederation, that would set up a legal government, until these lands were ceded to the central government. The states with land titles finally yielded their claims, and thus was the Public Domain created. The area of public land was to be augmented by subsequent acquisitions, but the pattern of management was established in dealing with this first section.

C. EARLY POLICY REGARDING THE PUBLIC LAND

The weak and degenerating Congress under the Articles of Confederation, prompted by lobbyists interested in Western lands, roused itself to enact two great pieces of legislation.

1. The Ordinances of 1785 and 1787. The first of these was the Land Law of 1785, which set up the system of rectangular surveys, and provided for division of the land into townships six miles square and into sections of one square mile, or 640 acres. It also initiated the policy of giving land for public purposes, by setting aside section 16 of each township for the support of education.

With the second measure, the famous Ordinance of 1787, the Congress abandoned the colonialism that had characterized nations and empires of the past, and launched a policy that would provide entire equality for the subject territory. Brief periods of tutelage would lead by quick successive steps to incorporation of Territories into the Union with complete equality in the sister-hood of states.

105

2. Early Policy on Land Sales. Involved with these two important laws were acts for the sale of large tracts of land in the Northwest Territory to interested parties. The first sale, in October 1787, to the Ohio Company, was for about 1,500,000 acres at $1 per acre, with one-third reduction for swamp and other undesirable land. Marietta was settled on this tract. The Scioto Company, in which Congressmen held stock, obtained an option on some 4,000,000 acres on similar terms. This company never took up its option. Judge John C. Symmes, in October 1788, contracted for 1,000,000 acres at 66-2/3 cents per acre. Upon this tract Cincinnati, Ohio, was founded.

-5-

Miscellaneous smaller tracts also were sold, the price averaging $1.60 per acre.[1]

The public land policy of the nation immediately following adoption of the constitution considered land as a resource which should be utilized for payment of the national debt incurred by the Revolutionary War. The plan adopted was to sell the land at auction to the highest bidder; and thus obtain the maximum amount from the land. A minor voice was raised in behalf of selling the land cheap and thus promoting settlement and rapid development of the country. Westerners felt that they were doing a national service by pioneering, and should be rewarded by receiving land cheaply or free. Their voice was to gain in force until ultimately it would triumph as public policy in the Homestead Act of 1862.

The land law of 1796 provided for sale of surveyed land at auction to the highest bidder; with a minimum price of $2 per acre. The relatively high price was fixed to discourage the land speculator and to increase the revenue. Inasmuch as state land was then selling for 30 cents to $1 per acre, little federal land, less than 50,000 acres, was sold in four years.[2]

In 1800 William H. Harrison, new Delegate from the Northwest Territory, presented the settlers' demand for more favorable terms of land procurement. The result was the Harrison Land Law of 1800. It reduced the size of a saleable tract from 640 to 320 acres, and permitted installment buying (over a period of four years). The minimum price remained at $2, and interest at 6 percent was charged on the deferred payments.[3]

Inasmuch as many people bought more land than they could make the later payments for, and the Panic of 1819 having made matters worse, the Government passed the Land Law of 1820. It abolished installment buying, reduced the

-6-

size of the saleable tract to 80 acres, and set the minimum price at $1.25 per acre. This price was to remain standard for several decades.[4]

II. ECONOMIC BACKGROUND AND UNITED STATES DEVELOPMENT TO 1865

Interwoven with the enactments regarding land policy, and helping to cause and to explain them, was the general material progress of the nation.

A. TRANSPORTATION AND COMMERCE

1. By Rivers, Roads, and Canals. Waterways were the first highways. In birch bark canoes and pirogues the American Indians skimmed the streams and lakes that threaded the wide primeval forest area of America. When the white man came to the eastern shores, he followed the same water courses into the interior. On land, also, he followed trails first made by the wild animals and the red men. White pioneers widened these Indian paths into packhorse trails and later converted them into wagon roads.[5]

The vanguard of the white advance into the West were the explorers and traders in canoes. Then followed flatboats down the Ohio, carrying homeseekers to new lands or floating produce to a New Orleans market. Then keelboats ascended the great rivers and their branches, propelled by poles, cars, sails, and the taut tow line, or cordelle. But it remained for the steamboat to usher in the great days of water transportation. John Fitch launched his crude steamboat, the first in American waters, in 1786. The next year he offered it to the Congress of the Confederation, but the lawmakers and people generally failed to see its possibilities. Not until Fulton's Clermont churned its way up the Hudson in 1807 did the era of commercial steam navigation begin.

In 1811 Nicholas Roosevelt built a steamboat at Pittsburgh. This 116-foot stern-wheeler, with a capacity of 100 tons, was the first steam craft to operate on the inland waters of the United States. As steamboats increased, they pushed further up the rivers. By 1823 a steamer arrived at St. Anthony Falls, Minnesota, and nine years later one ascended the Missouri to the mouth of the Yellowstone. Thereafter steamboats increased on the ocean lanes and multiplied upon our inland waters. By 1842 there were 450 steamboats on our Western rivers; and these were to increase to 1000 by 1860.

The ease and cheapness of water transportation suggested the supplementing of natural waterways by the construction of canals. The remarkable success of the Erie Canal, built by New York state and completed in 1825, gave great impetus to canal building throughout the country. Especially were these inland waterways constructed in the old Northwest, connecting the Great Lakes with the Mississippi drainage area.

For land travel the saddle horse and pack animal were the chief reliance during the early years. Wheeled vehicles began to come into general use in the early eighteenth century, but roads were so limited and poor that carriages and wagons were largely confined to the towns. Before the American Revolution, stagecoaches had made their appearance, and one that covered the distance from New York to Philadelphia in a day and a half was called the "Flying Machine." Contemporary stages running between Boston and New York were more than a week on the way.

The need for roads was felt, not only to connect towns and cities, but to link the Ohio country of the West with the Atlantic seaboard. In response to

-8-

Western demands, the Ohio Enabling Act of 1802 provided that five per cent of the proceeds from the sale of land in Ohio be set aside for the building of a road to connect that region with Atlantic waters. Subsequent legislation provided for the survey and construction of such a road. It became known as the Cumberland, or National Road, and extended from Fort Cumberland on the Potomac to Wheeling on the Ohio. This road was built in conformity with the techniques of John McAdam and the best engineering standards of the day. A graded roadbed, covered with layers of gravel upon crushed rock, and the bed slightly arched for effective drainage, produced an excellent macadamized highway. Soon emigrant vehicles, stagecoaches, and great Conestoga freight wagons were rumbling along the busy thorofare. The popularity and success of the first section of the National Road caused the building of successive extentions until it had spanned Ohio, Indiana, and Illinois. There it stopped, strict construction of the federal constitution being largely responsible for discontinuance of federal appropriations for the project.

Of course, the building and extension of roads continued, but now it was largely done by private initiative and by county and state action.

The great arteries of the Far West pushed out beyond the wide Missouri. The Santa Fe Trail, leading southwestward from Independence to Santa Fe, became the distinctive highway of commerce. Caravans of freight wagons lumbered across the prairies laden with trade goods for the markets of New Mexico and Chihuahua.

The Oregon Trail, leading up the Platte River and through South Pass, became the major emigrant road. The womb of the covered wagon delivered the future citizens of Oregon, California, and Utah.

The federal government did make some grants of public land to aid in building specific wagon roads. The first such act, of 1823, gave a mile strip on each side of a road across Ohio. The land was to be sold for not less than $1.25 per acre. In 1827 Indiana was given a similar grant on a road the full length of the state. These two grants amounted to 251,353.88 acres.

Such federal wagon road aid was to be revived in the 1860's. It was now in the form of alternate sections of land in a six-mile strip along the road. The land given, in Michigan, Wisconsin, and Oregon, 1863-69, amounted to over 3,000,000 acres.[6]

Federal aid to canal building in a similar pattern was given about the same time. At first (in 1827) it amounted to one-half of the land in a five-mile strip; later it was increased to half of a ten-mile strip. About ten canals were federally aided; the total land given in alternate sections, 1827-66, amounted to 4,598,668.32 acres. Similar grants for river improvements, 1828-46, amounted to 2,245,252.31 acres.[7] The Wisconsin-Fox River Canal Act of 1846, for the first time introduced the provision that the government-retained sections should be sold at $2.50 per acre--"double the minimum."[8]

2. Early Railroad Development. The canal era was shortlived; and wagon road development, principally financed by local taxation, survived on a starvation diet. Then a new giant was born--the railroad. The earliest cars were drawn by horse power and ran on wooden rails. The application of steam motive power was to work a revolutionary change and inaugurate a new era in transportation history. In 1830 the first twelve miles of the Baltimore and Ohio Railroad were opened. The earliest railroads were built to connect

important cities or to supplement water routes. Gradually they became competitors of canal boats and river steamers. Short sections of track were then consolidated into trunk lines. Wooden rails were covered with strips of iron and then displaced with rails or iron. The diversity in widths of track was eliminated and the English standard gauge of four feet eight and one-half inches was adopted. Iron rails climbed the Appalachians and nosed westward.

Railroads were looked upon as public benefactions, their promotion a civic duty. Meetings were called to promote the enterprise and develop enthusiasm. Railroad conventions in the late forties became epidemic. The Camp Meeting technique was employed, vigorous exhorters preaching the new gospel of salvation via the iron rail. But efforts were more productive of converts than cash. Corporate finance in America was yet in swaddling clothes, with accumulations of capital inadequate to such an enterprise. Advocates turned to governmental units for aid, with cities, counties, states, and the nation being asked to subscribe stock. All were finally induced to render aid, as we shall note later. But the new policy was not inaugurated until 1850.

B. POPULATION GROWTH AND LAND SALES

1. Early Immigration and Growth. During the first hundred years of settlement along the Atlantic seaboard the colonists came almost entirely from England, and settled on the Tidewater area. The next half century (1700-1750) saw the settlement of the Piedmont region and the introduction of sizeable blocks of non-English stock, especially German and Scotch-Irish. The French and Indian War and the American Revolution discouraged and almost stopped immigration, but with the return of peace and the establishment of the United

States, foreigners began to come again to our shores.

The first census of the United States was taken in 1790. It showed a population of nearly 4,000,000, almost evenly divided between the North and South. Almost 70 per cent were native whites of English descent; nearly 20 per cent were Negroes. Philadelphia was the largest city, with a population of 42,444; New York was second, with 33,131; and Boston third, with 18,028.

During the next seventy years the population was to grow rapidly, increasing about 35 per cent each decade, and thus doubling about every 25 years. By 1820 the population of the nation was 9,600,000; by 1840, it was 17,000,000; and in 1860 it had reached 31,000,000.[9] Most of this was natural increase of native stock, for marriages occurred early and families were large. But immigration made sizeable contributions.

112

Prior to 1820 no official records of immigration were kept, but the estimate of alien arrivals in this country from 1789 to 1820 is 234,000, or an average of 7,700 per year. The French Revolution, the Napoleonic Wars, and our War of 1812 so interferred with normal intercourse that immigration was small.

2. <u>Frontier Expansion.</u> The year 1816 opened a new era in our history. The United States turned its back on Europe, faced westward, and concentrated upon the development of its own vast resources. There was rapid growth in manufacturing, enlargement of transportation facilities, and extension of internal improvements. National pride mounted, a national literature arose, and a vision of Manifest Destiny of the nation seized the minds of the people. Population moved impressively westward as a flood.

In the two decades following 1800 public land was sold at auction, with $2 per acre as the minimum price. In 1814 for the first time the amount sold per year exceeded 1,000,000 acres. In 1818 the sales exceeded 3,490,000 acres. The total sales up to the year 1820 amounted to 19,399,158, and the receipts totaled $47,689,563.[10]

The hard times following the Panic of 1819 materially reduced the sales of public land, even though by the Act of 1820, the price of land had been reduced to $1.25 per acre minimum, and the size of the saleable tract was reduced to 80 acres. Not until 1829 did sales again reach the one million acre mark. They continued to mount until in the boom year 1836 the sales reached the peak of over 20,000,000 acres. The Specie Circular of that year, which stopped the acceptance of wildcat bank currency and required specie, or hard money, in payment for land, pricked the bubble of inflation and speculation, and reduced land sales by three-fourths. Depressed conditions prevailed for several years. For the period 1820 to 1841 the total sales amounted to 87,538,346 acres, and the receipts were $122,172,013, an average of about $1.28 per acre.[11]

The General Pre-emption Act of 1841, allowed squatters to procure their land at $1.25 per acre. The Graduation Act of 1854 provided for sale of less desirable land for less than the previous $1.25 minimum. This arrangement, combined with the good times then prevailing, resulted in large public land sales. Thus in the years 1854, 1855, and 1856, the sales were over 7,000,000, 15,000,000, and 9,000,000 acres respectively. For the two decades, 1842 to 1862, the total sales amounted to 69,198,547 acres, and the receipts were $64,125,589.[12]

The middle west was rapidly peopled during this period before the Civil War. From 1816 to 1819 the four new states of Indiana, Illinois, Mississippi, and Alabama were admitted to the Union. Missouri, Arkansas, Michigan, Wisconsin, Iowa, and Texas became states, 1820-50. Canal-building and other internal improvements were pushed in the earlier years; manufacturing increased; cities grew; and westward migration of settlers continued.

The generally good times prevailing in America during most of this period combined with hard times in Europe to bring a swelling tide of immigrants to our shores. Industrial depression in Britain during the 1830's caused a heavy immigration. The potato famines in Ireland in the '40's drove a million and a quarter destitute Irish to America in ten years. During the same decade political oppression and business depression in Germany caused

114 a large exodus to this country.

C. FISCAL POLICY AND FINANCIAL HISTORY TO 1850

Affecting the value of land and the growth of the country was the fiscal policy of the nation.

1. Currency and Banking. The reckless issue of paper money during the American Revolution caused a rapid decline in its value. Soon this scrip was "not worth a continental," and went out of circulation. Upon creation of a stable government under the constitution, an early concern was for financial credit and a sound currency. Under Alexander Hamilton, chief architect of the new fiscal structure, a decimal system and free coinage of both gold and silver were established, and a National Bank was created.

-14-

During the twenty years of the Bank's existence the monetary system was sound and adequate. But when the charter expired and we had to fight the War of 1812 without its bolstering influence, financial weaknesses developed. With an almost complete lack of metal for coins, and with the First National Bank dissolved, state banks rushed in to fill the currency vacuum. Between 1811 and 1816 the number of these institutions, chartered by the states, increased from 88 to 246. With the restraining influence of the National Bank removed, and with a great demand for currency, these state banks issued their notes with reckless abandon. Between 1812 and 1817 the bank-note circulation rose from $45,000,000 to $100,000,000. [13]

At this period much of the business speculation was in land. Installment buying, permitted under the Harrison Land Law of 1800, encouraged people to contract for more land than they could pay for. The increased number of banks and their expanded issues of notes made borrowing easy. So the result was an orgy of land buying. In 1815 the government sold over 1,300,000 acres of land; in 1818, more than 3,490,000 acres. [14]

2. <u>Boom and Bust Periods.</u> The Second Bank of the United States, chartered in 1816 for twenty years, was poorly managed during its first three years. It over-issued its notes, as state banks were doing. When the United States Bank contracted its loans and its circulating notes in 1819, it helped precipitate the Panic of that year. Too-rapid commercial expansion, and unstable position of manufacturing industries, and speculation in Western lands helped bring on the financial crisis. Specie payments were generally suspended, many banks failed, factories shut down, and laborers were thrown out of employment.

115

-15-

The recovery was fairly rapid, and soon the National Bank was acting as a regulator of the currency. This action was unpopular in the South and West, where there was great need for more money for capital investment and to pay the unfavorable trade balance with the East. Opposition to the Bank was spear-headed by President Andrew Jackson. The question of a re-charter of the Bank got into politics, and Jackson defeated the Bank. He now had the federal money withdrawn and placed in "Pet Banks." This gave these favored private institutions added deposits. And these deposits were very large in the early '30's, for the federal government, with its large revenue from the tariff and from the sale of public land, was able to completely pay off the national debt and had a large surplus. The affluence of the Pet Banks made them optimistic lenders; and easy credit sent land speculation to new heights. Federal land sales soared from an average of less than $2,000,000 a year before 1830, to $25,000,000 in 1836.[15] At this time the expression, "doing a land office business," came to mean great commercial activity. Prices rose, trade flourished, and speculation went wild. Then the boom collapsed, the "Specie Circular" being the pin that pricked the bubble. Over 600 banks failed; prices plunged. The Panic of 1837 and a depression ensued.

The federal government, having much of its money "frozen" in the Pet Banks, now adopted the safe, if not sane, expedient of placing its money in vaults. Though none was lost under this "Independent Treasury System," the money was withdrawn from the channels of trade, and business suffered from a shortage of currency.

With the federal government withdrawn from the banking field, banking

regulation was left to the states. Some managed well; the majority did rather

poorly. For a decade bank capital, loans, and note circulation did not reach

the figures attained before the Panic of 1837. But confidence gradually returned,

and by the late 1840's business was thriving and Europeans were again making

large investments in America. The credit of the national government was so

good that the Mexican War was financed without difficulty. The bonds, for

$65,000,000, were sold at a premium and for specie.[16] The acquisition of the

enormous Mexican Cession, and presently the discovery of gold in the California

portion of it, raised national morale, stimulated business, and helped to produce

the expansion of the next decade.

D. THE BOOM OF THE FIFTIES AND SIXTIES

1. Business and Industrial Expansion. The discovery of gold in Cali-

fornia in 1848, and the mighty rush of argonauts in 1849 stirred the nation. The

great production of gold, and the consequent large accessions of hard money to

the United States currency, infused new life into the channels of trade.

The gold from California and from Australia stimulated credit expansion.

The unusual demand for our products resulting from the famines in Ireland and

the Crimean War created business prosperity. Rising prices produced

speculative optimism. There was marked iron and coal production in Pennsyl-

vania, and increased industrial growth throughout the nation. The textile and

iron industries grew two-thirds in the 1850's, and general manufacturing approx-

imately doubled, rising in value from about one billion to nearly two billion dollars.

"During the decade ending with 1860 the country made the most remarkable in-

dustrial progress in its history."[17]

117

The rise of manufacturing, the building of railroads, the growth of cities, and expanding area of farms, promoted the economic boom. The number of banks in the United States increased from 750 in 1853 to 1562 in 1860, and their capital more than doubled in the same seven-year period.[18]

European investors who had suffered losses in the Panic and Depression of 1837, regained their confidence in America during the 1840's, and again were making large investments here.[19] Bogart and Kemmerer state:

> Down to 1845 England supplied nearly all our iron rails and loaned us the money to buy them. By 1838 Europeans had close to $200,000,000 invested here, much of it in state bonds that had been issued to finance internal improvements. Large firms importing drygoods, investment houses like Baring Brothers of London, and the Second Bank of the United States were some of the channels through which these securities reached the English investors. It is said that on a single trip in 1836, the cashier of the Second Bank took $30,000,000 of American securities to London. Englishmen were tempted by the profit possibilities of canals and railroads in this growing nation and by the higher rates of interest. By 1860 some $400,000,000 of foreign money was invested here. Despite some disgraceful defaults in the late 1830's the average nineteenth-century English investor got his money back and a generous return on his American investments...

> As a consequence of all these developments, the evolution of the corporation and of investment banking, the birth of stock exchanges, and the growing interest of foreign investors in this country, capital grew rapidly before the Civil War. Census figures for capital invested in manufactures alone indicate a growth from $50,000,000 in 1820 to $250,000,000 in 1840 and $1,000,000,000 in 1860.[20]

Life insurance company assets were beginning to grow; and savings bank deposits were $150,000,000 in 1860.

2. Transportation Progress. Before railroads nosed out from the Missouri frontier, the transport of settlers and of freight was provided by wagons and stagecoaches. The famous covered wagons were the conveyors

of the pioneer settlers into the West. The wheels of these vehicles cut deep the ruts of the Santa Fe, Oregon, and California Trails and carried the settlers to new homes on the Pacific Coast and to the Rocky Mountain region.

The big freighting outfits carried supplies to these settlers, to the mining camps of the Rockies, and to the military forts in the West. One of the freighting outfits--Russell, Majors, and Waddell--employed 3,500 wagons, 40,000 oxen, 1,000 mules, and 4,000 men in its operations of 1858.[21]

The Butterfield Overland Mail line, inaugurated in 1858, carried mail and passengers in a swaying Concord stagecoach from St. Louis to San Francisco. The stage ran semi-weekly, and covered the distance in 25 days and nights of continuous travel. The government payed the company $600,000 per year for the transport of the mail. Several other stagecoach lines ran overland to California.[22]

In 1860 the Pony Express was launched, carrying letters at $5 per half ounce, and making the trip from St. Joseph, Missouri, to San Francisco in ten days. This famous and speedy carrier continued in operation but eighteen months--until the overland telegraph was completed in October, 1861.[23]

The fast American clipper ships of the 1840's began to give way to iron steamers in the 1850's. American ships were carrying a larger proportion of the world's commerce than ever before. All of our coastwise trade and about 70 per cent of the total foreign trade of the United States flew the American flag. The shipping on our rivers and other inland waters was enormous before the Civil War.

The railroad was coming into its own at mid century. Its expansion
was in large part made possible by the creation and growth of the corporation.
This economic entity was especially adapted for financing the railroad, which
was a costly undertaking and was then looked upon as a novel and risky enterprise. The pooling of domestic savings and offering of attractive securities
to foreign lenders was necessary for the financing of the early railroads. The
Baltimore and Ohio cost $20,000,000, the New York Central and the Pennsyl-
vania each $25,000,000. Between 1850 and 1860, $1,250,000,000 were invested
in American railroads. [24] The railroad mileage of the United States in 1850
was 9,021 miles; in ten years it more than tripled, to 30,626 miles in 1860. [25]
The Mississippi was reached in 1854; and five years later the railroad reached
the Missouri at St. Joseph.

120

Railroad construction was enormously helped by government aid.
Stephen A. Douglas, the great railroad senator, won for the Illinois Central
federal aid in the form of alternate sections of land in a 12-mile strip along the
track. [26] The price of remaining sections was raised to double the minimum,
or to $2.50 per acre; the United States would thus lose no cash as a result of
the contribution.

Congressional Acts of 1856 and '57 granted, in the same pattern, land
to aid railroad construction in the states of Iowa, Alabama, Florida, Louisiana,
Wisconsin, Michigan, Mississippi, and Minnesota. The grants to these eight
states were along 4,650 miles of line and amounted to 11,775,484 acres. [27]

The largest grants were made in 1862 and 1864 to the four Pacific
railroads--the Union Pacific, Northern Pacific, Southern Pacific, and the

Santa Fe. By the grants from 1850 to 1871--the only period during which this land grant policy was in effect--a total of about 129,000,000 acres was eventually allotted to railroads. Additional land granted directly by the states amounted to 55,000,000 acres.[28] The total land granted in aid of railroad construction thus amounted to 184,000,000 acres.

These railroad lines were to play a great part in the opening of the West, promoting the sale of land and the peopling of the frontier.

3. <u>Agricultural Development.</u>   An agricultural revolution had taken place in America before the Civil War. Not only was there a rapid expansion in arable land, but farming machinery and techniques had wrought marvelous changes. In the 1840's the John Deere steel plow and the McCormick reaper came into use. The mechanical thresher was widely used in the 1850's. These machines not only greatly reduced the cost of production, but by saving time the reaper and the thresher made possible the harvesting of large grain crops at the moment of maturity, and this accomplishment made large-area farming possible.

Cotton production, given such impetus earlier by invention of the cotton gin and improvement in spinning and weaving, continued to increase. From an annual output of about one billion pounds in 1850, it increased to double that amount in 1860.

Farm production in other lines showed similar advances. "By 1860 the transition from a self-sufficient economy, in which a farmer produces practically all that he needs, to commercial agriculture, in which he specializes on a money crop, and buys most of his supplies with the proceeds, had been generally accomplished."[29]

Three great economic transformations--the Industrial Revolution, the Transportation Revolution, and the Agricultural Revolution--occurred before the Civil War. They were interdependent and simultaneous. The Industrial Revolution could not have taken place had there not been a Transportation Revolution to bring in raw materials and distribute products. Nor could industrial cities have risen and expanded had not an Agricultural Revolution produced more food, and a new transportation system been able to bring the food to the cities. None of the three Revolutions could have occurred without the other two. No one came first; they interacted as cause and effect; they occurred together--and had to.

4. **Population Growth.** The boom of the 1850's was reflected in the population growth of the nation. The large immigration from Ireland and Germany produced by famines and oppression, swelled the incoming tide. It was also encouraged by the alluring opportunities beckoning in America. Labor was in demand at high wages. Ocean transport had been speeded and cheapened. The production of gold in California had quickened and stimulated our economy. Annual immigration averaged about 300,000 between 1845 and 1855, and reached 427,833 in 1854--the high mark for a quarter century. And two-thirds of these newcomers were in their most productive years, between 15 and 40 years of age.

Another significant factor in population change and growth was the rapid rise of the industrial city. The movement toward urban centers, noticeable in the 1820's, was most marked after 1840. The number of cities (then classified as centers with a population of 8,000 or more) increased from 44 in 1840, to 141 in 1860. City population grew five times as fast as that of the country as a whole. The mushrooming factory towns of New England and growing commercial cities like New York and Chicago, made a great market for farm products.

City growth slackened somewhat in the 1850's. This was because the annexation of Texas, the opening of the Oregon country, and our acquisition of the enormous Mexican Cession after the War with Mexico provided new land for eager settlers. Also, much of the region once thought of as the "Great American Desert," was found to be productive farm land. So the growth of rural America was notable in the decade before the Civil War.

E. EFFECTS OF THE CIVIL WAR

The immediate effect of the Civil War was to divert energies toward military needs.

123

1. Boom in Industry and Agriculture. The armies required huge quantities of manufactured goods of all kinds--arms and amunition, clothing, blankets, wagons, ready-to-eat rations. Ready-made clothing now came into general use for the first time.

The mining of coal, lucrative in itself, but also a measuring stick of manufacturing progress, increased three fold. Lumber was in great demand. Iron ore and copper production increased; and the new gold and silver mines of the West added their wealth to the nation.

Railroads, overbuilt during the fifties, were turned into profitable investments by the heavy traffic of the war. Internal waterways did an enormous volume of business.

Agriculture was equally stimulated. With the new farming machinery larger crops could be planted and harvested. Crop failures in Britain produced an added market for grain. Between 1861-63 American farmers furnished more than 40 per cent of the wheat and flour imported into Britain, and the total United States export of wheat rose to over fifty million bushels annually, three times the previous amount. Wool production more than doubled from 1860 to 1865.

2. Expansion of Business. The urgency of demand and shortage of supply produced a rise of prices and an active market. Business boomed. With man power drawn into the armies, a demand for labor was created on the home front. So wages rose. Despite heavy property destruction and the terrific loss of life during the War, trade flourished and business boomed. War contracts netted large profits, for the Government was a dependable and generous purchaser. Big earnings stimulated freer spending. War profits bred a spirit of extravagance and frivolity among non-combatants that was quite in contrast to the suffering and sacrifice on the fighting front.

3. Enlargement of Available Capital. There was call for more capital for new and expanding industry. This need, combined with the Government's heavy borrowing, raised interest rates. The Government borrowed over two billion dollars during the War. The high interest rate attracted large loans from Europe.

J. Cooke and Company, beginning in 1862 as general agent for the United States government in the sale of bonds, made a reputation and a fortune. They publicized the bonds and appealed to small investors as well as to the large

-24-

purchasers. British investors, who in the mid-nineteenth century had a surplus

of capital which they were placing throughout the world, bought heavily in govern-

ment bonds and industrial securities. These bonds and securities proved to be

such good investments that European capitalists were encouraged to place still

more money in the United States.

William Blackmore, a British promoter who later became prominently

connected with western land sales, came to America in 1863 and laid before

Lincoln and Congress a plan for lending the United States one-half billion

dollars. The loan was to be secured by 500,000,000 acres of the public domain. [30]

The plan, at first favorably considered, was finally rejected as politically in-

expedient, inasmuch as it might permit procurement of large segments of the

public domain by foreigners, and at $1 per acre, while citizens were being charged 125

a minimum of $1.25 per acre.

With failure of this plan to materialize, Blackmore and other European

investors turned to the purchase of Mexican Land Grants and other large areas in

the United States, and to opportunities in the open range cattle industry of the West.

In addition to the large Government bond sales at increased rates of

interest, the Government resorted to the questionable expedient of issuing non-

interest-bearing Treasury Notes. The issuance of some $450,000,000 of these

"greenbacks" greatly inflated the currency. This paper money, together with

war spending caused prices to more than double. Gold was driven from circula-

tion, and before the end of the war, a gold dollar would buy $2.50 in currency.

III. DEVELOPMENTS ON THE ARAPAHO-CHEYENNE LAND AREA

A. EARLY EXPLORATION AND TRADE AND INDIAN AFFAIRS

1. Spanish and French Explorations. The Arapaho-Cheyenne Land of
our present interest early became a region of conflicting international claims.
Spaniards were the first white men to reach it. Coronado, the sixteenth-century
knight in shining armor who penetrated from Mexico far into the interior of
North America in 1540, did not explore the area. Others who followed him did,
and in 1706 Ulibarri visited the land, took formal possession of it for Spain, and
named the region San Luis.

In the meantime explorers of the rival nation of France ascended the St.
Lawrence, penetrated to the Great Lakes, and then crossed the portages to the
Mississippi Valley. When La Salle descended the mighty river to its mouth in

126

1682, he claimed the whole drainage basin of the Mississippi as French
territory and named it Louisiana in honor of his king, Louis XIV. Soon other
French explorers were pushing westward from the Mississippi towards the Rocky
Mountains. And the Spaniards ;, firmly entrenched in New Mexico after 1598,
marched out onto the eastern plains to turn back the Frenchmen. There was an
actual clash of arms in the Arapaho-Cheyenne land on the banks of the Platte
River in 1720. Villasur and his soldiers from Santa Fe were defeated and nearly
annihilated by Frenchmen and their Indian allies. In 1739 the French became so
bold that they crossed our Land Area and reached Santa Fe. International trade
between France and Spain across this land was well on the way to becoming
regular traffic when in the great French and Indian War Britain brought France
to her knees and expelled her from North America. When this result became

-26-

imminent, France quickly ceded (in 1762) her claims west of the Mississippi to

Spain, to avoid losing this area to England. Spain retained control and developed

this Louisiana Territory for about forty years.[31]

    2. Purchase and Official Exploration of Louisiana Territory. In 1800

ambitious Napoleon Bonaparte forced Spain to re-cede the Louisiana territory

west of the Mississippi to France. He had hardly taken possession of it before

its capture by Britain was imminent. So to prevent that loss to his enemy,

Napoleon quickly sold it to friendly United States.

    With this great Purchase, at a bargain price, the area of the United States

was doubled, a new field for American expansion was provided, and the future

greatness of the nation was assured.

    By the Louisiana Purchase of 1803, control of the Arapaho-Cheyenne

Land Tract was acquired by the United States. The official exploration of the

127

Louisiana Territory was undertaken for our country by three notable expeditions--

those of Lewis and Clark, Pike, and Long. Lewis and Clark's journey was north of

our Arapaho-Cheyenne territory, but the other two leaders traversed it.

    In 1806 Captain Zebulon M. Pike led his exploring party up the Kaw River

and its Republican Fork, moved southwestward to the Arkansas, and ascended

that river to the Rocky Mountains. He contacted the Pawnee Indians of the

Nebraska region, but did not meet with the Indians of the high plains. After un-

successfully attempting to reach the summit of the peak that later bore his

name, Pike explored the upper Arkansas, the headwaters of the South Platte,

crossed the Sangre de Cristo Mountains, and journeyed south into New Mexico

and Chihuahua. His report was published in Philadelphia in 1810. Interest in the nature and resources of the region was so great in Europe that Pike's book went into English, French, German, and Dutch editions within three years.

Major Stephen H. Long's exploratory tour of 1820 led him up the Platte River to the Rockies and south along the Front Range to the Arkansas. He then divided his company into two parts; one went down the Arkansas River, while the other descended the Canadian. Captain Bell, of Long's party, held councils with the Arapahoes and Cheyennes on the Arkansas River. Chief Bear's Tooth of the Arapahoes, was the big leader of that time and region, dominating several large bands of various tribes. Major Long's report of his trip was first published in the United States and then in England.

3. <u>Fur Trade Exploration and Exploitation.</u> Captain Pike and Major Long were not the first men from the United States to explore the Arapaho-Cheyenne land. The earliest American explorers were trappers and fur traders. Setting their steel-jawed traps in the beaver-ponded streams, these adventurers were rewarded for their trail-blazing by the catch of furry pelts. The trappers were the first whites thoroughly to explore the land of our present interest. They had friendly relations with the Arapahoes and Cheyennes, and such famous Mountain Men and trappers as William Bent, Thomas Fitzpatrick, and John Smith married into the Arapaho and Cheyenne tribes.

The first large trapping party in the region was led by Auguste Chouteau and Julius De Mun. They ascended the Arkansas to the mountains and trapped the region of the upper Platte and Arkansas. They attended a big trading fair on the South Platte (just south of present Denver) in 1816. Here the Arapahoes and Kiowas held a council with the Cheyennes who had recently obtained supplies from

British traders on the upper Missouri and had brought these goods south to trade for horses which the Arapahoes had obtained from the Spaniards of New Mexico.[32]

In 1821 Hugh Glenn and Jacob Fowler came up the Arkansas River to trade with the Arapahoes and Cheyennes. They built a temporary log house on the site of modern Pueblo, Colorado. In 1831 Gantt and Blackwell launched a fur trade venture in the region. They established Gantt's Post (about five miles east of Pueblo). Gantt is reputed to have been the first to introduce whiskey to the Arapahoes, making it palatable to them by diluting and sweetening it. In 1833 William Bent and his partners built Bent's Fort on the north bank of the Arkansas. Bent, who married into the Cheyenne tribe, became the most important person dealing with the Arapahoes and Cheyennes for the next 35 years.

The beaver skin business of the early trappers was short-lived. The country was soon over-trapped. Then came the silk hat, displacing the high-topped beaver headgear in the fashion centers of the world, and the beaver business was ruined. Some of the trappers turned to the buffalo robe trade, procuring these less valuable skins from the Indians. Forts Bent and Pueblo on the Arkansas, Forts Vasquez and St. Vrain on the South Platte, and Fort Laramie near the North Platte were all active trading posts located in the Arapaho-Cheyenne Land Area during the 1830's or '40's. Arapahoes and Cheyennes brought their nicely tanned buffalo robes to these trading centers and bartered them for white man's blankets, knives, beads, and gewgaws. The Buffalo robe business never showed great profits, so most of the trading posts were abandoned before permanent settlers came to occupy the land.

129

4. Trails and Travel through the Area. In the meantime the attractions and resources of New Mexico, Oregon, and California lured prospective settlers to those distant areas. The trails of these emigrants traversed our Arapaho-Cheyenne Land. By 1822 wagons were cutting the ruts of the Santa Fe Trail; in 1830 wagons marked the Oregon Trail as far as the Rockies, and soon they were pushing on to Oregon, California, and Utah. In addition to the emigrant companies on the Oregon Trail and the freight caravans on the road to New Mexico, there were several military and official exploring expeditions through our Indian Land.

In 1835 Colonel Henry Dodge led the First United States Dragoons up the Platte and its South Fork to the mountains, and back along the Arkansas. Ten years later Colonel Stephen W. Kearny led a larger contingent of Dragoons over the same general route. Both of these military expeditions held councils with our Indians, endeavored to win their good will, and impress them with white man strength. All five of the famous Fremont western explorations (1842-53) traversed the Arapaho-Cheyenne land.

In 1846 came the War with Mexico, and over the Santa Fe Trail, along the southern edge of the Arapaho-Cheyenne land, marched General Kearny and his "Army of the West." Cavalry, infantry, and supply trains pushed up the Arkansas River to Bent's Fort and took over for military and hospital purposes this famous trading post and assembly point for the Arapahoes and Cheyennes. Then with New Mexico conquered and with United States forts established there, the Indian owners of the route saw continual freight caravans, military contingents, and then stagecoaches traversing their land and interfering with the buffalo herds.

-30-

The covered-wagon emigrant trains that first went to Oregon and to California in 1841, were augmented annually thereafter. In 1847 the Mormon migration to Utah swelled the tide, and then the flood came with the California-bound argonauts of 1849 and '50. Our Arapahoes and Cheyennes let the white caravans pass in peace, but they began to fret at the killing or the frightening away of the buffalo--the Indians' cattle.

Then came the search for a trans-continental railroad route. The three railroad explorations of 1853, led respectively by Lieut. E. F. Beale, Captain J. W. Gunnison, and Col. J. C. Fremont, all went over our Indians' land.

5. The Fort Laramie Treaty of 1851. Thomas Fitzpatrick, early trapper, trader, and friend of the Indians, was appointed the first United States Indian Agent to the Arapahoes and Cheyennes, in 1846.[33] He traveled much among his Indian wards, and counseled with them. In 1851 he gathered these Indians, along with some other tribes, to the great Fort Laramie Treaty Council. On this occasion the lands of the various tribes were first legally described and recognized by the United States and the areas specifically defined. It is the land as described in this treaty, and now accepted as defined, that is the subject of our present Case. Representatives of the tribes were taken to Washington to be impressed with the numbers and power of the white men. In addition to describing the boundaries of tribal lands and recognizing the Indian title thereto, the Fort Laramie Treaty of 1851 permitted white transit over the Indian land and stipulated that for this concession the Indians were to receive specified annuities.

6. Indian-White Conflicts. The Arapahoes and Cheyennes observed the terms of the treaty. But the Sioux, also signers of the agreement, became involved

131

-31-

in difficulties, especially the Grattan Massacre, in 1854. General W. S. Harney led a punitive expedition against the Sioux and inflicted a severe defeat upon them in 1855. The following year he made a treaty with these Indians at Fort Pierre, present South Dakota.

Thomas Fitzpatrick's Indian Agency of the Upper Arkansas and Platte, which he served faithfully until his death in 1854, was thereupon divided. John W. Whitfield became Agent to the Southern Arapahoes and Southern Cheyennes with headquarters at Bent's Fort on the Arkansas. Thomas S. Twiss served the Northern Arapahoes and Northern Cheyennes from Fort Laramie.

The first collision between the Cheyennes and the United States government occurred in 1856 and led to the "Cheyenne Campaign of 1857." The friction began with a minor incident, when a Cheyenne band returned some stray horses to a military camp above Fort Laramie. One Indian refused to return an alleged stray, so the military commandant ordered the arrest of three braves. As the three were being put in irons, two made a break for freedom. One of these was shot down, the other escaped. Relatives and friends of the Indians fled; and coming upon a lone trapper, killed him in retaliation for the loss of their relative. The remaining Cheyennes fled southward and joined those on the Arkansas. [34]

In August, 1856, a Cheyenne band, encamped on the Platte near Fort Kearny, saw a stagecoach coming up the road. A young half-breed and companion in the band went out towards the coach to ask for tobacco. The driver, becoming frightened, whipped up his horses and fired at the Cheyenne youths. They shot arrows at him, wounding him in the arm. Next day soldiers from the fort made a surprise attack on the Indian village and killed several persons. The fleeing

Cheyennes, coming upon small emigrant trains killed several whites. Some other Cheyennes, unaware of this clash, came in to Fort Kearny. One Indian was arrested, the others fled. Soldiers pursued the Indians and captured thirteen horses. These the Chyennes later recaptured.

In the fall of 1856 the Southern Cheyennes, in response to the call of William Bent, came in to Fort Bent and received their regular annuities. The Northern Cheyennes went to Agent Twiss at Fort Laramie and expressed regret at what had occurred. Twiss pledged the Indians to cease further depredations, and then reported the Cheyennes "perfectly quiet and peaceable."[35]

Most of the Cheyennes, both Northern and Southern, gathered on the upper Solomon River of western Kansas. During the winter they discussed their experiences of the preceding summer, and their grievances grew with the telling. Medicine men worked up fervor and assured the warriors that with the power of their medicine the balls from white man guns would fall powerless. With spring grass and improved horseflesh, enthusiasm for battle mounted. Necessary ceremonies were performed and preparations made to insure victory in war.

Reports of Cheyenne raids on the great emigrant road during 1856 convinced the military leaders and the government at Washington that the Cheyennes must be punished. Accordingly, a campaign was launced in the spring. Colonel E. V. Sumner set out from Fort Leavenworth on May 20th. He divided his command, sending Major John Sedgwick with some troops up the Arkansas, while he led the rest of the command up the Platte. They found no Indians on their march, and joined forces on the South Platte, July 4th.

Now leaving behind the wagon train and cutting supplies to what could be carried on pack animals, Sumner and Sedgwick pushed into the Indian country between the Platte and Arkansas Rivers. On July 29th they contacted the Cheyennes, drawn up for battle. A surprise cavalry charge with drawn bayonets spoiled the Indians' medicine and put them to flight. In the running battle that ensued, most of the Indians escaped on their fresh horses. Sumner followed, found their hastily deserted village, and burned the abandoned tepees and accoutrements. He then moved up the Arkansas River to Bent's Fort, where he took over the annuity goods intended for the Cheyennes and gave most of these to the peaceful Arapahoes. [36]

In July, 1858, Sumner with six companies of the First Cavalry marched into the Arapaho-Cheyenne country again. The Cheyennes offered no resistance, and the troops remained in the Indian country until September.

In the summer of 1858 Agent R. C. Miller of the Upper Arkansas Agency, made his official visit and distributed annuities to the Arapahoes and Cheyennes. He found them peaceful, and requesting help in learning to cultivate the soil. Agent Twiss of the Upper Platte also reported his Indians peaceably inclined.

This year 1858 marked the beginning of a great change for the Indians and for the land of the Arapahoes and Cheyennes--the discovery of gold in their domain. To the story of this we now turn.

B. THE PIKES PEAK GOLD RUSH AND ITS IMMEDIATE EFFECTS

1. Initial Discoveries. Rumors of gold in the Rockies had been afloat for many decades. Spaniards had been lured northward by visions of the yellow metal. American trappers and explorers had heard of gold, but the evidence

134

was vague or meager. Then in 1849 thousands of eager goldseekers hurried overland to the California fields.

Many of these argonauts passed through or along our Arapaho-Cheyenne land. One of these parties was made up of Cherokee Indians who had done mining in the gold fields of north Georgia. This Cherokee party traveled up the Arkansas River, moved northward, and descended to the South Platte. At Ralston Creek, in the vicinity of present Denver, they found "color", and stopped to do some panning. But the placer was not rich enough to hold them while their minds were filled with visions of limitless gold in California.

After they had reached the Pacific Coast and then returned home, they thought again of the prospects at the foothills of the Rockies. John Beck, a Cherokee preacher, urged the formation of a party to prospect thoroughly the foot of the Rocky Mountains. After correspondence and consultations, two parties were formed--one in Georgia, composed mostly of whites, and the other of Cherokees in Indian Territory of present Oklahoma. The two agreed to meet on the Arkansas River enroute. This was done, and the combined parties made their way to Ralston Creek. The prospectors, over 100 strong, searched the stream beds and gullies for about two weeks without finding anything rich. Discouraged, all the Indians and most of the whites turned homeward. Only Green Russell, leader of the Georgians, and twelve men remained to search further.

The very next day the thirteen hopefuls moved up the South Platte and found a placer. While making good wages at this site they were visited by some traders from Fort Laramie, who carried a sample of the gold-bearing sand back

135

to Kansas City. There it was washed before an eager crowd. The promising results were published in the newspaper; and the gold excitement began its sweep of the country. Some hurried out to the mines that fall, but many more controlled their eagerness and made preparations to journey the next spring.

The goldseekers who went to the mines in the fall of 1858 learned that little gold had yet been found. But the hopeful staked out townsites at likely locations and waited for spring.

2. <u>Pikes Peak Rush of 1859</u>. With the first appearance of grass the rush began.[37] In covered wagons, on horseback, afoot, and with packs on their backs they hurried westward. When the advance companies of '59ers reached the mouth of Cherry Creek they found the diggings far too poor to justify the mad rush. Soon the disillusioned turned back over the trail and sent forth the cry of the Pikes Peak Humbug."

136

But all were not disheartened. Some pointed to the placers and argued that the gold there had been washed down from veins in the mountains and that these would surely be found. Just as the whole uncertain structure was about to collapse, a gold vein was discovered by John Gregory on May 6, 1859. Other lodes were found and the future of the country was assured. Men flocked to the district and their gold recoveries were gratifying. O. J. Hollister gives specifics:

It was not unusual for four or five men to wash out from the Gregory, Bates, Bobtail, Mammoth, Hunter, and many other lodes, then newly discovered, one hundred and fifty dollars a day for weeks together. Single pans of dirt could be taken up carefully from any of a dozen lodes that would yield five dollars. Zeigler, Spain & Co., ran a sluice three weeks on the Gregory, and cleaned up 3,000 pennyweights, their highest day's work yielding $495, their lowest $21. Sopris, Henderson & Co. took out $607 in four days, and on a subsequent day, $280.

Shears & Co., two days, $852, -- all taken from within three feet of the surface. Brown & Co., one and a half days, $260; John H. Gregory, five days, $942; Casto, Kendall & Co., one and a half days, $135; Colman, King & Co., one-half day, $75; Defrees & Co., twelve days, with one sluice, $2,080. In one day Leper, Gridley & Co. obtained $1,009 from three sluices One sluice washed out in one day $510. Foote & Simmons realized $300 in three days. The Illinois Company obtained $175 in their first day's sluicing from the Brown Lode in Russell District. Walden & Co. took in one day, from a lode in the same district, $125. Jacob Pogue took $500 from a lode in the same district in three days. Three men took from the Kansas Lode, in two days, $500. Kehler, Patton & Fletcher averaged with five hands on the Bates Lode, $100 a day for two months. Day & Crane, on the same lode, with seven or eight hands, sluiced for ten weeks, their smallest weekly run being $180, their largest, $357. J. C. Ross & Co., with four hands, averaged $100 a day on the Fish Lode for four months. F. M. Cobb & Co., on the Bobtail Lode, with four men, averaged from $75 to $100 a day for two months. Heffner, McLain & Cooper worked four men at a sluice on the Clay County Lode, averaging $100 a day for ten weeks. Shoog & Co. averaged $100 a day for three months, sluicing with five men on the Maryland Lode. [38]

Goldseekers by the hundreds rushed into the various areas as mines were discovered. To secure order and protect property rights mining districts were organized. These spontaneous democratic governments enacted laws and regulations not only concerning mining claims, but upon civil and criminal matters as well. Numerous mining districts were created on the North and South Forks of Clear Creek, on Boulder Creek and in South Park. Several of these printed their constitutions and bylaws and all wrote out their rules and kept records of claims and title transfers.

To supply the numerous mining camps in the hills, supply depots were established near the base of the Front Range. These developed into the cities of Denver, Boulder, Colorado City, and Pueblo. Soon sluices, arrastras, and even stamp mills were operating at the mines. Gardens and farms were developed beside the streams and raised produce for the market. Trails were widened into roads, and these were soon lined with wagons freighting in supplies. Log houses in the towns gave way to structures of frame and brick. Before the year was out, schools, churches, and a theater were giving the settlements an air of civilization.

The year 1860 saw another rush to the new eldorado. There was now less wild excitement and more sober determination. More men came with their families, planning to build new homes. Shafts and tunnels pursued the veins deeper into the earth. Towns took on the look of stability.

3. <u>Governmental Development</u> . Kansas and Nebraska Territories had been created by Congress in 1854, and the settling of their eastern areas had proceeded rapidly. Western Kansas, extending to the continental divide and co-terminal with the Arapaho-Cheyenne land, contained most of the new mines. As a result of the heavy emigration, the Kansas legislature created new counties in the gold region. But the ambitious miners visioned a mountain state of their own, and set about to organize the State of Jefferson. The more moderate element won control of the convention and the citizenry was satisfied with creation of the spontaneous government of Jefferson Territory. Officers were elected; a legislature convened; and laws were enacted and published. [39]

But this extra-legal general government was not so fully respected as were the spontaneous and also extra-legal local governments. In the camps, Mining Districts were organized, with codes of laws and regulations adopted in that great democratic institution, the mass meeting. In the agricultural areas the squatters formed Claim Clubs, joining together in the well known frontier

138

pattern, to protect their squatter claims. Neither of these governments was legal; the property claims under them were maintained by physical force. In the towns, similar vigilante action was resorted to on occasion to establish order and mete out criminal justice.

Finally, after repeated urgings by the residents of the mining country, Congress acted to create Colorado Territory, on February 28, 1861. The regular governmental machinery was soon in operation--counties created and organized, towns chartered, courts in session, schools established, and roads constructed.

Paralleling this was growth in the towns--residences multiplying, businesses built and expanded, newspapers published, mail and express service provided, banks founded, and even mints established for coining the gold from the mines.

C. INDIAN REACTION TO THE WHITE OCCUPANCY OF THEIR LAND, 1858-65

1. White Intrusions and Efforts at Treaty Making . The Arapahoes and Cheyennes appeared to be not greatly disturbed at the eager whites digging in the gravel beds in 1858. Then as the intruders increased, staked out mining claims and town sites, grazed their animals on the prairie grass, and began to act as though they were exclusive owners of the land, the Indians became concerned for their own property rights.

On December 17, 1858, William Bent wrote from his trading post on the Arkansas to the Superintendent of Indian Affairs at St. Louis:

> The Cheyenne, Arapaho and other Indians of this River are now very uneasy and restless about their country, the whites coming into it, making large and extensive settlements and laying off and

building towns all over the best part of their country, on this
river, also on the South Fork of the Platt & Cherry Creek.
This is their principle hunting ground. This movement they
do not understand, as they have never been treated with for
it. . .

        The emigration to the Gold Diggins this fall has been
very large, and they still continue to come. They have all
passed unmolested by the Indians, although they have stolen
several horses from them already, this they do not think
much of, but losing the favorite hunting ground and their
only place to get their summer and fall provisions, that
goes rather hard with them, although I hope it may turn out
well. . . .[40]

The following summer William Bent, as Indian Agent, held councils with

the Southern Arapahoes and Cheyennes. They expressed a willingness to settle

on the Fountain and Purgatory branches of the Arkansas, provided the Govern-

ment would teach them to farm and give equipment. They wanted a treaty with-

140 out delay and they asked "for pay for the large district known to contain gold."[41]

        Agent Twiss of the Upper Platte Agency went back to Washington in the

winter of 1858-59 to present the problems of his Indians. While there he wrote

to Commissioner of Indian Affairs, James W. Denver (who had been Governor

of Kansas in the summer of 1858, and for whom the town at the mouth of Cherry

Creek had been named), offering to submit a plan for a treaty. Apparently he

was encouraged to go ahead, and he did so. At a council with the Northern

Arapahoes and Northern Cheyennes and the Sioux on September 18, 1859, he

submitted a treaty to the Indians and obtained their acceptance. It provided a

reservation for the Northern Arapahoes on the Cache la Poudre and annuities

of $20,000 per year. For the Northern Cheyennes it gave a reservation on the

Laramie River and annuities of $16,000.[42] The agreement was never approved by

Congress or ratified by the Senate.

In the meantime the great Pikes Peak gold rush of 1859 had swept over the Indian land. The whites came in by the thousands and took possession, ignoring entirely the rights and title of the Indians. B. D. Williams, the Delegate from the mining region (self-organized as Jefferson Territory), wrote to Secretary of Interior Thompson telling of the large white emigration. On May 18, 1860, Williams wrote to the Commissioner of Indian Affairs and said that on the day previous Senator S. A. Douglas had said in the Senate: "Every man in Pikes Peak is there in violation of law; every man of them has incurred the penalty of $1,000 fine and six months imprisonment for going in violation of the Indian intercourse law," and seizing without authority upon land to which the Indian title is not extinguished. (Wants to know interpretation of the Department. Big Roll Summary, page 13)

141

In the year 1860 there was another great white migration onto the area. The summer of 1860 saw also a campaign led by Major Sedgwick against the Kiowas and Comanches of the plains. As winter approached, he settled on the north bank of the Arkansas, occupied Bent's New Fort, and built Fort Wise near it.

2. Fort Wise Treaty and the Question of its Acceptance. On August 11, 1860, the Secretary of the Interior instructed A.B. Greenwood, Commissioner of Indian Affairs, to go to the Arapahoes and Cheyennes and hold a treaty council with them. He reached Bent's Fort on September 8th and found there most of the Southern Arapahoes and a few Cheyennes. The runners sent out to bring in the Cheyenne villages had failed in their object. Finally some Cheyenne chiefs came in and Greenwood held a council with them and the waiting Arapahoes. He

told them that the Great Father wanted them to settle down and to reduce their reservation. The Cheyennes wanted to consult the other chiefs and their people before agreeing. Greenwood wrote: "It should be remarked that a portion of the Cheyenne and Arapahoe bands reside north of the fort, upon the Platte River, and belong to Agent Twiss's agency, and receive their annuities from him; ..."[43]

Greenwood proposed a reservation on both sides of the Arkansas and wanted the Fort Wise military reservation reduced to give more good land to the Indians. Greenwood left Fort Wise on September 20, before he had completed the agreement. He directed that A. G. Boone, who succeeded William Bent as Agent, should proceed to consumate the treaty.

Agent Boone induced the "confederated tribes of Arapahoe and Cheyenne Indians of the Upper Arkansas River" to sign the Fort Wise Treaty on February 18, 1861. They ceded their rights to "all lands now owned, possessed, or claimed by them, wherever situated," except a tract to be reserved for the use of said tribes located within the boundaries described in the treaty and to be "known as the Reservation of the Arapahoes and Cheyennes of the Upper Arkansas."[44]

The Northern Arapahoes and Northern Cheyennes of Agent Twiss's Agency on the North Platte, refused to come in and were not parties to this treaty.

Strong efforts were made by Governor Evans of Colorado Territory to induce them to sign. He and Loree and Colley, Indian Agents respectively of the Northern and the Southern bands of Arapahoes and Cheyennes, were appointed Commissioners to treat with the Northern bands. They sent Elbridge Gerry and Antoine Janise, old Mountain Men and Indian traders, to go to the Northern bands and invite them to a council on the Arickaree Fork of the Republican River on

September 1, 1863. The Northern Arapahoes and Cheyennes refused to meet the Commissioners and the plan for a treaty failed. The Cheyennes said, "The whites are all at war in the States and will kill one another, and the Indians will take this county in the spring."[45]

3. The Indian War and the Sand Creek Massacre. Intelligent Indians saw in the white man's Civil War their opportunity. Perhaps the Great Manitou had caused the white men to war among themselves, so that the Indians might drive the intruders back to the land of the rising sun. In 1862 and '63 Indians began to collect firearms. In the spring of 1864 they clashed with Colorado troops on the South Platte and Arkansas Rivers. In June Indians stampeded horses from freight trains along the Platte River road. They killed a rancher and his family thirty miles east of Denver. In July and August general attacks on the emigrant road brought destruction to the stagecoach line and freight trains. All white travel was stopped on the Platte River road.

Gov. Evans issued a call for volunteers to fight the Indians, and the Rocky Mountain News added: "A few months of active extermination against the red devils will bring quiet, and nothing else will."[46] In the meantime the Indians planned a concerted attack upon the Colorado settlements for August 22, but the news leaked out, the settlers were warned, and the attack did not take place.

In late August, 1864, a letter from Black Kettle and other chiefs of the Cheyennes proposed peace and an exchange of prisoners. Major Wynkoop went to their village on the Smoky Hill, recovered four white prisoners, and brought the chiefs to Denver for a parley. Orders came from the head of the military forces that no peace was to be made until the Indians had suffered more. The chiefs returned to their tribes.

About the middle of October, Left Hand's band of Arapahoes came in to Fort Lyon (formerly Fort Wise) and announced their peaceful intentions. They came in response to Gov. Evans' earlier order for all peaceful Indians to gather at designated military forts for protection. After being fed at Fort Lyon for some days the Arapahoes were sent to establish camp on Sand Creek, about forty miles northeast, and within their Reservation as defined by the Fort Wise Treaty of February 18, 1861. Here they were joined by Black Kettle's Cheyennes to form a village of six or seven hundred. They considered that they had complied with the Governor's directives and were secure from attack. In the meantime plans were afoot which were to make their position far from safe.

A regiment of "Hundred Days Men," recruited for three months' service against the Indians, was anxious to strike a decisive blow. Col. J. M. Chivington, with most of these recruits and some companies of the First Colorado Regiment (Civil War troops), set out on their campaign. Moving rapidly and cautiously they moved to Fort Lyon and then toward the Indian encampment on Sand Creek, taking care that no wind of their approach reached the Indian village. After an all-night march the soldiers swooped down upon the unsuspecting camp at sunrise, November 29, 1864. The United States flag flew from one of the tepees, and a chief who ran out holding up his hand in sign of peace was shot down. The slaughter was terrible, men, women, and children being killed indiscriminately as they ran.

Estimates of the Indian losses vary from 100 to 500. Others escaped by flight. The military commander is reputed to have said: "Nits make lice"; and in accord with orders, no prisoners were taken. Of the troops, ten were killed and thirty-eight wounded.

The "Sand Creek Massacre" is one of the most notorious affairs in the history of the West.[47] The terrified fugitives from Sand Creek told their story to other tribes. A thousand Indians joined them and moved north to make a counter attack. Early in January, 1865, they plundered the mail station and supply stores at Julesburg on the South Platte and killed soldiers at nearby Fort Sedgwick.

Acting Governor Elbert telegraphed to Washington: "We must have 5,000 troops to clean out these savages or the people of this Territory will be compelled to leave it."[48] Martial law was proclaimed in Colorado and more local troops were raised.

The Indians again raided the South Platte in February and carried off supplies of flour, sugar, and rice to their winter encampment on Powder River. The following spring and summer they raided stations and trains on the North Platte, and engaged in the Platte Bridge Fight near present Casper, Wyoming.

Additional troops, including "Galvanized Yankees" (Southern war prisoners employed to fight Indians), marched out from the East and opened the lines of communication and protected the settlements.

4. The Treaties of 1865 and 1868. Finally the Southern Arapahoes and Southern Cheyennes were induced to come in to a peace council. The outcome was the Treaty of the Little Arkansas, of October 14, 1865. By this agreement these Indians relinquished their rights and claims to the territory which is the subject of this case, being the land described by the Fort Laramie Treaty of 1851 as belonging to the Arapahoes and Cheyennes. They were removed from their homeland to a Reservation of less desirable land in present Oklahoma.

145

The Northern Arapahoes and Northern Cheyennes continued to roam free, associating principally with the Sioux north of the Platte River. Finally some of their leaders were induced to sign a treaty on May 10, 1868, giving up their claims to the Arapaho-Cheyenne Land of our present concern.

IV. STATUS AND PROSPECTS OF THE ARAPAHO-CHEYENNE AREA IN OCTOBER, 1865

INTRODUCTION

Among the whites on the Arapaho-Cheyenne Land Area a definite optimism existed in the summer of 1865. It resulted from the following conditions:

The termination of the Indian War of 1864 and the acceptance of the Little Arkansas Treaty of 1865 gave promise of an end to Indian conflicts in the region.

The close of the Civil War had released thousands of soldiers and other potential settlers to seek homes and jobs in the West.

Mining development, heretofore retarded by refractory ores and lack of machinery, was now ready for a boom.

The railroads pushing out across the plains were beginning to carry passengers and freight and were giving promise of easy and rapid transportation soon to be available.

The farming area was extending westward from the region of eastern Kansas and Nebraska, and along the Platte and Arkansas Rivers.

Profits and capital accumulated in the brisk wartime business were available for investment in the new country, and the new National Banks were providing loans and currency.

These various conditions and prospects, which were stimulating emigration into the region, we shall describe more fully in turn.

A. INDIAN REMOVAL AND END OF THE CIVIL WAR

As a result of the Indian War of 1864 and of the Peace Treaty of October 14, 1865, the Arapaho-Cheyenne Land Area was nearly cleared of Indians. Only Friday's peaceful band of Northern Arapahoes in the Fort Collins area and some Northern Cheyennes and Arapahoes in the Fort Laramie region remained. The military forts previously established on the Arapaho-Cheyenne land--Forts Laramie, Collins, Sedgwick, Lyons, and Larned--were still manned by United States troops, as guarantees against possible return of the natives. Fears of Indian attacks were allayed, and the whites now felt secure in possession of the land they had wrested from the original inhabitants.

147

The Civil War, that had practically stopped immigration from Europe, was now at an end, and migration to the Promised Land could be resumed. Many could look again with hope to our shores and to the large areas of procurable land in the West.

The War had also curtailed the normal westward flow of our own citizens. Now the gates were raised and the pent-up reservoir could flood the land newly made available.

B. MINING DEVELOPMENT

When the original placer gold finds of 1858 were supplemented by discoveries of veins the next spring in the Central City region, definite assurances of mining wealth were at hand. Other rich mining districts on Clear Creek, Boulder Creek, and in South Park brought enthusiasm this year. The outstanding new di strict opened in 1860 was in California Gulch, near later Leadville, where about 5,000 miners worked. Over the divide, on the Blue River and its branches new mines were opened. Immigration to the mining region was heavy this year. In July there were sixty mills and thirty arrastras in the Gregory District. The placers paid well in 1861 and '62. [49]

The Civil War and the Indian conflict which stopped most of the emigration to the Colorado region helped cause the slump in mining. The depression was furthered when the tunnels and shafts in lode mines grew deeper and more costly to drive and operate, and when the miners encountered refractory sulphide ore which known processes could not treat successfully.

A detailed description of lodes and of mining districts, with operating companies and productions of each, is given in Hollister's The Mines of Colorado (Springfield, Mass., 1867). Such statistics are being presented by other witnesses in this case. Suffice it here to say that by the end of 1865 conditions were improving. Various smelting processes were meeting with success. Silver had been discovered on South Clear Creek, and Georgetown and Silver Plume were to develop into rich silver camps. Prospects in other areas gave promise of the great mining developments yet to come.

C. TRANSPORTATION PROGRESS

1. Stagecoach and Freight Lines. The Leavenworth and Pikes Peak Express that ran its stagecoaches up the Republican Fork of Kansas River and westward into Denver in 1859, moved its line to the Platte River after a few months to consolidate with the mail route to Utah and California. This service was improved to a daily schedule in 1861, with a Government contract at $1,000,000 per

year. Ben Holladay, "the stagecoach king." took over the line in 1862 and ran

his California stages through Denver. Later he was to sell out to Wells Fargo,

who continued operation until displaced by the railroad. [50]

In 1864 the Butterfield Overland Dispatch came up the Smoky Hill River

Route, right through the heart of the Arapaho-Cheyenne land area. Stagecoaches

and fast freight wagons operated on this route.

A stagecoach line also operated over the Santa Fe Trail, across our

Indian land and to New Mexico. The ox-drawn freight trains and the emigrant

wagons wore ruts along this Trail beside the Arkansas, and also along the favored

route beside the Platte.

The big freight outfits being lugged across the plains usually consisted

of 26 wagons, each drawn by two or three yokes of oxen or by two or three span

of horses or mules. It is reported that in 1865 there were 7,240 wagons, 57,002

oxen, 6,887 mules and horses, and 7,700 men employed in freighting goods to

Colorado from the shipping point of Plattsmouth on the Missouri River. Much

freight was being hauled from other points as well. It was estimated that 62,500

tons of freight were carried to Colorado that year. [51] All of this was carried across

our Arapaho-Cheyenne Land and to settlers upon this same land. Heavy mining

machinery, dry goods, and food supplies constituted the major part of this freight.

2. Railroads. In 1862 Congress passed the Act which provided for the

building of the Union Pacific and the Kansas Pacific railroads across the Arapaho-

Cheyenne tract. Alternate sections of land in a 20-mile strip along the track were

given to the railroads, and the Government increased the price of retained sec-

tions to a minimum of $2.50 per acre. The railroads also received a loan of

Government bonds at the rate of $16,000 to $48,000 per mile. In 1864, the
Government loan was changed from a first to a second mortgage upon the road,
and the land grant was doubled. Now the Union Pacific began actual construction.[52]

With the War on, both labor and capital for railroad construction were
scarce. But ground was broken at Omaha in December 1863. Building went
slowly at first; only forty miles of track were completed by the end of 1865.
Now, however, all was ready for rapid construction. By July 1866, the road
would stretch 300 miles westward from the Missouri and would reach Cheyenne in
the fall of 1867.

What came to be known as the Kansas Pacific was a second railroad
across the Arapaho-Cheyenne Land--one through the heart of the area. Originally
chartered as the Leavenworth, Pawnee, and Western in 1855, it was to become
one of the eastern branches of the Union Pacific. Its route was later changed
to run west to Denver and then north to connect with the Union Pacific at
Cheyenne. Its course was through the better settled area of Kansas and was
finally completed to Denver and Cheyenne in 1870.

A third railroad affecting the Arapaho-Cheyenne Land was the Santa Fe.
Chartered as the Atchison and Topeka in 1859, it later received the usual federal
land grant and under the vigorous leadership of Cyrus K. Holliday, pushed on
towards Santa Fe. It ran along the Arkansas River, and its land grant included
a 20-mile strip along the southern part of our Indians' land.

The Burlington and the Rock Island, that were to run across the Arapaho-
Cheyenne country in the early 1880's, were not yet visioned by most people in 1865.

D. RAILROAD LAND SALES AND PROMOTION

The railroads, building and projected to the Arapaho-Cheyenne land, were very potent forces by the end of 1865. These roads would soon place the products of millions of acres of new land within the reach of markets. The rails would bring cheaper machinery and supplies to Western farms and towns. With the large areas of land granted to them by the Government, these railroad companies were owners of vast estates.

The land grant railroads employed various policies in the disposal of their lands, but all obtained considerable revenue from the sale of their government tracts. The first of these railroads, the Illinois Central, sold its land at the highest figure. Writes Dr. B. H. Hibbard, in his History of the Public Land Policies (New York, 1924), p. 257:

151

> Little land was sold by the Illinois Central road prior to
> 1855. By 1864 somewhat over half of the whole amount had been
> disposed of at an average price of $10.77. Sales were fairly
> brisk till about 1871 at which time all but a third of a million
> acres had been sold. The price remained about as usual, the
> average for the two million acres sold before 1871 being $10.61.
> The small amount of land remaining was a long time on the mar-
> ket, but by 1890 an unimportant area was left. The price rose a
> little, despite the fact that much of the later sales were of land
> not very high in quality, making the average price on the total
> sales up to that date, 2,457,000 acres, $11.70. Thus the gross
> receipts from the land were not far from thirty million dollars,
> or about six-sevenths the first cost of the road.

The Chicago and Northwestern sold its land in Iowa in fairly small tracts (73 to 112 acres). Writes Dr. Hibbard (p. 258):

> The railroad did not push sales while government land was open
> for homesteads or on sale at a dollar and a quarter or two dollars
> and a half an acre, but they waited till the government land was gone
> and then sold at a figure two to four times as great.

The Union Pacific, Kansas Pacific, and Denver Pacific were the principal railroads with extensive land areas on the Arapaho-Cheyenne tract. The Kansas Pacific, running from Kansas City to Denver, received a land grant of about 6,000,000 acres. Approximately one-half of this lay in the Arapaho-Cheyenne land. The railroad was completed to Denver on August 15, 1870.

This railroad's land, that east of Ellsworth, Kansas, only, was first offered for sale in 1869. This year 384,185 acres were sold for a total of $1,008,191.47, or about $2.61 per acre. The railroads policy was to sell at a moderate price to induce settlement and promote ultimate business for the road.[53]

The Fourth Annual Report of the Kansas Pacific Railroad (Exhibit A), p. 11, shows 124,168 acres sold in 1870, for $389,105.68, being an average of 3.13 per acre.

The Fifth Annual Report shows sales in 1871 of 121,743.18 acres at an average of $3.56 per acre. In the area from the 380-mile post (west of Kansas City) to Denver, wholly within the Arapaho-Cheyenne area, 21,690.8 acres were sold that year at an average of $5.62 per acre (Exhibit B, p. 10).

Byers and Parker, who became the sole agents of all Kansas Pacific and Denver Pacific railroad land in Colorado, put out a 24-page pamphlet describing this land and the conditions of its sale. This booklet (Exhibit C) is entitled 3,000,000 Acres of Choice Farming, Grazing, Coal and Timber Land Along the Kansas Pacific and Denver Pacific Railway, for Sale at Low Prices upon Long Time, with Nominal Rates of Interest, by Byers and Parker.

152

-52-

It tells how the lands were to be sold, with appraisers setting a fair price. "Agricultural lands generally range from $3.50 to $6.00; timber lands from $5.00 to $10.00; coal lands from $10.00 to $100.00 and grazing lands from $2.00 to $4.00 per acre (p. 15).

The Weekly Rocky Mountain News of Denver of January 8, 1873, (Exhibit D) gives the number of acres of Denver Pacific railroad land sold during 1872 as 19,242, at an average of $4.08 per acre; and Kansas Pacific land sold by W. N. Byers the same year as 1,358 acres at $6.29 per acre.

Sales of Denver Pacific and Kansas Pacific land by Byers and Parker for 1873 were reported in the Rocky Mountain News of January 8, 1874 (Exhibit E), as 42,882 acres at an average of $5.46 per acre.

The Report to the Stockholders of the Union Pacific Railroad for the Year 1875 (Boston, 1876), p. 5 says:

153

> The total amount of Land Sales for 1875 was 111,049.55 acres, purchased by 705 different persons, at an average price of $3.36 per acre, amounting to $404,462.

> The total amount of land sold since organization of Department was 1,082,893.36 acres at an average price of $4.47 per acre, amounting to $5,336,044.02.

The Union Pacific Annual Report to Stockholders for 1877 pages 13-14, gives the land sales of 1876 as 125,905.21 acres at an average of $2.98 per acre; for 1877 as 69,015.87 acres at $4.98 per acre.

The Annual Report to Stockholders of the Union Pacific for 1880, p. 12, gives for 1878, sales of 318,903.47 acres at an average of $4.88-1/4 per acre; and for 1879, sale of 243,337.31 acres at an average of $4.141 per acre.

The Kansas Pacific and Denver Pacific railroads organized the National
Land Company to dispose of the land received from the Government. This
company sold large tracts to "colonies" that settled in Colorado. The colony
plan of settlement, extensively used, was a method whereby prospective settlers
in the East organized to select and secure a tract for occupancy. Through cooperative effort they could procure desirable land, obtain cheap railroad transportation to the selected location, and have community life from the start. The
Union Colony that founded Greeley, and the Chicago-Colorado Colony that settled
Longmont, were among the successful Colorado colonies established in this way.
They bought land from the National Land Company for $3 to $6 per acre, and were
able to obtain the alternate sections from the Government for the fixed price of
$2.50 per acre. [54]

In the Daily Rocky Mountain News of April 13, 1870, we read:

> The Union Colony has just completed through the National
> Land Company, a purchase from the Denver Pacific Railway &
> Telegraph Company of over 60,000 acres of land, upon which they
> paid in cash over $31,000. Another payment will be made inside
> of 60 days. For some of this land they pay $5 per acre, and the
> average is over 3-1/3 dollars. They also apply to government
> for an equal amount, and have paid to individuals for improved
> and entered lands within the last week almost $30,000. Their
> purchases entire will cover at least 150,000 acres, and amount
> to more than $400,000. Mr. Meeker left today for Greeley to
> commence work actively, in surveying the town, digging ditches
> and getting in crops. He will in a few days start for New York.

The Executive Committee of the Union Colony issued a statement on
May 16, 1870, regarding their first purchases. It showed the purchases from
the Denver Pacific Railway at $3 to $5 per acre, and from private individuals at
from $8 to $10 per acre. [55] This is Exhibit F.

Most of the railroads did well with their land. The Northern Pacific obtained from the sale of its granted lands almost double the total cost of the road. The land sales approximated $136,000,000; the railroad cost about $70,000,000.[56]

Dr. Hibbard summarizes:

It is all but impossible to assemble the information for all sales, but a close approximation may be made from the reports of several roads which in the aggregate represent the bulk of land grants within the area readily available for agriculture. The average price of substantially all railroad land sold prior to 1881 was $4.76 per acre. Until that time most sales consisted of land to be used for ordinary farming within the humid district. The sales of the Illinois Central road were about all of the kind to take place in Illinois, and, as stated above, these lands brought about $11.70 per acre.

For the state of Iowa a very complete report is at hand, from which it appears that 3,724,801 acres were granted to nine roads. This land substantially all sold prior to 1893 at an average price of $5.50 per acre.

The Union Pacific was one of the greatest land grant beneficiaries, and its sales up to and including 1894 were 7,141,000 acres, at an average price of $3.14 per acre. Later sales have been such as three-quarters of a million acres in 1905 at $3.44 per acre; a million and a quarter acres at $2.72 in 1906, and a very small amount in 1911 at $4.08.

The Chicago, St. Paul, Minneapolis and Omaha between the years 1882 and 1907 sold 1,502,000 acres of land at $5.23 per acre. The Northern Pacific between 1875 and 1895 sold 4,352,000 acres of land, largely in North Dakota, at an average price of $3.90 per acre.[57]

The total grants to railroads which ran through our Arapaho-Cheyenne land were as follows:

Union Pacific, 11,935,121.46 acres
Union Pacific, (Kansas Pacific Division, Kansas City to Denver) 6,175,660.63 acres
Union Pacific (successor to Denver Pacific, Denver to Cheyenne) 821,164.15
Atlantic & Pacific (now the Santa Fe), 9,878,352.14.[58]   (Exhibit G)

155

The railroads building westward, in addition to affecting the sale and price

of land, were to affect greatly the mining and town building in the West. The

cheaper and more ready procurement of equipment and supplies for the mines

through railroad transportation would add to the value of the mining property.

Real estate in the towns would increase in value with railroad service to bring

in supplies and more settlers.

William J. Palmer, who surveryed the route of the Kansas Pacific rail-

road, presently became the chief organizer, promoter and builder of the Denver

and Rio Grande Railroad. The scandal associated with the Credit Mobilier and

the Crocker Construction Company in the building respectively of the Union Pacific

and the Central Pacific, induced the United States Government to stop the giving

156 of land grants and loans to promote the building of railroads. So the Denver

and Rio Grande and other railroads launched after 1869, had to depend on their

own resources and resourcefulness. The activities of W. J. Palmer and his

Denver and Rio Grande exhibited the importance of the promotion and sale of land.

He was to locate and promote town sites along his railroad and this was done

on an extensive scale. Colorado Springs, West Pueblo, Alamosa, and Durango

were among the towns so promoted.

From the Palmer Collection of documents preserved in the State Histor-

ical Society of Colorado archives, we take some documents to illustrate land

sales and promotion.

First, as Exhibit H, we submit the confidential letter of Palmer to

W. A. Bell, English capitalist and promoter and associate of Palmer. In this letter, of November 19, 1869, Palmer proposes the purchase of land in the "Pinery," southeast of Denver. "The Denver Pinery lands," he writes, "now to be had from $2.50 to $5 per acre probably will in selected positions be worth I think at least $20 per acre pretty soon after our Road reaches Denver (next summer)." He says there are between 150,000 and 200,000 acres in the Pinery. Bell procured capital in the East and purchases were made of Pinery lands.

Exhibit I, from the Palmer Collection, is a letter of E. M. Stone to Governor A. C. Hunt of Colorado, September 12, 1870, proposing the purchase of 33,000 acres of the St. Charles Mexican Land Grant, immediately south of the Arkansas River and adjoining Pueblo, Colorado. This land, he says, "can be had for $150,000, or about $4.50 per acre." "The price of Ranches all over our country is from five to twenty dollars per acre," he says.

157

Exhibit J, from the same Collection, is Governor Hunt's letter of November 9, 1872, to W. J. Palmer. It refers to the one and one-half million acres of land owned by the Denver and Rio Grande Railroad, and proposes plans to induce emigration from rural Switzerland, Germany, and elsewhere in Europe, to settle upon it. Sell the land in 40-acre tracts at $15 per acre, he advises.

Exhibit K, is "Inducements offered to the Agriculturalist of England to remove to the State of Kansas." It describes the fine resources of the region and then says: "The prices of land vary from $4 to $9 per acre, and are sold in farms of 40, 60, 80, 120, and 160 acres and upwards on payment of 1/3 cash, and the remainder in yearly installments within 3 years." This is signed by Chris Long of New York and was drafted for W. J. Palmer's inspection. It is undated, but the internal evidence indicates it was written in 1867 or 1868.

E. AGRICULTURAL AND INDUSTRIAL EXPANSION

1. **Early Farming**. While prospectors and miners in 1859 were digging in the gravel or examining mountain slopes for signs of gold, other pioneers were selecting likely plots of farming land. In the established frontier pattern these men staked out farms, and organized Claim Clubs for the registering of their holdings. In 1859 and 1860 farms were developed along the South Platte and such branches as Clear, Cherry, St. Vrain, and Boulder Creeks. Along the Arkansas River and Fountain Creek also, farms were established. [59]

This was irrigation agriculture, a type of farming practiced by the Indians of the Southwest for centuries; and which the Spanish settlers of New Mexico had adopted. Among the Colorado pioneers were men familiar with irrigation practices in New Mexico, California, and Utah, so they began at once to apply the principle. Diversion dams were constructed, irrigation ditches dug, and soon water was supplied to thirsty land. Garden vegetables were first produced then followed yields of such crops as corn, wheat, barley, and potatoes.

In his message to the legislature in July 1862, Governor Evans called attention to the development of agriculture: "The crops now standing on the farms in the valleys of the various branches of the South Platte and Fontaine-qui-Bouille afford most encouraging prospect. In the latter valley alone there will be produced this year, according to careful estimates, 25,000 bushels of wheat, 40,000 bushels of corn, and 20,000 bushels of potatoes, and other produce in proportion."[60]

The first threshing machine was brought to the South Platte Valley in the fall of 1861. Others came the next year. Mr. J. McAuley, owner of one of the machines, is quoted in the Rocky Mountain News of January 19, 1864:

From Mr. McAuley, who has been engaged in thrashing ever since last harvest and has doubtless better means of knowing than any other man in Colorado, we learn that the small grain crop of the Platte watershed the past year was about 50,000 bushels. Of this total about 33,000 bushels was wheat, equivalent to 13,200 sacks of flour, provided all of it was ground. A large share of this amount, however, must be counted out; a part for seed, and a very considerable quantity for feed for stock. The remaining 17,000 bushels is mainly barley and oats, with a little rye and buckwheat. The Arkansas country, including the Fontaine-qui-Bouille and Huerfano Valleys, probably produced an equal quantity, giving a grand total of 100,000 bushels of wheat, barley and oats as the crop of 1863. Considering the newness of the country, its small farming population, and the very unfavorable season, the result is quite satisfactory. This year will doubtless see it doubled, as the season bids fair to be favorable, and our farmers have gained much valuable experience.[61]

The Surveyor General of Colorado in his official report of October 1, 1863, said: "The emigration to this Territory during the present summer has been unusually large, and consists mostly of persons intending to enter into agricultural pursuits. . . . One ditch alone now completed, reclaims over 10,000 acres of land."[62]

159

Grist mills were in operation in the region in 1860 and thereafter.[63]

In November, 1861, delegates from the various Claim Clubs had met in Denver and petitioned Congress to recognize their claim lines, which ran in conformity with the topography beside the streams.[64] This request was not complied with, but instead the regular Government system of quadrangular survey was followed.

Among the first officials appointed for Colorado Territory in March, 1861, was F. M. Case to be Surveyor General. He set up his office in Denver on June 17, 1861. In his report to the General Land Office on September 1, 1862, he told of the land being taken up along the streams flowing from the mountains. .

"The 'claims' upon the following streams," he reported, "are nearly all taken up by actual settlers: Cache la Poudre Creek, Platte River to mouth of Cache la Poudre, Big Thompson Creek, Little Thompson Creek, Bear Creek, Fountain qui Bouit, Arkansas River."

He soon began surveying and marking the public domain, and a United States Land Office for the registery and sale of land was opened October 5, 1863.

An Agricultural Society for promotion of farming interests was organized in Denver in March 1863, and plans were laid for the holding of an agricultural fair. The first fair was to be held in 1866. [66]

The Surveyor General of Colorado officially reported on August 15, 1865, that 260,000 acres in Colorado were then in cultivation, and that 2,500,000 acres were capable of cultivation. He reported that 56 townships, totaling 1,197,282.99 acres had been surveyed. [67]

160

The farm area expanded, and the enduring and fullest wealth of the region was to be found in the soil.

2. <u>Cattle Industry</u>. The millions of buffalo and other game which covered the high plains and provided food for the Indians gave ample proof of the grazing potential of the region. Domestic cattle and sheep had been a major feature of the economy of New Mexico for more than 200 years when the first white men settled on the Arapaho-Cheyenne Land area.

Thomas Fitzpatrick, first Agent to the Arapahoes and Cheyennes, had written in his report of 1853 of the land between the Arkansas and the South Platte Rivers: "On the high table lands a short but nutritious grass affords excellent grazing, and will cause this country to be some day much prized for pastoral purposes."[68]

Some of the early freighters on the Oregon Trail wintered stock on the Arapaho-Cheyenne land. In 1852 Seth E. Ward, sutler at Fort Laramie, wintered his animals on the Chugwater, a southern branch of the North Platte, and two years later Alexander Majors, outstanding freighter, kept several hundred head of work cattle in the same area.[69]

The draft animals that pulled the emigrants across the plains to the central Rockies subsisted on the grass enroute. And when the pioneers settled down in the region they turned their stock out to shift for themselves. Many draft cattle from the freight outfits were similarly treated. To the surprise of many, these cattle thrived on the short, curly, nutritious buffalo grass that carpeted the plains.[70]

The Colorado mining camps and outfitting towns were a market for beef in 1859 and thereafter. John C. Dawson drove cattle from Texas to the Colorado region in 1859.[71] Samuel Hartsel herded cattle in South Park, on the upper waters of the South Platte, in 1860 and the next year brought out from Iowa registered Shorthorns with which he improved his herd in South Park.[72]

F. M. Case, the Surveyor General of Colorado, said in his official report of September 1, 1862:

> Thousands of cattle, horses, mules, and sheep are now subsisted upon the plains, and the time is not far distant when the herds of Colorado will rival in number and quality those of any other country upon this continent.[73]

John Pierce, Surveyor General of Colorado in 1863, reported:

> Enormous herds of cattle and sheep have been brought to this Territory during the past year and the transportation of goods to this Territory from the States employs about 15,000 head of cattle a year, a great portion of which remain here.[74]

-61-

In 1864 Charles Goodnight, one of the great western cattlemen, drove Texas cattle to Colorado.[75] John W. Iliff, who was to become the "Cattle King of Colorado," began his stock business in the Denver area in 1861. He accumulate holdings in northeastern Colorado and soon held hundreds of acres along the South Platte and by his control of the river front, had the use of thousands of acres of upland back from the stream. He ultimately (in 1878) owned over 15,000 acres, controlled 65,000 additional acres, and ran 35,000 cattle. Iliff's biographer writes:

> Iliff's lands were scattered across the range for 100 miles or more from the eastern boundary of Colorado and for more than sixty miles north and south. Most of the land was appraised in 1878 at $2.00 per acre, with the exception of the 80 acres at the LF headquarters ranch, on which a value was placed of "$860 with improvements."[76]

While Iliff was the largest individual cattleman in Colorado, the largest cattle corporation of the region was the Prairie Cattle Company, organized in 1881, and dissolved in 1915. Professor Steinel writes:

> The property lay in three divisions, the Colorado holdings comprising 2,242,000 acres, and embracing a territory of 3,500 square miles. On this range in the early eighties there were nearly 54,000 cattle, in the management of which 300 horses were required. . . .
>
> This division (the second) embraced 4,032 square miles or 2,580,480 acres, with 57,799 cattle at the time of its first stocking up under the Prairie ownership. Five hundred horses were used on this division, the range being northeast New Mexico and a part of the neutral strip, or No Man's Land, which later became the Oklahoma Panhandle.
>
> The third division comprised principally the L I T Ranch, purchased from the original owner, Littlefield, with headquarters at Tascosa, Texas, with its main range along the Canadian in the Texas Panhandle. The area was 400 square miles, or 256,000 acres, with about 30,000 cattle.[77]

By 1865 various factors existed that gave rise to the range cattle industry and were to promote its rapid development:

1. A big reservoir of surplus stock had built up in Texas and was ready to invade the northern plains.

2. The extension of the railroads westward would provide transportation of beef eastward to the centers of population.

3. The rapid growth of cities made large concentrations of people who needed to be fed. And the increased wages and prevailing prosperity enabled workers, heretofore unable to buy meat, to now make meat a part of their regular diet.

4. Canning and refrigeration were developed, and these new processes expanded the domestic demand and opened up a large new European market.

163

In 1866 the large movement northward of Texas cattle began. It was estimated that 260,000 head went north that year. During the next two decades the numbers driven north totaled nearly 6,000,000 head.[78]

The number of cattle in Colorado were to show the following figures and increases: 147,000 in 1867; 271,000 in 1870; 488,000 in 1875; 809,000 in 1880; and 1,240,000 in 1885.[79] Most of these were on the Arapaho-Cheyenne Land tract.

In 1871 there were between 60,000 and 80,000 head of cattle within 100 miles of Cheyenne, Wyoming;[80] this would be within the Arapaho-Cheyenne land. The number of cattle reported in Wyoming were: 90,000 in 1874; 110,000 in 1875; 136,000 in 1876; 176,000 in 1877; 260,000 in 1878; 450,000 in 1879; and 530,000 in 1880.[81]

Foreign and domestic capital poured into new cattle herds and land, and boomed the industry. Dr. Ernest S. Osgood, authority on the cattle business, writes in his The Day of the Cattleman (Minneapolis, University of Minnesota Press, 1954):

> Deals involving thousands of head of cattle and millions of dollars were common. In 1883, for example, the Swan Land and Cattle Company was organized through combining three ranch properties with a range from Fort Steele, Wyoming, on the west, to Ogallala, Nebraska, on the east, and from the Union Pacific to the Platte River (thus within our Arapaho-Cheyenne land area). These companies sold to the new company some 30,000 acres of land, part in full title and part in process of title; over a hundred thousand head of stock and rights on a range, one hundred miles long and fifty to one hundred miles wide, for a purchase price of $2,588,825. The new company was capitalized at $3,000,000, which was raised to $3,750,000 to provide for the purchase of over half a million acres of Union Pacific alternate sections.[82]

3. Industrial Beginnings. Manufacturing in the region was in its infancy in 1865. However, saw mills, flour mills, brick yards, and breweries were in operation. Salt works were producing in South Park, pottery works and a fire-brick kiln were operating in Golden. Stone was quarried and coal mined in a number of places. Oil was being obtained near Canon City. Iron manufacturing was being attempted. All of this was in addition to the milling and smelting of ores from the mines.

F. BANKING AND INVESTMENTS

1. Pioneer Banking and Exchange. Before trade can flourish an acceptable medium of exchange must be established. In the fur trade days the beaver skin served as a medium of exchange, and with these hairy banknotes trade was carried on. With the discovery of mines in the Colorado region, gold became the measure of value. Since gold dust and nuggets were of varying richness, the

-64-

Denver Chamber of Commerce in May , 1861, undertook to fix the value of gold from various gulches at rates from $15 to $20 per ounce. [83] With difficulty in evaluating accurately, business was greatly aided when mints were established. Clark, Gruber, and Company put their Denver mint in operating in July 1860. They minted coins of $2.50, $5, $10, and $20 denominations. Their coinage to April 1862, when the Government bought out the establishment, amounted to $3,000,000. [84] Two other mints also coined Colorado gold in the region. [85]

Some business houses that at first purchased and shipped gold, soon went into general banking. Beginning in 1860, these institutions extended their activity and increased in number. Some issued bank notes and scrip "shinplasters." After the passage of the National Bank Act in 1863, one bank complied with the federal legislation and became a National Bank; others remained as private concerns. The First National Bank of Denver, chartered in April, 1865, had in October of that year $162,000 in deposits, and total assets of $427,000. [86] Figures on the holdings of the other banks are not available.

Greenbacks, issued by the National Government, soon came into circulation. In terms of this currency, gold was at a premium and rose rapidly in price.

By 1863 Fifteenth Street, Denver, was becoming the local Wall Street, with four banks near the intersection of Fifteenth and McGaa (Market.) Other banks and mints served Central City, Pueblo, and the South Park area.

2. Investment Capital. While these banks aided in the conduct of local business, money for investment came largely from older sources of capital in the East and in Europe. Many Colorado mines were sold in the East during

1863-64, gold mines being considered good investments during this period of
greenback issues and the consequent rise in the price of gold. O. J. Hollister
writes:

> There is no necessity for a history in detail of the trans-
> fer of the quartz-mines of Colorado to Eastern men. It is suf-
> ficient to say that a mania for Colorado mining property was
> created in New York and Boston about the end of 1863, and fabu-
> lous prices,--in several cases a thousand dollars a foot, were
> given for improved mines. Surely that was temptation enough;
> we need look no further for the causes of the mania for selling
> out which responded in Colorado to the mania for buying, in
> the East.[87]

Foreign capital was becoming interested in investments in the Western
country, especially beginning in 1865, when boom conditions as indicated above,
were developing.

Dr. E. S. Osgood writes:

166

> There was nothing new in the investment of foreign capital
> in far-western enterprises. Western railroads had sold large
> blocks of securities to English, German, and Dutch investors.
> Land companies, financed abroad, had purchased millions of
> acres of the public domain, which had either been settled
> through some colonization scheme, or were being held as a
> speculation. The arrival of cheap American beef in the
> European market and the stories of the profits that could be
> made in its production turned the attention of investors to this
> new field.[88]

The London Economist, in a table, gave the extent and character of English
and Scotch investments and the dividends paid (Osgood, p. 102).

The "Ordinary Share Capital" of these eleven companies thus totaled
2,314,505 pounds, or well over $11,000,000. The land they owned exceeded two
million acres and their leased land almost 1-1/2 million acres.

Financial figures on the larger British land and cattle companies operating in the American West are contained in the Statement from the Scottish Banking and Insurance Magazine, VI(July 5, 1884), p. 260. (Frink, Jackson, and Spring, p. 187).

It is to be noted in this table that the reported cost of the range land was from $1.62 to $2.83 per acre.

The availability of foreign capital for purchase of large tracts of land is also demonstrated by the history of such transactions as the purchase of the Maxwell and the Sangre de Cristo land grants in Colorado and New Mexico. The former, comprising about two million acres, sold in 1870 for $1,350,000. The property was then mortgaged for 750,000 pounds sterling. In 1872 a second mortgage was placed against the property to secure a loan of 275,000 pounds sterling. Both mortgages were foreclosed on March 11, 1878. The Grant was sold at foreclosure sale on March 1, 1880, for $2,000,000.[89]

The Sangre de Cristo Grant was procured from the Mexican heirs by Governor William Gilpin of Colorado. The United States Freehold Land and Emigration Company, chartered under Colorado laws and by a special Act of Congress (July 8, 1870), acquired one-half of the Grant (the Costilla Estate) for $500,000; it capitalized its holding at $2,500,000; and sold $1,000,000 of the stock to a Dutch banking syndicate for a lump sum of $500,000 in cash. The land was to be sold at appraised value, but in no case below $5. per acre. Objections of actual settlers on the tract, hesitancy of the owners to spend money in promotion, and lack of sufficient water for irrigation were factors that caused failure of the big project.[90]

167

F. MATERIAL AND CULTURAL STATUS

The population of Colorado had shown little or no growth during the Civil. War period. Men had returned to the East to enter the Union or the Confederate military forces. Some miners had been lured to the new goldfields in Montana and Idaho. The forces previously listed, which retarded development in Colorado, were operative.

But despite discouragements, progress was being made. Roads were built between towns and mining camps. Bridges were constructed and ferries were in operation. Ditches were dug for irrigation of the land and to provide water power for mills and mining machinery.

Log houses had given way to frame structures and buildings of brick and stone in the towns. Large stores were stocked with merchandise. Blacksmith shops, barber shops, markets, livery stables, and boarding houses were serving the townspeople.

Private schools had been operated since 1859, and in 1862 tax-supported schools were provided. The Colorado Seminary (later Denver University) and St. Mary's Academy were founded in 1864, as the first institutions above the grade school level. A Territorial University had been created by statute in 1861, but did not go into operation until after 1865.

Churches of several denominations were serving the people in a number of towns. Fraternal organizations and various cultural societies were in existence.

CONCLUSION

By 1865 prospects were bright. The new factors discussed above were now ready to exert their potential force. The end of the Civil War and the Indian

168

removal had opened the gates for an emigrant tide. Railroads were coming in to boom the economy. Refractory ores were being conquered, and mining was to experience a great upsurge. Farming was expanding, and the range cattle industry was beginning. Wartime profits and European capital were ready for investment in the new region.

That great developments were imminent is proved by the phenomenal growth that Colorado did experience. Her population, which was 39,864 in 1870, increased to 194,327 in 1880, and during the following decade more than doubled, to reach 413,249. Truly the region was on the verge of great development and increased values in 1865.

169

170

FOOTNOTES

1. B. H. Hibbard, A History of the Public Land Policies (New York, The Macmillan Company, 1924), pp. 45-55.
2. Ibid., pp. 67-68.
3. Ibid., p. 83.
4. L. R. Hafen and C. C. Rister, Western America (New York, Prentice-Hall, 1950), pp. 109-10.
5. For the history of transportation see Seymour Dunbar, A History of Travel in America (4 vols., Indianapolis, 1915).
6. B. H. Hibbard, op. cit., pp. 234-36.
7. Ibid., pp. 237, 41.
8. Ibid., p. 238.
9. E. L. Bogart and D. L. Kemmerer, Economic History of the American People (New York, Longmans, Green and Co., 1951), pp. 362-64.
10. Table printed in Hibbard, op. cit., p. 100.
11. Ibid., pp. 102-103.
12. Ibid., p. 106.
13. Bogart and Kemmerer, op. cit., pp. 321-22. For a general fiscal account see D. R. Dewey, Financial History of the United States (New York, 1918).
14. Hibbard, op. cit., p. 100.
15. Ibid., p. 103.
16. Bogart and Kemmerer, op. cit., p. 337.
17. Ibid., p. 466.
18. Ibid., p. 326.
19. Ibid., p. 337.
20. Ibid., pp. 355-56.
21. Hafen and Rister, op. cit., p. 469.
22. L. R. Hafen, The Overland Mail (Cleveland, Arthur H. Clark Co., 1926).
23. Arthur Chapman, The Pony Express (New York, 1932).
24. Bogart and Kemmerer, op. cit., p. 332.
25. Ibid., pp. 286-90.
26. Ibid., p. 533.
27. "Report of the Commissioner of the General Land Office, 1858," in House Executive Documents 2, 35th Cong. 2d sess. Vol. I (Serial 997), p. 116-20.
28. Bogart and Kremmerer, op. cit., p. 534.
29. Ibid., p. 266.
30. H. O. Brayer, William Blackmore: The Spanish-Mexican Land Grants of New Mexico and Colorado, 1863-1878 (Denver, 1949), pp. 35-46.
31. For an account of early explorations of the region see Hafen and Rister, op. cit.
32. Early Explorations and trade in the Colorado region are treated in L. R. Hafen, Colorado and its People (2 vols., New York, 1948).
33. For his biography see L. R. Hafen and W. J. Ghent, Broken Hand, the Life of Thomas Fitzpatrick (Denver, Old West Pub. Co., 1931).
34. The best account of relations between the Cheyennes and the whites is G. B. Grinnell, The Fighting Cheyennes (New York, 1915).

171

FOOTNOTES (Cont'd)

35. Agent Twiss's report of Oct. 13, 1856, in Report of the Commissioner of Indian Affairs. . . 1856 (Washington, 1857), p. 101.

36. Col. Sumner's report of his Cheyenne Campaign of 1857 is found in House Executive Documents 2, 35th Cong., 1st Sess. (Serial 943), pp. 96-99. See also Grinnell, op. cit., pp. 107-17.

37. For accounts of the gold rush see L. R. Hafen, Editor of volumes IX to XI in the Southwest Historical Series (Glendale, Arthur H. Clark Co., 1940-41).

38. O. J. Hollister, The Mines of Colorado (Springfield, 1867) pp. 66-67.

39. L. R. Hafen, Colorado and Its People, op. cit.

40. Indian Department Records, National Archives in Washington, D. C. (big roll, microfilm prints summary., p. 12).

41. Bent's letter of October 5, 1859, in Report of the Commissioner of Indian Affairs . . . 1859, p. 137.

42. Microfilm prints from Indian Department Records, op. cit.

43. Report of the Commissioner of Indian Affairs . . . 1860, p. 229.

44. See the Fort Wise Treaty of February 18, 1861.

45. Loree's report of October 24, 1863, and the statements of Governor Evans and others in Commissioner of Indian Affairs Report of 1863.

46. Rocky Mountain News (Denver), Aug. 10, 1864.

47. See the "Massacre of Cheyenne Indians." in Report of the Joint Committee on the Conduct of the War at the Second Session Thirty-eighth Congress (Washington Government Printing Office, 1865). See also the account in Grinnell, Fighting Cheyennes, op. cit.

48. Rocky Mountain News, January 9, 1865.

49. O. J. Hollister, The Mines of Colorado, op. cit., pp. 110, 122. See also C. W. Henderson, Mining in Colorado; a History of Discovery, Development, and Production (Washington, Government Printing Office, 1926).

50. L. R. Hafen, The Overland Mail, op., cit.

51. L. R. Hafen and A. W. Hafen, The Colorado Story, a History . . . (Denver, 1953), pp. 226-27.

52. R. E. Riegel, The Story of the Western Railroads (New York, 1926).

53. Third Annual Report of the Board of Directors of the Kansas Pacific Railway Company to the Stockholders for the Year Ending Dec. 31, 1869 (St. Louis, 1870), p. 10.

54. J. F. Willard and C. B. Goodykoontz, Experiments in Colorado Colonization (Boulder, 1926), pp. 259, 343.

55. Reproduced in J. F. Willard (Ed.), The Union Colony at Greeley, Colorado 1869-71 (Boulder, 1918), p. 27. The National Land Company's advertisement in the Boulder County News (Colorado) of May 25, 1870, said that 1,200,000 acres were then ready for sale. The figure given to illustrate the time payment plan was $5 per acre. The Daily Central City (Colorado) Register of August 6, 1870, reported the sales of Denver Pacific land at their office in this city to the end of July, as 21,202.75 acres at the average price of $4.01 per acre.

56. Hibbard, op. cit., p. 260.

57. Ibid., p. 261-62.

58. Ibid., p. 264.

FOOTNOTES (Cont'd)

59. A. T. Steinel and D. W. Working, History of Agriculture in Colorado (Fort Collins, 1926).

60. Message of the Governor to the Legislature, 1862.

61. Steinel and Working, op. cit., p. 50.

62. Report of the Commissioner of the General Land Office, 1863.

63. Steinel and Working, op. cit., pp. 31-36.

64. Rocky Mountain News, Nov. 4, 1861.

65. Report of the Commissioner of the General Land Office, 1862 (Serial 1157), p. 112.

66. Steinel and Working, op. cit., pp. 55-60.

67. Report of the Commissioner of the General Land Office, 1865 (Serial 1248), pp. 102-109.

68. Hafen and Ghent, Broken Hand, op. cit., p. 255.

69. M. Frink, W. T. Jackson, and A. W. Spring, When Grass Was King; Contributions to the Western Range Cattle Industry Study (Boulder, University of Colorado Press, 1956), p. 36.

70. This discovery of the value of the grass was made as early as the winter of 1858-59. See Steinel and Working, op. cit., pp. 108-109. Also Frink, Jackson, and Spring, op. cit. p. 346.

71. Ibid., p. 35.

72. Steinel and Working, op. cit., p 111.

73. Report of the Commissioner of the General Land Office, 1862, p. 114.

74. Report of the Commissioner of the General Land Office, 1863.

75. Frink, Jackson, and Spring, op. cit., p. 36.

76. A. W. Spring, "'A Genius for Handling Cattle': John W. Iliff," in When Grass Was King, op. cit., p. 385. Also Steinel and Working, op. cit., p. 136.

77. Steinel and Working, op. cit., pp. 137-38.

78. Second Annual Report of the Bureau of Animal Husbandry, 1885, p. 300.

79. U. S. Department of Agriculture, Bureau of Agricultural Economics, Livestock on Farms, January 1, 1867-1935 (Washington, 1938), pp. 117, 121, 123, 125; and Frink, Jackson, and Spring, op. cit., p. 26.

80. Cheyenne Daily Leader of Sept. 2, 1871, quoted in E. S. Osgood, The Day of the Cattleman (Minneapolis, University of Minnesota Press, 1929), pp. 49-50.

81. Osgood, op. cit., p. 53.

82. Ibid., pp. 97-98.

83. Rocky Mountain News, May, 1861.

84. R. F. Niehaus, Seventy Years of Progress; History of Banking in Colorado, 1876-1946 (Federal Deposit Insurance Corporation, 1948), pp. 7-8.

85. L. R. Hafen, "Currency, Coinage, and Banking in Pioneer Colorado," in the Colorado Magazine, X, pp. 81-90

86. Niehaus, op. cit., p. 13.

87. Hollister, op. cit., p. 122.

88. Osgood, op. cit., pp. 99-100.

89. See W. A. Keleher, Maxwell Land Grant; a New Mexico Item (Santa Fe, 1942).

90. For the history of the Sangre de Cristo Grant see Brayer, op. cit., pp. 59-123.

174

CHEYENNE AND ARAPAHO INDIANS **v.**
THE UNITED STATES, DOCKET NO. 329-A,
BEFORE THE INDIAN CLAIMS COMMISSION

<u>Historical Background</u>

175

Arthur A. Ekirch, Jr.

176

TABLE OF CONTENTS

178

Part I

SOCIAL AND ECONOMIC CONDITIONS
IN THE UNITED STATES IN 1890

The generation after the Civil War saw the settlement of the last American frontier of the Far West. This
was the region between the first tier of states beyond
the Mississippi River and the Rocky Mountains. It included most of the original Louisiana Purchase and cessions
from Mexico except for the state of California. Compared
with the older frontiers to the east, it was a plains
region-- level, treeless, and semi-arid. It was well
suited to cattle grazing and, with proper rainfall, to grain
crops. The railroads pushing steadily into the area made
it possible for farmers to send their beef and wheat to
markets in the East and in Europe. Although the price
level of most agricultural commodities was declining after
1873, the world market for American agricultural produce
held up well until the mid-1880's. Western farmers in
this period also enjoyed the considerable advantage of
cheap land. The Homestead Act and other federal legislation made it possible for them to secure a quarter section
or more of land for only nominal fees or for a minimum
price of $1.25 an acre.

In 1890 United States population including Indians
was just under 63 million persons, a gain of some 12½
million compared with 1880. In 1889 the six new states

179

of North and South Dakota, Montana, Washington, Idaho,
and Wyoming were admitted to the Union, while only Utah,
Arizona, New Mexico, and the area of present-day Oklahoma
remained in the status of territories. The population of
the West South Central states of Arkansas, Louisiana, and
Texas increased from 3,334,220 in 1880 to 4,740,983 in
1890. The latter figures included 258,657 in the Indian
Territory and Oklahoma, of which some 60,000 were Indians.
Immediately to the north, the state of Kansas grew from
996,096 persons in 1880 to 1,428,108 in 1890. Added to
the considerable natural domestic increase in the population after the Civil War, was the stream of immigrants
pouring into the United States from Europe. In the decade
of the 1880's, almost five million immigrants came to
American shores, a figure more than double the numbers of
the preceding ten years and not surpassed until the first
decade of the 1900's.[1]

Despite the declining prices and increasing immigration after the Civil War, wage rates held up remarkably
well. By 1890 the total labor force had grown to some
23 million persons, of which just under 10 million were
engaged in agriculture. Average hourly wages in industry
in 1890 were around 21 cents with the following subdivisions:[2]

>   Manufacturing $ .19
>   Building Trades   .34
>   Unskilled Labor   .14

Average wages for farm labor in the United States since the

Civil War were estimated by the Department of Agriculture as
follows:

	1866	1869	1875	1879	1882	1885	1888	1890
per month without board	$26.87	25.92	19.87	16.42	18.94	17.97	18.24	19.10
with board	17.45	16.55	12.72	10.43	12.41	12.34	12.36	12.45
per day in harvest without board	2.20	2.20	1.70	1.30	1.48	1.40	1.31	1.30

For Oklahoma no figures were compiled until 1893 when wages
per month without board were $21.47, compared with a national
average of $19.10. Wages with board were $14.85 in Oklahoma and $13.29 in the United States, while wages per day
in harvest without board were $1.18 in Oklahoma and $1.24
in the United States.[3]

The boom conditions of the 1880's were not destined to
continue indefinitely. There were signs even before the
close of the decade that the prosperity of the West was
about to suffer a prolonged interruption. The collapse of
good times began in the late 1880's. A combination of
abnormally cold, snowy winters and hot, dry summers proved
ruinous for cattlemen and farmers alike. The hard winter
of 1886-87 was succeeded in the summer of 1887 by the first
of a long series of dry seasons. Settlers attracted to the
Great Plains by the mild weather and above-average rainfall of the preceding decade, now learned that they had
optimistically put too much land to the plow. At the same

time that natural conditions worsened, the world market for
American agricultural products declined. Better transportation facilities abroad and high costs in the United States
resulted in keen competition for American wheat from Australia,
Canada, and Russia.[4] Driven by drought and hard times,
settlers began to move back to the East. A noted historian of
this period in the West has pointed out that the census takers
of 1890 felt obliged to pad their figures to conceal this
exodus, and he concludes that is not unlikely that the Plains
States of the West had as many or more people in 1887 than
were claimed for it in 1890.[5] Another scholar estimates that
179,000 persons, most of them probably farmers and their
families, left Kansas between 1887 and 1891.[6]

In the face of bumper crops abroad, poor harvests in
the United States in these years did not cut supplies enough
to bolster prices. The hard times in the West by the late
1880's were illustrated by the course of prices for key
agricultural commodities. In the Chicago Cattle Market the
prices paid for good and choice steers between 1200 and
1500 pounds, in terms of yearly averages, ranged from $4.67½
per hundredweight in 1886, to $3.95 in 1889.[7] The value
per head of livestock in 1884 and in 1890 was as follows:[8]

all cattle	$25.26	16.95
hogs	5.64	4.80
sheep	2.40	2.29
horses	73.80	69.27
mules	83.53	77.61

Corn prices for the decade dropped from a high of 63 cents in

1881 to a low of 28 cents in 1889, provoking the comment
that it was cheaper to burn corn than to buy coal. Wheat
production, exports, and prices are illustrated in the table
below, which shows that after 1882 wheat dropped continuously
below the farmer's traditional break-even point of one dollar
a bushel.[9]

Wheat Crop

year	total production in millions of bushels	exports	export price per bushel	domestic price
1879	448	122	$1.07	$1.11
1880	498	153	1.24	.95
1881	383	150	1.11	1.19
1882	504	95	1.18	.88
1883	421	106	1.13	.91
1884	512	70	1.07	.65
1885	357	84	.86	.77
1886	457	57	.87	.69
1887	456	101	.89	.68
1888	415	65	.85	.87
1889	490	46	.90	.70
1890	399	54	.83	.84

183

The demand for land in the West followed roughly the
trend in the prices of agricultural commodities, although
there is evidence that some farmers looked to recoup in
land speculation what they had lost on their crops. Thus in
the 1870's and 1880's cheap land encouraged the farmer to
acquire still more land either for cultivation or speculation.
The number of farms in the United States just about tripled
in the fifty years from 1850 to 1890:[10]

	No. Farms in millions	Av. size in acres
1850	1½	203
1860	2	199
1870	2½	153
1880	4	134
1890	4½	137

Sometimes declining agricultural prices could be overcome by
putting more acres under cultivation, or the land could become a source of credit. Many farmers were able to avoid
bankruptcy as a result of falling prices only by mortgaging
their lands or by selling what equity they still had in their
farm. The post-Civil War land boom reached its peak between
1884 and 1886 and then declined steadily. Original homestead
entries in the 1880's ranged from 9,145,135 acres in 1886 to
a low of 5,531,678 acres in 1890. For railroad land
selections, the top year was 1884 when over 8 million acres
were sold, and the low was 1890 with less than 2 million.
Public lands sold for cash ranged from 26 million acres in

1884 to 12 million in 1890.[11]

Both speculation and hard times contributed to a rapid
turnover in western homesteads, and to a sizeable increase
in mortgage debt. By 1890 on the farms of Kansas, Nebraska,
the Dakotas, and Minnesota, there were as many mortgages as
families in the five states.[12] In Kansas the real estate
mortgage debt in force on January 1, 1890, totaled
$243,146,826-- sixth highest of all states. With $170 of
mortgage debt per person, Kansas was the fourth highest state
on a per capita basis. It had the highest per cent of taxed
acres covered by mortgages, 60%, and the second highest per
cent of mortgage debt to true value of real estate, 26%.
The interest rate on mortgages for all types of land in
Kansas averaged out at 8.68%. The interest rate in the United

States in 1890 for acres only ran at about 7½%. In the 1880's
the amount of real estate mortgage debt on such tracts had
been increasing slowly. For acres and lots combined, however,
mortgage debt had more than doubled in the decade, growing
from 700 to 1,750 million dollars.[13]

The various statistical indices of the period all indicate that the late 1880's and early 1890's were a period
of economic depression. This judgment is reflected in the
contemporary and historical literature. It is well summed
up in Hibbard's standard work on public land policies, in
which the author comments:

> During the latter portion of the nineteenth century all
> prices were low, but agricultural prices were relatively lower
> than prices of general commodities as compared with the
> period just before the Civil War, and distinctly so as com-
> pared with prices for some years just before the World War.
> Agricultural products were higher, absolutely, in price
> before the Civil War than for several decades following.
> The general commodity price level, taking 1856-60 as the
> base; rose to 205 at the close of the war, stood at 135 in
> 1870, and at 101 in 1880, agricultural prices being below
> this level by ten to thirty points, the greatest discrepancy
> occurring about 1880. The lowest prices for farm produce
> were reached in 1896, although in purchasing power the
> farmer was somewhat better off then than in 1880.[14]

Notes
Part I

SOCIAL AND ECONOMIC CONDITIONS
IN THE UNITED STATES IN 1890

1 U.S. Bureau of the Census: Historical Statistics of the United States 1789-1945 (Washington, 1949), Population Schedules; Statistical Abstract of the United States 1949 (Washington, 1949), p. 33.

2 Historical Statistics of the United States, pp. 63, 67.

3 "Wages of Farm Labor in the United States," U.S. Dept. of Agriculture, Bureau of Statistics, Bulletin No. 26 (Washington, 1903), pp. 14-16.

4 David A. Wells, Recent Economic Changes (New York, 1893), p. 166.

5 John D. Hicks, The American Nation (Boston, 1941), p. 238.

6 Harold U. Faulkner, Politics, Reform and Expansion 1890-1900 (New York, 1959), p.54.

7 U.S. Bureau of Statistics, Statistical Abstract of the United States 1890 (Washington, 1891), p. 340.

8 Historical Statistics of the United States, p. 101.

9 Statistical Abstract of the United States 1890, pp. 186, 316-317.

10 U.S. Census Office, Compendium of the Eleventh Census: 1890, Part III (Washington, 1897), p. 605.

11 Statistical Abstract of the United States 1890, pp. 243-245.

12 John D. Hicks, The Populist Revolt (Minneapolis, 1931),pp. 23-24.

13 U.S. Census Office, Statistical Atlas of the United States (Washington, 1898), pp. 66-69.

14 Benjamin H. Hibbard, A History of the Public Land Policies (New York, 1924), p. 544.

Part II

THE EARLY HISTORY
OF OKLAHOMA

The area of the present state of Oklahoma like most
of the rest of North America was inhabited originally by
a number of primitive Indian tribes. Before the coming
of the first white man, the Osage, Caddo,, Quapaw, Wichita,
Kiowa, Commanche, and Apache ranged freely over the region.
In the 16th and 17th centuries, the Spaniish and the French
explored parts of the Oklahoma country, amd in 1803 the
United States acquired its possession witth the purchase of
Louisiana. The purchase added 827,192 square miles or
529,911,680 acres to the public domain att a cost of approximately 3.6 cents per acre to make what wass surely one of
the greatest real estate bargains in histtory. Later the
Florida Purchase Treaty of 1819 correctedl the southeastern
boundary of the Louisiana Purchase, and tthis also became
the Oklahoma southeastern boundary, but tthe narrow western
rectangle known as the Oklahoma Panhandlee was not acquired
until after the War with Mexico.

Although the Louisiana Purchase securred to the American
people territory of inestimable value forr the future, for
several generations a good part of the lamd was regarded as
unsuitable for cultivation by the white mman. In 1819 Major
Stephen Long explored the High Plains reggion of the Louisiana
Purchase from the Platte to the Canadian River and in his
report to the United States government comndemned it as a

dessert "hardly fit for man or beast." Thus the idea
developed that much of the country between the Mississippi
River Valley and the Rocky Mountains was a "Great American
Dessert," the caption Long had placed on the map accompanying his report.[1]

Meanwhile the pressure of the advancing frontier of
American civilization was forcing the Indians westward.
In 1830 the policy of assigning lands in the West to the
Indians in return for their removal from east of the Mississippi was given formal approval of Congress, which
authorized the President to undertake such transfers.(4 Stat.
411) Already in the 1820's the Five Civilized Tribes had
begun their trek to present-day Oklahoma, while other tribes
were removed to areas farther north. Congress in 1832
provided for the appointment of a Commissioner of Indian
Affairs within the War Department, (4 Stat. 564) and in the
Indian Act of June 30, 1834, Congress stipulated that "all
that part of the United States west of the Mississippi, and
not within the states of Missouri and Louisiana, or the
territory of Arkansas... be taken and deemed to be the
Indian country." For legal purposes that part of the Indian
country between the Platte and Red Rivers was annexed to the
territory of Arkansas. (4 Stat. 729)

Since the Dakotas as well as the more specific Indian
country to the south were not open to white settlement, in
effect there was a barrier to the American westward movement

Map of Indian Territory

1836-1856

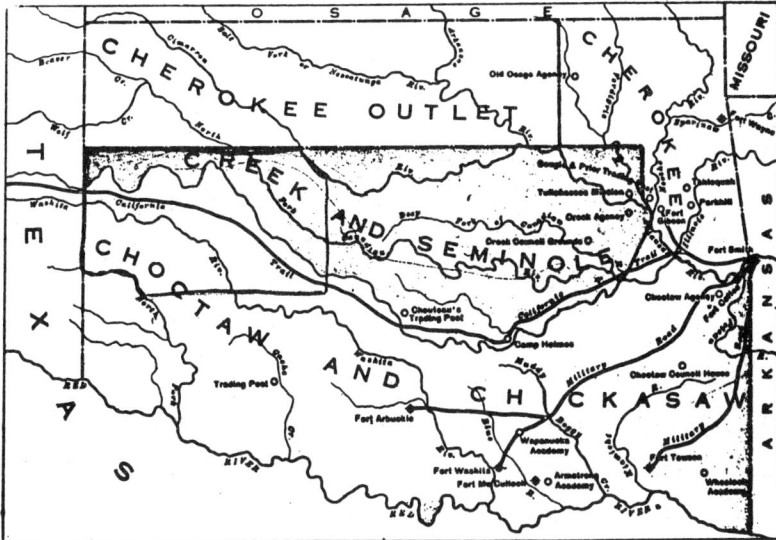

Indian Territory, 1836-1856

Thoburn and Holcomb, "History of Oklahoma" - Page 48

extending from Canada to Texas. Although pioneers crossed
this region on their way to Oregon, none of the area was
formally or officially organized as a political territory
until 1854 when the first break in the Indian barrier came
as a byproduct of the sectional conflict over slavery.
Anxious to settle new western lands and to make possible
a northern or central route for a railroad to the Pacific,
Senator Stephen A. Douglas introduced his fateful Kansas
Nebraska territorial bill in 1854. Meanwhile the Indian
Office was busy making treaties with the Indians to extinguish
their title to lands within the limits of Douglas' proposed
territories. The Kansas Nebraska Act (10 Stat. 277) repealed
not only the Missouri Compromise but also, in effect, the
Indian Act of 1834, defining the Indian country. It divided
what had come to be known as the Indian Territory on the line
of the 37th parallel or the present-day Oklahoma Kansas
boundary, opening Kansas and the territories to the north for
white settlers. The Kansas Nebraska Act thus spelled the end
of the notion of the Great Plains region as a perpetual
Indian Territory unsuited to white occupation.[2]

The Civil War occasioned the next major revision in the
status of the Indian Territory. During the war most of the
Indians in Oklahoma had been driven by the course of events
into alliance with the Confederate States. This fact, plus
the changing needs and way of life of both the Indians and
whites west of the Mississippi, made it desirable that the

Map of Indian Territory

1856-1866

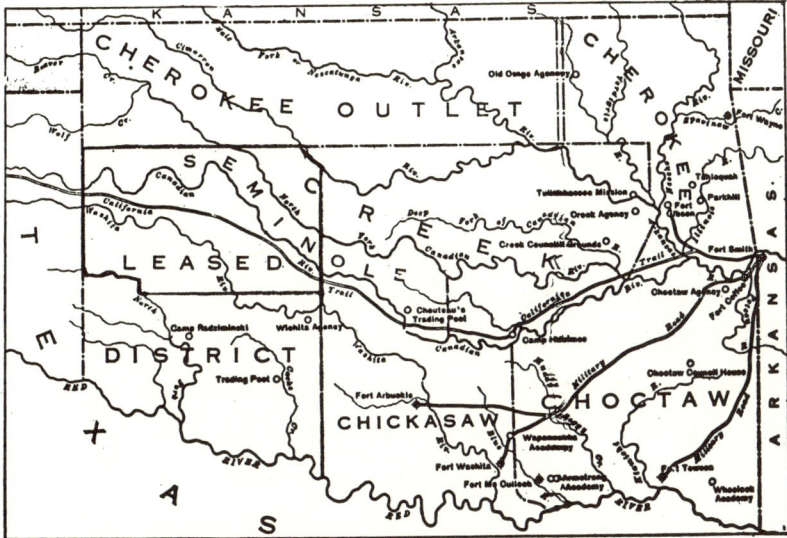

Indian Territory, 1856-1866

Thoburn and Holcomb, "History of Oklahoma" — Page 64

United States enter into new treaty relationships with the
Five Civilized Tribes that had been dwelling in eastern
Oklahoma. In 1866 therefore in a series of treaties, the
Oklahoma tribes ceded their western lands to the United
States for the use of other Indians scattered throughout
the trans-Mississippi West. (14 Stat. 755-809)

The federal government now undertook to remove as
many as possible of the western Indians to reservations
in the Indian Territory of Oklahoma. On March 3, 1871,
Congress as a part of its annual appropriation act declared
that henceforth no Indian tribe could be considered as an
independent nation with which a treaty could be signed.
(16 Stat. 566) President Grant in his annual messages in the
1870's stressed the importance of some permanent abode for the
Indians and suggested the advisability of reserving all of
the Indian Territory south of Kansas, or present-day Oklahoma,
for their future use. He also cited the possibility that the
Indian in such a territory could achieve the necessary degree
of civilization to enable him to compete equally with the
white man.[3]

Behind the government policy sketched out by President
Grant was the economic and political pressure being created
by the westward advance of the frontier. The construction of
the transcontinental railroad lines after the Civil War
helped to swell the tide of white settlement in the West. At
the same time the buffalo herds, on which the Plains Indians

depended for their food and whole way of life, were being
rapidly killed off. In 1875 the southern herd was gone, and
by the 1880's only a few thousands remained of the millions
of buffalo that had roamed the plains after the Civil War.
Thus the Indians had little choice but to give up their
nomadic ways and accept the government's policy of
concentrating them upon reservations located for the most
part in the Indian Territory of Oklahoma.

THE MIGRATION OF THE CHEYENNE
AND ARAPAHO INDIAN TRIBES

Prominent among the tribes that the United States desired to settle in the Indian Territory were the Cheyenne and Arapaho. The earliest known habitat of the Cheyenne was in western Minnesota, but by the early 1800's they were being constantly pushed farther westward into the High Plains country by the Sioux Indians. The Arapaho, who were closely associated with the Cheyenne throughout the 19th century, originally inhabited the area around the Red River Valley in northern Minnesota. Then they too moved in a southwesterly direction across the Missouri River at the same time as the Cheyenne. The Wichitas, who eventually were settled on the Cheyenne Arapaho reservation in Oklahoma, originally ranged from Kansas to Texas across the middle reaches of the Arkansas River. Much decimated by disease, they fled to Kansas during the Civil War. Primarily a sedentary and agricultural people, they were never as nomadic or warlike as the Cheyenne.[4]

In 1851 on September 17 at Fort Laramie, the United States entered into its first important treaty with the migrating Southern Cheyenne and Arapaho Indians. The two tribes were assigned to territory on the Upper Arkansas River subject to the right of the whites to establish roads through the country. The treaty, however, although proclaimed in force, was never ratified, and the discovery of gold in Colorado soon afterward resulted in white population overrunning the region, destroying the

wild game and threatening the Indians with starvation. By
anot her treaty on February 18, 1861, at Fort Wise Kansas, the
Chey enne and Arapaho therefore agreed to accept a smaller
rese rvation on the Upper Arkansas River farther to the east
and south in the "short-grass" country of eastern Colorado.
(12 Stat. 1163) Up until now the Cheyenne had been at peace
witbh the whites, but henceforth they became prominent in the
inte rmittent border warfare that persisted for some fifteen
yearrs from 1862 until 1877. At Chivington or Sand Creek,
Colorado, 1864, and again at Washita, Oklahoma, in 1868, the
Sout hern Cheyenne suffered severe d efcats by the United States
Army . In between these engagements, at Camp on the Little
Ark ansas River, Kansas, a peace treaty was negotiated with
the Cheyenne and Arapaho by which they agreed to give up
the ir lands on the Upper Arkansas River in return for a
tem porary reservation in southern Kansas adjacent to the
Che rokee lands in northern Oklahoma. (14 Stat. 703) On
October 28, 1867, at Medicine Creek Lodge, Kansas, still
ano ther treaty was negotiated with the Cheyenne and Arapaho
set tling them south of Kansas in the tract known as the
Cherrokee Outlet.[5] (15 Stat. 593)

The Cheyenne and Arapaho, however, refused to take up
the lands granted them in the Outlet, and in 1869 the United
ta tes selected for them still another reservation. On the
as is of a recommendation by the Commissioner of Indian
ff airs approved by the Secretary of the Interior, President

195

Grant issued an Executive Order dated August 10, 1869, which
superseded in effect the earlier treaty of 1867 and set
apart a new site immediately south of the Cherokee Outlet.[6]
Despite President Grant's order, the government did not
give up its efforts to settle the Cheyenne and Arapaho tribes
on the original reservation planned for them in the Cherokee
Outlet by the 1867 treaty. Accordingly in 1872 and 1873,
three agreements were made with the tribes, together and
separately, which related to the lands in the Outlet. These
agreements, however, were not ratified by Congress, and the
Cheyenne and Arapaho were later settled on the lands indicated
in the 1869 Executive Order.[7]

196   The 1869 Cheyenne Arapaho country, on which the tribes
were eventually settled, was in the western part of Oklahoma
within the northern portion of what was known as the Leased
District. The Cheyenne Arapaho reservation had been created
from the cessions of part of their lands in the Indian Territory by the members of the Five Civilized Tribes, excepting
only the Cherokee all of whose lands lay north and east of the
subject area. The original cession of what was called the
Leased District was made on June 22, 1855, by the Choctaw and
Chickasaw Indians who leased that part of their lands west
of 98°, amounting to 7,713,239 acres, for the use of the
Wichita dnd other western Indians.[8] (11 Stat. 611) By the
unratified agreement of October 19, 1872, a small section of
743,610 acres from the Leased District was assigned to the

Map of Indian Territory
1875

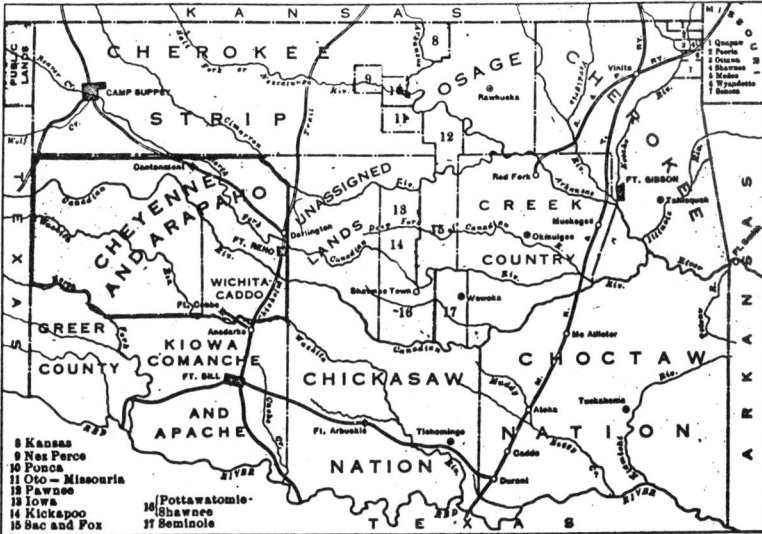

Indian Territory, 1875

197

Thoburn and Holcomb, "History of Oklahoma" - Page 128

Wichitas. Although these lands were never officially ceded
to them, because of their longtime occupancy of the area
the Wichita were conceded to have an interest in this section
of the Leased District, which was actually the southeastern
corner of the Cheyenne Arapaho reservation.[9]

The Cheyenne Arapaho reservation lands in the Leased
District included 2,489,160 acres from the original 1855
grant of the Choctaw and Chickasaw Indians. (11Stat. 611)
On April 28, 1866, the Choctaw and Chickasaw completely ceded t
to the United States whatever remaining rights they might
still have had to this Leased District for the use of other
tribes. (14 Stat. 769) In addition the Cheyenne and Arapaho
tract included the unoccupied western lands of the Creeks,
ceded June 14, 1866, (14 Stat. 785) plus additional Creek
land which they had ceded to the Seminoles on August 7, 1856,
(11 Stat.699) who then ceded it to the United States on
March 21, 1866. (14 Stat. 755) From all these cessions, the
Cheyenne and Arapaho received a total of slightly over
5 million acres, including the 743,610 acres of the Wichita,
divided as follows:[10]

Creek cession of 1866	·619;450.59 acres
Seminole cession of 1866	1;189;194.15
Choctaw & Chickasaw	2,489;159.84
Wichita lands	743,610.00

The boundaries of the Cheyenne Arapaho reservation, including the corner occupied by the Wichita, were officially
defined as follows:

Commencing at the point where the Washita River crosses
the ninety-eighth degree of west longitude; thence north on

a line with said ninety-eighth degree to the point where it
is crossed by the Red Fork of the Arkansas (sometimes called
the Cimarron River); thence up said river, in the middle of
the main channel thereof, to the north boundary of the
country ceded to the United States by the treaty of June 14,
1866, with the Creek Nation of Indians; thence west on said
north boundary and the north boundary of the country ceded
to the United States by the treaty of March 21, 1866 with the
Seminole Indians, to the one hundredth degree of west longitude; thence south on the line of said one hundredth degree
to the north boundary of the country set apart for the Kiowas
and Commanches by the second article of the treaty concluded
October 12, 1867 with said tribes; thence east along said
boundary to the point where it strikes the Washita River;
thence down said Washita River, in the middle of the main
channel thereof, to the place of beginning...." (26 Stat. 1022)

The corner of the above occupied by the Wichitas was

bounded as follows:

    Commencing at a point in the middle of the main channel
of the Washita River, where the ninety-eighth meridian of
W. longitude crosses the same; thence up the middle of the
main channel of said river to the line 98 40' W. longitude;
thence up said line of 98 40' due N. to the middle of the
main channel of the main Canadian River; thence down the
middle of the main Canadian River to where it crosses the
ninety-eighth meridian, thence due S. to the place of beginning. [12] (26 Stat. 1023; 28 Stat. 895)

    In the years following the Civil War, the Cheyenne

were engaged in almost constant warfare with the United

States. Although one small group surrendered in February

1869, the remainder refused to stay on their reservation

until their final defeat at the close of the general uprising

of 1874. Thus the immigrant Cheyenne and Arapaho, who had

travelled widely since their days in Minnesota, were finally

settled in 1875 on their reservation in Indian Territory, of

which the government tried to grant them exclusive possession

until they were induced to make the cession of 1891, per-

mitting allotment and sale of the larger portion of their

lands. [13] Although not part of our story, it is interesting to note that those of the Northern Cheyenne who were not settled in Oklahoma fought hard at the side of the Sioux in the bitter outbreaks of the 1870's. After a failure to unite them with their southern brethern in Oklahoma, the Northern Cheyenne finally accepted by Executive Order of November 26, 1884, a reservation in Montana.[14]

THE COMING OF THE CATTLEMEN
AND THE RAILROADS

By the time the Southern Cheyenne were finally settled on their reservation in Indian Territory, the Western
Plains country was in the midst of an economic revolution
that was to make it increasingly difficult to keep the
Territory exclusively for the red man. Unless the Indians
could be concentrated in sufficient numbers in Oklahoma,
white pressures for the cession of part of their lands
would increase, and the maintenance of a separate Indian
Territory would become impossible. The initial economic
interest in the Indian Territory came from the railroads
and the cattle ranchers. After the Civil War it became
profitable to drive surplus cattle up from Texas to the head
of the railroad lines being built across Kansas. From there
it was a relatively swift and easy trip to the slaughter-
houses of Kansas City, St. Louis, and Chicago. The routes
taken by the cowboys in "the long drive" from Texas to
Kansas were subject to change, but the Chisholm and other
famous cattle trails cut directly through the Indian
Territory.

At first the cattlemen paid little or nothing to the
Indians for the privilege of crossing their lands, or for
grazing and watering their cattle en route. Indeed much of
the prosperity of the early cattle industry rested on the
ranchers' free possession or use of the unfenced and unsettled parts of the national domain and of the Indian country.

201

Gradually Indian protest and increasing competition of
homesteaders outside Indian Territory forced changes upon
the ranchers. The cattlemen also were concerned over the
protection and classification of their livestock and hence
were more willing to enter into leases with the Indians by
which they could erect fences and temporary buildings.
Although the sale or leasing of Indian lands was forbidden
by the government, there was little United States inter-
ference as long as the leasing arrangements were satisfactory
to the respective Indian tribes. The most important of the
ranchers' agreements with the Indians was that of the
Cherokee Strip Live Stock Association, which in 1883 arranged
202 to pay the Cherokees $100,000 a year for five years for the
use of lands in the Cherokee Outlet.[15]

Immediately to the south of the Cherokee Outlet, the
Cheyenne Arapaho lands extended across the major cattle
trails from Texas. By the 1880's cattle were trespassing
on these lands, and several ranchers made arrangements for
grazing rights, retaining the Indians' goodwill by gifts
of beef or money. The cattlemen were eager to regularize
these arrangements, and in January 1883 a council of
Cheyenne and Arapaho chiefs authorized the United States
agent, John D. Miles, to lease their lands to a group of
seven ranchmen, who were to receive a total of 3,117,880
acres for a term of ten years in consideration of an annual
rental of two cents an acre, payable semi-annually in advance.

23

Fencing and improvements were to become the property of the Indians when the leases should expire.[16]

This grant of an exclusive lease by Agent Miles in behalf of the Cheyenne Arapaho chiefs brought forth a storm of protest from other cattlemen not included in the syndicate. The lessees, on the other hand, sought government protection on their lands rented from the Indians. Dubious of the leases' legality, and yet sympathetic with the Indians' desire to secure some economic return, Secretary of the Interior Teller ruled that, although it was not the policy of the Department to recognize such leases, there was no immediate objection on his part to allowing the Indians to grant the use of their lands to outsiders on fair and reasonable terms.[17] However, two years later in 1885, Attorney General A.H. Garland ruled that the cattlemen's leases in Indian Territory were illegal.[18]

Meanwhile the government's hands-off policy resulted in open warfare on the range between rival groups of cattlemen. The Indians also took sides and conditions on the Cheyenne Arapaho reservation steadily worsened. In December 1884 Congress launched an investigation of the situation, and in July 1885 General Sheridan was sent to the Cheyenne lands with orders to take charge and restore peace.[19] Before Sheridan could report, President Cleveland on July 23, 1885, resolved the matter by a proclamation declaring all leases on the Cheyenne Arapaho reservation void and ordering all

203

persons to remove their cattle, horses, and other property
within forty days. (24 Stat. 1023)

Cleveland's order provoked consternation among the
ranchers who had over 200,000 head of cattle on the
Cheyenne lands. The season was late to drive the cattle
to ranges in the North, and most of the animals were not yet
sufficiently fattened for slaughter. As a result many of
the cattle, together with additional thousands from the
Kiowa Commanche reservation to the south, were thrown at the
beginning of the winter upon the already overstocked ranges
of Kansas or Texas. Since the winter of 1885-86 was severe
in the Southwest, cattle died by the thousand, and ranchmen
blamed Cleveland's order for depressing prices. The peak of
prosperity for the cattle industry had already been reached
in 1884. Although a decline began in the summer and fall of
1885 after Cleveland's order, it was not until 1887 that
conditions became so bad as to show almost universal distress
in the cow country. Meanwhile cattle began to drift back,
illegally of course, into the Cheyenne reservation, and a
considerable number were again pastured there when the lands
were opened to settlement in April 1892.[20]

The relative isolation of the Indian Territory, already
broken by the cattle trails and range cattle industry, was
further disrupted in the 1870's by the coming of the
railroads. Oklahoma was almost literally a creature of the
railroads, which encouraged and aided white settlement. In
1871 the Missouri, Kansas, and Texas was constructed to run

north and south across the eastern part of the Indian
Territory. That same year the Atlantic and Pacific was
extended from the southwest corner of Missouri to connect
with the other road at Vinita. In 1882 work began on the
further westward extension of the Atlantic and Pacific, now
called the St. Louis and San Francisco. During the 1880's
railroad mileage in the Indian Territory grew rapidly: from
289 miles in 1880; 428 miles in 1886; 887 miles in 1887;
975 in 1889; and 1,155 in 1889; to 1,258 miles in 1890.
Finally one line of the Sante Fe ran through the heart of the
central part of Oklahoma from north to south, while in the
Cherokee Outlet another Sante Fe line just barely dipped
down to cut across the extreme northwestern corner of the
Cheyenne and Arapaho tract. Except for the few miles of this
last line of the Sante Fe, there was no railroad in 1890 in
any part of the Cheyenne Arapaho reservation, nor in that
portion of it occupied by the Wichita.[21]

205

THE OPENING OF THE
INDIAN TERRITORY

As the economic development of the West brought the
white man into closer contact with the Oklahoma country,
demands increased upon Congress for the opening up of the
unassigned and unoccupied parts of the Indian Territory
to white homeseekers. The "Boomers," as the enthusiastic
advocates of white settlement were called in the 1880's,
adopted the slogan "On to Oklahoma." The relative lack
of density in the Indian population of the area excited
the desires of these potential speculators and homesteaders.
At the beginning of the 1880's, it is estimated that there
were a quarter of a million Indians in the United States.
The vast majority were located west of the Mississippi,
dwelling on over a hundred scattered reservations in an
area as large as Texas. The survivors of over twenty tribes
dwelled in the unorganized Indian Territory, where the population was estimated in 1870 to be 68,152 persons, and ten
years later in 1880 only 79,769. This amounted to a little
more than one person to the square mile. In 1886 the General
Land Office reported that of a total of over 40 million acres
in Indian Territory, over 17 million acres were unsurveyed
and almost 10 million were unoccupied. Varying estimates of
the Cheyenne and Arapaho population in Oklahoma in the 1880's
ranged from 3000 to 6000, while the Wichitas numbered only a
few hundred, but over a thousand with their associated
tribes.[22]

The first official sign that Congress was ready to
give up the policy of keeping the Indian Territory closed
to whites was a provision in the Indian Appropriation Act
of March 3, 1885, which authorized the government to negotiate for the sale of the remaining unoccupied Indian lands.
(23 Stat. 362,384) No action was taken in regard to this law,
and two years later it was followed by the Dawes Severalty
or General Allotment Act of February 8, 1887. (24 Stat. 388)
This measure provided a means by which the communal
organization of the Indian tribes of the West could be
dissolved, the reservations broken up, and individual Indians
admitted to American citizenship. By the terms of the act,
individual Indians qualified for homestead grants of 160 acres
to heads of families, 80 acres to single adults, and 40 acres
to each dependent child. In 1891 this was amended so that
each member of a tribe regardless of age or sex received
equally 80 acres of land (26 Stat. 794) The remainder of the
reservation lands of each tribe were to be held in trust for
the tribe with the understanding that if the lands were
opened to white settlement, the Indians would receive an
adequate payment. Citizenship was conferred upon all Indians
who accepted the benefits of the Dawes Act, but it was
stipulated that no Indian might dispose of his land for
twenty-five years.

Although the Dawes Act was so drawn that it did not
apply to the Five Civilized Tribes or other Indians in
eastern Oklahoma, the measure did provide the basis on which

the government could begin negotiations with the remaining
Oklahoma tribes for the sale of the western part of the
Indian Territory. By Act of March 1, 1889, Congress
established the Indian Territory as a partially organized unit
of government with boundaries identical with those of the
present state (25 Stat. 783) The first Oklahoma area actually
opened to white settlement was the strip in the central part
of the present state, unoccupied by Indians, and known as the
Unassigned Lands, which Congress authorized for sale by Act of
March 2, 1889. (25 Stat. 1004) When the Creek and Seminole
tribes relinquished any remaining claims they might have to
this territory, President Harrison announced on March 23 that
it would be opened to homesteaders at twelve noon April 22,
1889. (26 Stat. 1544) This resulted in the first of the famous
Oklahoma land rushes. Within a few hours cities were staked
out at Guthrie and Oklahoma City, and by the end of the year
the central Oklahoma district had an estimated population of
60,000.[23]

208

The opening of the central Oklahoma district encouraged
the growing movement for the establishment of a separate
Oklahoma Territory, distinct from the Indian Territory. In
1890 a number of plans were proposed in Congress, and in
March a bill was approved to provide for a Territory of Oklahoma which should include all of the Indian Territory except
the districts in eastern Oklahoma occupied by the Five Civilized Tribes and several small reservations northeast of them.

The Cherokee Outlet was nominally excluded until 1893, but it
was attached to the Oklahoma Territory for judicial purposes.
Under the bill which became law May 2, 1890, (26 Stat. 81)
the new Oklahoma Territory included the Oklahoma district
just opened to settlement, the Indian reservations west of
96°, for which the government was negotiating cession
agreements, and the so-called No Man's Land or Oklahoma
Panhandle.[24]

Meanwhile the Indian Territory to the east, now diminished by the creation of Oklahoma Territory, was also being
subjected to the pressure of white homeseekers. In contrast
to the concentrated rushes that characterized the opening of
the central and western Oklahoma area, white settlers for a
long time had been gradually infiltrating eastern Oklahoma,
trespassing upon the Indian's lands. Varying reports of the
size of the white population in this Indian Territory in the
1880's indicate that the whites were becoming more numerous
than the Indians. During the 1890's Congress moved gradually
but consistently toward the dissolution of the Five Civilized
Tribes and the Indian Territory. The Tribes were eliminated
as political entities in 1898, and on March 3, 1901, all
Indians of the Indian Territory were made citizens of the
United States. (31 Stat. 1447) Although those in the Indian
Territory looked with some favor on separate statehood for
eastern Oklahoma, which would preserve something of the old
dream of an Indian state, the more influential population of

the Territory of Oklahoma preferred a united state. To
complete the story, it is sufficient to point out that on
June 16, 1906, an enabling act was passed,(34 Stat. 267)
and on November 16, 1907, Oklahoma statehood became a
reality.[25] (35 Stat. 2160)

Notes
Part II

THE EARLY HISTORY
OF OKLAHOMA, etc.

1 Roy M. Robbins, Our Landed Heritage (Princeton, 1942),
p. 139; Roy Gittinger, The Formation of the State of Oklahoma (Norman, 1939), Appendix B, p. 262.

2 J.C. Malin "Indian Policy and Westward Expansion,"
Bulletin of the University of Kansas Humanistic Studies, II
(November 1921), 101-103.

3 Robbins, Our Landed Heritage, p. 280.

4 Frederick W. Hodge, Handbook of American Indians (Washington, 1912), pp. 72, 251-253, 947-949.

5 For the location of the reservations and summaries of the
treaties, see Charles C. Royce, Indian Land Cessions in the
United States: Eighteenth Annual Report of the Bureau of American
ican Ethnology (Washington, 1899), pp. 786, 824, 838, 846;
Plates 426, 477, 489.

6 Ibid., pp. 852-853, Plates 525, 540A; Charles J. Kappler,
Indian Affairs: Laws and Treaties (Washington, 1904), I, 839-
841.

7 "Legal Status of Indians in the Indian Territory," Senate
Ex. Doc. No. 78, 51 Cong. 1 Sess., pp. 8-11.

8 Royce, Indian Land Cessions, p. 808; Plate 485.

9 Ibid., pp. 852, 856; Plate 540A.

10 "Legal Status of Indians in the Indian Territory," loc.
cit., pp. 21-30. See also Royce, Indian Land Cessions, pp.
808,816,840; Plates 404, 485, 486.

11 Quoted from the Executive Order as given in Kappler, Indian
Affairs: Laws and Treaties, I, 840. See also Royce, Indian
Land Cessions, p. 852.

12 Quoted as given in "Agreement with the Wichita and other
Indians," October 19, 1872, House Ex. Doc. No. 65, 42 Cong.
3 Sess., p. 2.

13 Grant Foreman, The Last Trek of the Indians (Chicago,
1946), pp. 296-300.

14 Royce, Indian Land Cessions, pp. 918-919; Plate 658A.

Notes
Part II

15 *Senate Ex. Doc. No. 17*, 48 Cong. 2 Sess., pp. 16-20.

16 *Ibid.*, pp. 12, 21ff.

17 *Senate Ex. Doc. No. 54*, 48 Cong. 1 Sess., p. 99.

18 18 *Opinions*, 235.

19 *Senate Ex. Doc. No. 16*, 48 Cong. 2 Sess., pp. 6ff.

20 Edward E. Dale, *The Range Cattle Industry* (Norman, 1930), pp. 144-146.

21 *Statistical Abstract of the United States 1890*, p. 274; Gittinger, *The Formation of the State of Oklahoma*, p. 215; Gaston Litton, *History of Oklahoma* (New York, 1957),II,102ff.

22 "Indian Territory," June 30, 1886, *House Misc. Doc. No. 15 Pt 2*, 49 Cong. 1 Sess., pp. 853ff.

23 Gittinger, *The Formation of the State of Oklahoma*, p. 190.

24 *Ibid.*, pp. 193-194; Solon J. Buck, *The Settlement of Oklahoma* (Madison, 1907), pp. 343-355.

25 Gittinger, *The Formation of the State of Oklahoma*, pp. 213-214, 231, 240-241.

Part III

OKLAHOMA, INCLUDING THE
SUBJECT AREA, IN 1890

Oklahoma in 1890 was divided into two parts. The
eastern portion was called the Indian Territory and embraced the homelands of the Five Civilized Tribes. The
western half, set apart as the Territory of Oklahoma by
the Organic Act of May 2, 1890,(26 Stat. 81) included the
Unassigned Lands later known as the Oklahoma District; No
Man's Land or the Oklahoma Panhandle; and the Indian
reservations in the Cherokee Outlet and in the old Leased
District, as well as Greer County which was claimed also by
Texas. The area of Oklahoma is 69,919 square miles or some
45 million acres, of which an estimated 27 million acres had
been surveyed by June 30, 1890. The six counties of the
Oklahoma District opened for settlement on April 22, 1889,
consisted of approximately 1,887,640 acres.[1]

In western Oklahoma the subject area was described
in a contemporary guide book for settlers as follows:

The surface of the Cheyenne and Arapahoe reservation,
in its leading features, is high, rolling prairie, rising at
some places into almost mountainous elevations. It is broken
by but little timber. Its lower bottom lands produce abun-
dantly. Its high prairies and cañons, in early spring, are
covered with beds of gorgeous flowers in great variety, and
their luxuriant nutritious grasses, with a plentiful water
supply from the Canadian and Washita rivers and their tributaries, create extensive ranges for horses and stock of all
kinds. Its soil, with the exception of the sand hills, is
naturally rich, and all it requires to make them productive
of all farm crops is the necessary rainfall or irrigation.
The climate is mild and equable, the nights being cool and
pleasant, and the rainfall is annually increasing.[2]

The total population of Oklahoma in 1890 according
to corrected census figures was 258,657.[3] This included
the Indian Territory which had a population of 180,182,
of which 51,279 were Indians, and Oklahoma Territory which
had a population of 78,475, of which 13,167 were Indians.
Divided into counties the population of Oklahoma Territory
was approximately as follows:

Beaver	2;674
Canadian	7;158
Cleveland	6;605
Greer(Texas)	5;338
Kingfisher	8;332
Logan	12;770
Oklahoma	11;742
Payne	7,125

The population of Oklahoma City was 4,151, and that of
Guthrie including the four separate townships was 5,883.[4]
The Oklahoma Governor's Report of October 1891 gave somewhat higher figures for the population of the counties in
1890, and estimated that at the time of his report the
population of Oklahoma Territory was around 80,000.[5] The
Governor's Report of the following year, 1892, estimated
the Oklahoma Territory population at 133,100 persons.[6]

The early Oklahoma Governor's Reports devoted considerable attention to the subject area. In 1891 the Governor
expressed the fear that, unless the Cheyenne and Arapaho
reservation was opened for settlement by the early part of
the next spring, there would not be time to plant crops and
avoid the hardships that had beset homesteaders following
the 1889 opening. At that time the United States government

had to be called upon to furnish help, and the railroads
had also come to the aid of the settlers by supplying seed
corn.[7] In 1892 the Governor noted that the taxable property
of the Territory could not be given as a whole because the
lands in the Cheyenne and Arapaho country were not yet
subject to taxation. There was no rush for these lands,
which were dry and far removed from any railroad, and the
Governor reported: "There has already been taken in the
Cheyenne and Arapaho country, since the opening April 19,
1892, 1,165,600 acres for homesteads, and a large quantity
remains yet to be taken." Otherwise most all the lands
available for settlement in the Territory had been occupied,
and in the Cheyenne and Arapaho area the eastern part had
been settled and was being converted to agriculture. In the
western part, the Governor pointed out, "there is still a
large amount of land unsettled. The experience of farmers
in western Kansas and Texas has caused an apprehension in
the minds of those seeking homes that these lands are located
too far west to receive sufficient rainfall during the crop
season to render them attractive for farms." Nevertheless,
the Governor predicted that in time on the basis of the
experience of Greer County, the Cheyenne and Arapaho country
"will prove to be fairly good as an agricultural country,
especially for wheat."[8]

Edward Everett Dale, a distinguished authority on

Oklahoma history, in his comments on the western Cheyenne

and Arapaho country, has written:

> During the late nineties western Oklahoma was rapidly
> changing from ranching to agriculture and by the first
> years of the twentieth century the transformation was
> about complete.
>   Western Oklahoma was at this time a very peculiar
> country. The general impression, even in the West, seems
> to be that Oklahoma was settled almost in a day. Strictly
> speaking, this is not true, and the stories of the great
> "rushes" are in some cases misleading. The newspapers of
> the time told of the great crowds gathered along the border,
> of how when the gun was fired at high noon on the day ap-
> pointed for the opening, these people dashed across the line
> and staked their claims, two or three men sometimes locating
> upon the same tract of land, so the casual reader is likely
> to get the impression that the entire country was taken up
> in this way.
>   This is quite erroneous. While it is true that the
> lands near the towns and the more fertile plains and valleys,
> especially in the eastern part of the Territory, were settled
> in this manner, it is also true that there were hundreds of
> acres of fertile agricultural land not settled until years
> after these "openings." This is particularly true of the
> Cheyenne and Arapaho reservation and of the Cherokee Outlet,
> opened to settlement in 1892 and 1893, respectively. In
> 1898 the author rode across this part of the country on
> horseback, and while there were settlements along the streams
> and in some cases on the level upland plains, yet it was
> possible to travel ten miles or more without seeing a house,
> though all of this land, except a little in each township,
> reserved for school purposes, was subject to homestead entry.
>   The greater part of this region was grazed over by the
> herds of the cattlemen.[9]

216

O. H. Day, one of the 89'ers and later a pioneer of

Day County in the northwest corner of the Cheyenne Arapaho

reservation, had recalled the region as "a Stockman's

paradise." When he went into the area in December 1897

seeking a location to go into the cattle business, he found

that "Settlers were few and far between, being located along

the streams. The principal industry was stock raising. The
cow man was supreme. Each cattleman located along a stream--
he placed his land filing so that he would control the water.
He then fenced off enough government land adjoining his
water rights to supply his needs."[10]

In 1890 much of Oklahoma was sparsely populated and
still undeveloped. Except for those areas owned by the Five
Civilized Tribes where some of the more progressive and
successful Indians were profitably growing crops, farm
improvements were generally meager and the acreages in
cultivation comparatively small. Early settlers were
familiar with the hazard of frequent drought periods, and the
1889 newcomers were hard pressed to get along. Despite the
fact that they could obtain their homestead free if they
stayed on it as long as five years, many gave up their claims
by selling "relinquishments" for as low as $25.00, or by
trading their lands off. Large areas owned by the Indians
were rented to ranchers or cattle companies for pasturing
for two or three cents per acre per year. In 1891 the
number and value per head of cattle in Oklahoma was estimated
as follows:[11]

all cattle	787;000	$14.10
hogs	26;000	3.70
sheep	40;000	1.95
mules	18,000	44.00

The existing market towns in Oklahoma and those along
the borders of the Territory of Oklahoma and the Indian
Territory, as well as the railroads, were all anxious to
have the Indian lands opened for settlement. They encouraged
the "Boomers" as well as a number of land speculators and
adventurers. The Boomers had been active prior to the
1889 settlement, and various groups of them had made efforts
at settlements only to be removed by the Army. Accordingly,
much of the demand for land for settlement was a result of
the agitation of the Boomers and of business interests,
rather than of the potential value of the land for farming.[12]

218 Although ranching and farming dominated Oklahoma in
1890, there were also some other economic resources. Bitumin-
ous coal was being commercially produced in fields around
McAlester to the east of the subject area. For several years
this coal had been used to supply the Missouri Pacific R. R.
No commercial oil had been discovered in either of the
Territories by 1890, but some lead and zinc were mined in the
northeastern corner of the Indian Territory.[13]

Oklahoma railroads included: (1) The Atchison, Topeka
& Sante Fe, the only road in the subject area which just
touched the northwestern tip of the Cheyenne country; and
another Sante Fe line completed in 1887 through the Territory
from north to south, from Arkansas City, Kansas, through
Oklahoma City and on to Texas.

(2) The St. Louis & San Francisco which crossed the southeast part of Indian Territory from Fort Smith, Arkansas, into Texas; and another line which ran southwesterly from Missouri through Vinita, Oklahoma, with a terminus at Red Fork, Oklahoma. (This railroad was operated in 1890 as the Atlantic & Pacific.)

(3) The Missouri, Kansas & Texas, a division of the Missouri Pacific started in 1870 and completed shortly thereafter, ran through the eastern part of the Indian Territory from Kansas to Texas through Vinita, Oklahoma.

(4) The Rock Island was just beginning to extend its Kansas lines into northcentral Oklahoma.

Total railroad mileage in operation in Oklahoma including the Indian Territory in 1890 was 1,258, but in the Oklahoma Territory proper in 1892 there was still only 172 miles in operation.[14]

219

One of the problems facing the first settlers in Oklahoma was that for a year there was no civil government within the area assigned for the initial opening. The lack of civil government encouraged crime and violence and weakened the protection of property. This situation was partly corrected when the Territory of Oklahoma was finally established on May 2, 1890. The Organic Act provided that there should be executive, legislative, and judicial departments. The Territorial Governor and Secretary were to be appointed by the President. Seven counties were created,

and Governor Steele, the first Territorial Governor,
appointed a full set of county officers for each county.
The statutes of Nebraska were adopted as laws of the
Territory until new laws could be provided by the Territorial
Legislature. In compliance with the terms of the Organic Act,
Governor Steele called for an election to be held August 5,
1890, to choose members of the first Territorial Legislative
Assembly, and by the end of the month it was organized for
business. The most lasting work of this first legislature
was the passage of bills to establish territorial schools
and colleges.[15]

   In general the political problems of Oklahoma were
those of all the new western territories in their formative
years. The economic problems of Oklahoma in 1890 were also
not dissimilar to those of other areas of the West which
were suffering from the hard times of the late 1880's and
early 1890's. But in Oklahoma the successive land rushes
after 1889 created an unusual situation which partly
modified the worsening economic conditions in the West and in
the United States generally.

Notes
Part III

OKLAHOMA, INCLUDING THE
SUBJECT AREA, IN 1890

1 Statistical Abstract of the United States 1890, p. 242;
Idem., 1959, p. 160; Grant Foreman, A History of Oklahoma
(Norman, 1942), p. 239; Gittinger, The Formation of the State
of Oklahoma, p. 194.

2 W.B. Matthews, The Settler's Map and Guide Book: Oklahoma (Washington, 1889), p. 7.

3 Statistical Abstract of the United States 1949, p. 33.

4 Compendium of the Eleventh Census: 1890, Part III, 1128-
1131; Part I, 36, 332, 446, 449.

5 House Ex. Doc. No. 1, Pt. 5, 52 Cong. 1 Sess., p. 449.

6 House Ex. Doc. No. 1, Pt. 5, 52 Cong. 2 Sess., p. 469.

7 "Report, " loc. cit., pp. 450-454.

8 "Report," loc. cit., pp. 470,474.

9 "The Passing of the Range Cattle Industry in Oklahoma,"
The Cattleman, XI (November 1924), in Dale and Rader,
Readings in Oklahoma History (Evanston, 1930), p. 581.

10 "Early Days in Day County," Chronicles of Oklahoma,
XXVI (Autumn 1948), 313.

11 Litton, History of Oklahoma, II, 42. For a summary of
economic developments, see Dale and Rader, Readings in Oklahoma History, ch. 18.

12 Gittinger, The Formation of the State of Oklahoma, ch. 7.

13 Matthews, The Settler's Map: Oklahoma, pp. 7-8.

14 Ibid., p. 8; Statistical Abstract of the United States
1890, p. 274.

15 Gittinger, The Formation of the State of Oklahoma, ch.10.

Part IV

THE CHEYENNE ARAPAHO
CESSION, 1891-1892

In the midst of the transition of the old Indian Territory into the state of Oklahoma, the United States government was negotiating with the various Indian tribes for the
cession of their surplus lands. Placement of the Indians
upon individual allotments and purchase of their remaining
surplus lands was a necessary prelude to white settlement.

At the same time that the Unassigned Lands were being
opened to settlement as the Oklahoma District in 1889, and
before the establishment of an official Oklahoma Territory
in May 1890, Congress in the Indian Appropriation Act of
March 2, 1889, provided for the establishment of a special
commission to deal with the Oklahoma Indians for the
relinquishment of their surplus lands west of 96°. (25 Stat.
1005,Sec. 14) This commission, generally known as the
Cherokee Commission, began its work in the summer of 1889,
and by the time it was dissolved four years later it had
secured the dissolution of Indian reservations embracing
more than 15 million acres.[1]

The Cherokee Commission was instructed to deal with
both the Cheyenne Arapaho and Wichita Indians at the
Cheyenne Arapaho Agency at Darlington. Negotiations with
the Cheyenne Arapaho Indians technically were over the
lands in the Cherokee Outlet by the treaty of 1867. Since
this treaty had been superseded by the Executive Order of

1869, the cession lands were actually those defined in 1869.
In any case, the Commission was warned that the Indians were
not to receive allotments on the basis of lands on two reservations.[2] The Cherokee Commission began its negotiations with
the Cheyenne Arapaho in July 1890. After forty days of fruit-
less discussions, the Commission adjourned and then resumed
its meetings in October when it was able to secure an agreement which was ratified by Congress on March 3, 1891. (26 Stat.
989)

The Cheyenne Arapaho agreement renounced the Indians'
rights to the Cherokee Outlet. The Cheyenne Arapaho ceded
to the United States, subject to allotment, all the territory
as defined and bounded in the 1869 Executive Order, and as
surveyed in the years 1858 and 1871. It was provided, however,
that no allotments to the Cheyenne and Arapaho were to be
made in the lands claimed by the Wichita and affiliated bands
of Indians. Each Cheyenne Arapaho received an allotment of
160 acres, with remaining surplus lands available for white
settlement.

The Indians were reluctant to take up their allotments
until the government made the first installments on the cash
payments due them for ceding their surplus lands.
Accordingly, on July 19, 1891, each Indian was paid 75 silver
dollars, and by October 1891 some 2,835 members of the tribes
had received $212,625. By March the task of apportioning the
allotments was completed with some 3,329 assignments of land

223

for a total of 529,682 acres, plus 32,344 acres for agency
and military purposes, and 231,829 acres for schools,
leaving 3,500,562 surplus acres for settlement, for which
the government paid $1,500,000.[3]

On April 19, 1892, the Cheyenne Arapaho lands were
opened to settlers, with an estimated 25,000 persons
participating in the run. In relatively dry country,
without railroad communication, and not contiguous to Kansas
or much of Texas, the opening of these lands failed to
generate the excitement of the rush of 1889 or the run in
1893 into the Cherokee Outlet. Thus in October 1892, six
months after the opening, the Governor of Oklahoma Territory
reported that only a little more than a third of the land
had been taken by white settlers, and the rest was still
available.[4]

Notes
Part IV

THE CHEYENNE ARAPAHO
CESSION, 1891-1892

1 Berlin B. Chapman, "Secret 'Instructions and Suggestions'
to the Cherokee Commission 1889-1890," Chronicles of Oklahoma,
XXVI (Winter 1948-49), 449-458.

2 Ibid.

3 Litton, History of Oklahoma, I, 397-398. The acreage
figures, differing slightly from those in Litton, are taken
from Kappler, Indian Affairs: Laws and Treaties, I, 1030.
Kappler's figures add up to 4,294,417 acres as the total
area of the Cheyenne and Arapaho reservation, in contrast
to the total sometimes used of 4,297,771 acres.

4 House Ex. Doc. No. 1, Pt. 5, 52 Cong. 2 Sess., p. 470.

226

COMMISSION FINDINGS

The following Findings and Opinion of The Commission include both title and value.

227

228

BEFORE THE INDIAN CLAIMS COMMISSION

CHEYENNE-ARAPAHOE TRIBES OF)
INDIANS, ETC., ET AL.)
)
                    Petitioners,   )
)
        vs.   )   Docket No. 329
)
THE UNITED STATES OF AMERICA   )
)
                    Defendant.   )

THE CHEYENNE AND ARAPAHOE TRIBES   )
OF INDIANS, ETC.,   )
)
        vs.   )   Docket No. 348
)
THE UNITED STATES OF AMERICA,   )
)
                    Defendant.   )

Filed: November 1, 1955

FINDINGS OF FACT

Certain documentary exhibits were received in support of petitioners' motion for summary judgment respecting the proper construction and effect of the Treaty of Fort Laramie, September 17, 1851 (10 Stat. 749). There is no substantial dispute as to the facts contained in these documents, the same having been stipulated to by the defendant in the case of the Crow Tribe of Indians v. The United States, Docket No. 54, 3 Ind. Cls. Comm. 147, and the defendant having opposed the consideration of the same in this case. The only question is as to the ultimate interpretation of the undisputed facts as respects the proper construction and effect of the Treaty of Fort Laramie. Accordingly, the Commission makes the following findings of fact in support of its order granting petitioners' motion for partial summary judgment.

1. On September 17, 1851, defendant and several Indian Tribes or nations, including the Cheyennes and Arapahoes, concluded a treaty by which a certain tract of land was therein designated as the "territory of the Cheyennes and Arrapahoes". The said treaty, insofar as applicable here, reads:

TREATY OF FORT LARAMIE WITH SIOUX, ETC., 1851

"Articles of a treaty made and concluded at Fort Laramie, in the Indian Territory, between D. D. Mitchell, superintendent of Indian affairs, and Thomas Fitzpatrick, Indian agent, commissioners specially appointed and authorized by the President of the United States, of the first part, and the chiefs, headmen, and braves of the following Indian nations, residing south of the Missouri River, east of the Rocky Mountains, and north of the lines of Texas and New Mexico, viz, the Sioux or Dahcotahs, Cheyennes, Arrapahoes, Crows, Assinaboines, Gros-Ventre Mandans, and Arrickaras, parties of the second part, on the seventeenth day of September, A.D. one thousand eight hundred and fifty-one.

"ARTICLE 1. The aforesaid nations, parties to this treaty, having assembled for the purpose of establishing and confirming peaceful relations amongst themselves, do hereby covenant and agree to abstain in future from all hostilities whatever against each other, to maintain good faith and friendship in all their mutual intercourse, and to make an effective and lasting peace.

230

"ARTICLE 2. The aforesaid nations do hereby recognize the right of the United States Government to establish roads, military and other posts, within their respective territories.

"ARTICLE 3. In consideration of the rights and privileges acknowledged in the preceding article, the United States bind themselves to protect the aforesaid Indian nations against the commission of all depredations by the people of the said United States after the ratification of this treaty.

"ARTICLE 4. The aforesaid Indian nations do hereby agree and bind themselves to make restitution or satisfaction for any wrongs committed, after the ratification of this treaty, by any band or individual of their people, on the people of the United States, whilst lawfully residing in or passing through their respective territories.

"ARTICLE 5. The aforesaid Indian nations do hereby recognize and acknowledge the following tracts of country, included within metes and boundaries hereinafter designated, as their respective territories, viz:

* * * *

"The territory of the Cheyennes and Arrapahoes, commencing at the Red Bute, or the place where the road leaves the north fork of the Platte River; thence up the north fork of the Platte River to its source; thence along the main range of the Rocky Mountains to the head-waters of the Arkansas River; thence down the Arkansas River to the crossing of the Santa Fe road; thence in a northwesterly direction to the forks of the Platte River, and thence up the Platte River to the place of beginning.

"It is, however, understood that, in making this recognition and acknowledgement, the aforesaid Indian nations do not hereby abandon or prejudice any rights or claims they may have to other lands; and further, that they do not surrender the privilege of hunting, fishing, or passing over any of the tracts of country heretofore described.

"ARTICLE 6. The parties to the second part of this treaty having selected principals or head-chiefs for their respective nations, through whom all national business will hereafter be conducted, do hereby bind themselves to sustain said chiefs and their successors during good behavior.

"ARTICLE 7. In consideration of the treaty stipulations, and for the damages which have or may occur by reason thereof to the Indian nations, parties hereto, and for their maintenance and the improvement of their moral and social customs, the United States bind themselves to deliver to the said Indian nations the sum of fifty thousand dollars per annum for the term of ten years, with the right to continue the same at the discretion of the President of the United States for a period not exceeding five years thereafter, in provisions, merchandise, domestic animals, and agricultural implements, in such proportions as may be deemed best adapted to their condition by the President of the United States, to be distributed in proportion to the population of the aforesaid Indian nations.

231

"ARTICLE 8. It is understood and agreed that should any of the Indian nations, parties to this treaty, violate any of the provisions thereof, the United States may withhold the whole or a portion of the annuities mentioned in the preceding article from the nation so offending, until, in the opinion of the President of the United States, proper satisfaction shall have been made.

"In testimony whereof the said D. D. Mitchell and Thomas Fitzpatrick commissioners as aforesaid, and the chiefs, headmen, and braves, parties hereto, have set their hands and affixed their marks, on the day and at the place first above written."

2. At the time that the Treaty of 1851 was negotiated and entered into all of the lands involved in and described in the Treaty were by the United States recognized generally to be lands held and occupied by Indians from time immemorial, held by them by aboriginal Indian title.

3. Immediately and for some years preceding the Treaty of Fort Laramie, because of the discovery of gold on the Pacific Coast, gold-seekers, emigrants and troops found it necessary to pass through this Indian country, the Indians bitterly resented their invasion and intrusion because the whites destroyed and depleted buffalo and game, the native grasses and forests, and threatened the livelihood and traditional means of subsistence of the Indians, bringing disease among them and causing starvation, suffering and great loss of life among the Indians. The hostility thus aroused manifested itself in the killing and massacre of the whites passing through the country, serving as a constant threat and hazard to any white people passing into or through said country. The Indian tribes or nations involved also fought among themselves, mostly on account of boundary disputes, the more warlike particularly preying upon and invading the territories of other tribes; these said internecine wars imperiling the whites who entered the country. (Ex. 3-A and 30).

4. The Indian nations and tribes, parties to said treaty considered themselves entitled to compensation for the right-of-way of white travelers through their country and for the resulting destruction of game, grass and timber committed by troops and emigrants. (Ex. 39).

5. The purpose and intent of the United States Government is seeking a treaty with the Indian nations and tribes here involved was to bring about peaceful relations among the Indian tribes themselves and stop internecine wars and to have the tribes agree among themselves, with respect to the vast territory

recognized as generally held by all of them by Indian title, to an exact definition of the national domain of each tribe and the establishment of fixed boundaries to that end, and to obtain from each tribe affected a right-of-way through their country for the peaceful passage of emigrants and troops; and otherwise to placate the Indians, satisfy their complaints and obtain agreement to avoid future depredations. (Ex. 3A, 30, 40).

6. The Government agents who negotiated the treaty with the Indians and who signed it for the United States as Commissioners understood the purpose and intent of the Government, as outlined in the previous finding, and in their extended negotiations with the Indian tribes at Fort Laramie, leading up to the execution of the treaty, so represented to the Indians, and the Indians so understood. (Exs. 25a, b, c, d and f).

7. By the treaty of Fort Laramie, the United States Government accomplished the purpose for which the appropriation of Congress was made and to which it desired the assent of the Indian tribes affected, whereby, for the consideration named, the United States obtained the right of passage through the territory and the promise from the Indians that they would keep the peace. The recognition that these lands were the lands of the Indian tribes affected, theretofore held in exclusive occupancy (except as invaded by whites) by these Indian tribes, was implicit throughout treaty and was understood by all of the negotiating parties. (Exs. 6, 41).

233

8. The Treaty of Fort Laramie is not merely a treaty of amity and an agreement between the Indian tribes themselves, but by said treaty and the manner of its negotiation and the acts and conduct of the defendant, the United States of America, immediately before and after the execution and ratification of said treaty, defendant accepted, acknowledged, ratified and confirmed petitioners'

aboriginal Indian title and right of occupancy, possession and use of the territory described in Finding 1.

9. That by order made and entered on May 5, 1952, the above cases were consolidated for trial, so the foregoing findings of fact are intended to apply to each insofar as either involves an interpretation of the Fort Laramie Treaty of September, 1851.

/s/ EDGAR E. WITT
Chief Commissioner

/s/ LOUIS J. O'MARR
Associate Commissioner

/s/ WM. M. HOLT
Associate Commissioner

234

BEFORE THE INDIAN CLAIMS COMMISSION

CHEYENNE-ARAPAHO TRIBES OF   )
INDIANS OF OKLAHOMA, et al.,)
)
            Petitioners,   )
)
      v.   )   Docket No. 329
)
THE UNITED STATES OF AMERICA,)
)
            Defendant.   )

THE CHEYENNE AND ARAPAHO   )
TRIBES OF INDIANS, et al.,   )
)
            Petitioners,   )
)
      v.   )   Docket No. 348
)
THE UNITED STATES OF AMERICA,)
)
            Defendant.   )

Decided: December 6, 1961

235

FINDINGS OF FACT

The Commission in a previous determination in these consolidated
cases made the following findings of fact, not previously published,
in support of its order granting petitioners' motion for partial
summary judgment on November 1, 1955.

Certain documentary exhibits were received in support of petitioners'
motion for summary judgment respecting the proper construction and effect
of the Treaty of Fort Laramie, September 17, 1851 (10 Stat. 749). There
is no substantial dispute as to the facts contained in these documents,
the same having been stipulated to by the defendant in the case of the
Crow Tribe of Indians v. The United States, Docket No. 54, 3 Ind. Cls.

Comm. 147, and the defendant having opposed the consideration of the same in this case. The only question is as to the ultimate interpretation of the undisputed facts as respects the proper construction and effect of the Treaty of Fort Laramie.

1. On September 17, 1851, defendant and several Indian Tribes or nations, including the Cheyennes and Arapahos, concluded a treaty by which a certain tract of land was therein designated as the "territory of the Cheyennes and Arrapahoes". The said treaty, insofar as applicable here, reads:

TREATY OF FORT LARAMIE WITH SIOUX, ETC. 1851

"Articles of a treaty made and concluded at Fort Laramie, in the Indian Territory, between D. D. Mitchell, superintendent of Indian affairs, and Thomas Fitzpatrick, Indian agent, commissioners specially appointed and authorized by the President of the United States, of the first part, and the chiefs, headmen, and braves of the following Indian nations, residing south of the Missouri River, east of the Rocky Mountains, and north of the lines of Texas and New Mexico, viz, the Sioux or Dahcotahs, Cheyennes, Arrapahoes, Crows, Assinaboines, Gros-Ventre Mandans, and Arrickaras, parties of the second part, on the seventeenth day of September, A.D. one thousand eight hundred and fifty-one.

"ARTICLE 1. The aforesaid nations, parties to this treaty, having assembled for the purpose of establishing and confirming peaceful relations amongst themselves, do hereby covenant and agree to abstain in future from all hostilities whatever against each other, to maintain good faith and friendship in all their mutual intercourse, and to make an effective and lasting peace.

"ARTICLE 2. The aforesaid nations do hereby recognize the right of the United States Government to establish roads, military and other posts, within their respective territories.

"ARTICLE 3. In consideration of the rights and privileges acknowledged in the preceding article, the United States bind themselves to protect the aforesaid Indian nations against the commission of all depredations by the people of the said United States, after the ratification of this treaty.

"ARTICLE 4. The aforesaid Indian nations do hereby
agree and bind themselves to make restitution or satisfaction for any wrongs committed, after the ratification of
this treaty, by any band or individual of their people,
on the people of the United States, whilst lawfully residing in or passing through their respective territories.

"ARTICLE 5. The aforesaid Indian nations do hereby
recognize and acknowledge the following tracts of country,
included within the metes and boundaries hereinafter designated, as their respective territories, viz:

* * * *

"The territory of the Cheyennes and Arrapahoes,
commencing at the Red Bute, or the place where the road
leaves the north fork of the Platte River; thence up the
north fork of the Platte River to its source; thence along
the main range of the Rocky Mountains to the head-waters
of the Arkansas River; thence down the Arkansas River to
the crossing of the Santa Fe road; thence in a northwesterly direction to the forks of the Platte River, and
thence up the Platte River to the place of beginning.

"It is, however, understood that, in making this
recognition and acknowledgement, the aforesaid Indian
nations do not hereby abandon or prejudice any rights or
claims they may have to other lands; and further, that
they do not surrender the privilege of hunting, fishing,
or passing over any of the tracts of country heretofore
described.

"ARTICLE 6. The parties to the second part of this
treaty having selected principals or head-chiefs for
their respective nations, through whom all national
business will hereafter be conducted, do hereby bind
themselves to sustain said chiefs and their successors
during good behavior.

"ARTICLE 7. In consideration of the treaty stipulations, and for the damages which have or may occur by
reason thereof to the Indian nations, parties hereto,
and for their maintenance and the improvement of their
moral and social customs, the United States bind themselves to deliver to the said Indian nations the sum
of fifty thousand dollars per annum for the term of ten

years, with the right to continue the same at the discretion of the President of the United States for a
period not exceeding five years thereafter, in provisions,
merchandise, domestic animals, and agricultural implements,
in such proportions as may be deemed best adapted to their
condition by the President of the United States, to be
distributed in proportion to the population of the aforesaid Indian nations.

"ARTICLE 8. It is understood and agreed that should
any of the Indian nations, parties to this treaty, violate
any of the provisions thereof, the United States may withhold the whole or a portion of the annuities mentioned in
the preceding article from the nation so offending, until,
in the opinion of the President of the United States,
proper satisfaction shall have been made.

"In testimony whereof the said D. D. Mitchell and
Thompas Fitzpatrick commissioners as aforesaid, and the
chiefs, headmen, and braves, parties hereto, have set
their hands and affixed their marks, on the day and at
the place first above written."

2. At the time that the Treaty of 1851 was negotiated and entered

into all of the lands involved in and described in the Treaty were by

the United States recognized generally to be lands held and occupied by

Indians from time immemorial, held by them by aboriginal Indian title.

3. Immediately and for some years preceding the Treaty of Fort

Laramie, because of the discovery of gold on the Pacific Coast, gold-

seekers, emigrants and troops found it necessary to pass through this

Indian country, the Indians bitterly resented their invasion and intrusion

because the whites destroyed and depleted buffalo and game, the native

grasses and forests, and threatened the livelihood and traditional

means of subsistence of the Indians, bringing disease among them and

causing starvation, suffering and great loss of life among the Indians.

The hostility thus aroused manifested itself in the killing and massacre

of the whites passing through the country, serving as a constant
threat and hazard to any white people passing into or through said
country. The Indian tribes or nations involved also fought among
themselves, mostly on account of boundary disputes, the more warlike
particularly preying upon and invading the territories of other tribes;
these said internecine wars imperiling the whites who entered the
country (Ex. 3-A and 30).

4. The Indian nations and tribes, parties to said treaty, considered themselves entitled to compensation for the right-of-way of
white travelers through their country and for the resulting destruction
of game, grass and timber committed by troops and emigrants (Ex. 39).

5. The purpose and intent of the United States Government in
seeking a treaty with the Indian nations and tribes here involved was
to bring about peaceful relations among the Indian tribes themselves
and stop internecine wars and to have the tribes agree among themselves,
with respect to the vast territory recognized as generally held by all
of them by Indian title, to an exact definition of the national domain
of each tribe and the establishment of fixed boundaries to that end,
and to obtain from each tribe affected a right-of-way through their
country for the peaceful passage of emigrants and troops; and otherwise
to placate the Indians, satisfy their complaints and obtain agreement
to avoid future depredations (Ex. 3A, 30, 40).

6. The Government agents who negotiated the treaty with the
Indians and who signed it for the United States as Commissioners understood

239

the purpose and intent of the Government, as outlined in the previous
finding, and in their extended negotiations with the Indian tribes at
Fort Laramie, leading up to the execution of the treaty, so represented
to the Indians, and the Indians so understood (Exs. 25a, b, c, d and f).

7. By the treaty of Fort Laramie, the United States Government
accomplished the purpose for which the appropriation of Congress was
made and to which it desired the assent of the Indian tribes affected,
whereby, for the consideration named, the United States obtained the
right of passage through the territory and the promise from the Indians
that they would keep the peace. The recognition that these lands were
the lands of the Indian tribes affected, theretofore held in exclusive
occupancy (except as invaded by whites) by these Indian tribes, was
implicit throughout treaty and was understood by all of the negotiating
parties (Exs. 6, 41).

8. The Treaty of Fort Laramie is not merely a treaty of amity and
an agreement between the Indian tribes themselves, but by said treaty
and the manner of its negotiation and the acts and conduct of the defendant,
the United States of America, immediately before and after the execution
and ratification of said treaty, defendant accepted, acknowledged, ratified
and confirmed petitioners' aboriginal Indian title and right of occupancy,
possession and use of the territory described in Finding 1.

9. That by order made and entered on May 5, 1952, the above cases
were consolidated for trial, so the foregoing findings of fact are intended
to apply to each insofar as either involves an interpretation of the
Fort Laramie Treaty of September, 1851.

240

The Commission now makes the following additional findings of fact which are supplementary to the above recited findings of fact 1 to 9, inclusive.

10. Jurisdiction and Identity

(a) The Cheyenne-Arapaho Tribes of Indians of Oklahoma, one of the petitioners in Docket No. 329, are a duly organized tribe of American Indians with a tribal organization, recognized by the Secretary of Interior as having authority to represent said tribe, and is authorized to maintain this action by the Indian Claims Commission Act of August 13, 1946 (60 Stat. 1049); and it is an identifiable tribe of American Indians residing within the territorial limits of the United States, having a common claim which it is authorized to have heard and determined by the Commission under Sec. 2 of the said Indian Claims Commission Act.

(b) The Northern Cheyenne Tribe of Indians of the Tongue River Reservation, Montana, one of the petitioners in Docket No. 348, is a duly organized tribe of American Indians with a tribal organization recognized by the Secretary of Interior as having authority to represent said tribe, and is authorized to maintain this action by the Indian Claims Commission Act of August 13, 1946 (60 Stat. 1049); and it is an identifiable tribe of American Indians residing within the territorial limits of the United States, having a common claim which it is authorized to have heard and determined by the Commission under Sec. 2 of the said Indian Claims Commission Act.

(c) The Northern Arapaho Tribe of Indians of the Wind River Reservation, Wyoming, one of the petitioners in Docket No. 348, is a

241

duly organized tribe of American Indians with a tribal organization
recognized by the Secretary of Interior as having authority to represent
said tribe, and is authorized to maintain this action by the Indian
Claims Commission Act of August 13, 1946 (60 Stat. 1049); and it is an
identifiable tribe of American Indians residing within the territorial
limits of the United States, having a common claim which it is authorized
to have heard and determined by the Commission under Sec. 2 of the said
Indian Claims Commission Act.

11. Treaties of Cession

(a) By the Treaties of February 18, 1861 (12 Stat. 1163),
October 14, 1865 (14 Stat. 703), and October 28, 1867 (15 Stat. 593),
petitioner, the Southern Tribes (Cheyenne-Arapaho Tribes of Indians of
Oklahoma) ceded to the United States all its interest in the territory
of the Cheyennes and the Arapahos described in Finding No. 1.

242

(b) By the Treaty of May 10, 1868 (15 Stat. 655), petitioner, the
Northern Tribes (Northern Cheyenne Tribe of Indians and Northern Arapaho
Tribe of Indians) relinquished, released and surrendered to the United
States all its interest in the territory of the Cheyennes and Arapahos,
described in Finding No. 1.

12. Evaluation Date - Notwithstanding the dates of the various
treaties of cession of the Cheyenne-Arapaho lands the value of the lands
is determined herein as of October 14, 1865, a date mutually agreed upon
among the parties hereto.

13. Topography - The ceded lands are in the heart of the western

part of central United States, bounded on the north by the North Platte

River; on the south by the Arkansas River; on the west by the Conti-

nental Divide of the Rocky Mountains; and on the east by a line roughly

midway between the 100th and 101st meridians. Plains lands make up at

least eighty-five percent of the total area; the remaining fifteen

percent is composed of mountain peaks, mountain parks and mountain

plateaus. The plains area has an average altitude of 4,500 to 5,000

feet and ranges from 3,500 feet on the eastern border to 5,000 or 5,500

feet at the base of the mountain plateaus; the mountain plateaus range

from 6,000 to 8,000 feet; some of the mountains in the mountainous

portion exceed 14,000 feet. The area contains three major watersheds;

the North Platte, South Platte and Arkansas Rivers, with incidental

drainage occasioned by the Cache la Poudre, Arikaree, Clear Creek,

Cherry Creek, North and South Forks of the South Platte, Boulder Creek,

South St. Vrain Creek, the Big and Little Thompsons, Chugwater Creek,

Laramie River, Medicine Bow River, and numerous smaller creeks.

14. The Cheyenne and Arapaho lands, which are involved herein and

will hereinafter be referred to as the subject tract, are located in

what are now the States of Colorado, Wyoming, Kansas and Nebraska. The

amount of land in each of these states has been estimated to be:

State	Acreage	Percent of Total
Colorado	26,447,516	51.64
Wyoming	9,960,748	19.46
Kansas	7,875,504	15.38
Nebraska	6,926,232	13.52
Total	51,210,000	100.00

243

15. <u>Highest and Best Uses</u> - The subject tract had multiple uses
for which parts of it were adaptable at the date of valuation. These
uses were grazing, mining, agriculture and townsites. The acreages of
each of the best uses of these lands are as follows:

Range or grazing	50,252,320 acres
Agricultural	400,000 acres
Mineral	550,000 acres
Townsites	7,680 acres

16. The Cheyenne-Arapaho lands, in 1865, had the following classi-
fications of vegetative cover:

River bottom	3,031,040 acres
Plains grassland	38,345,440 acres
Mountain parks and foothills	2,357,760 acres
Sagebrush-grass	1,745,920 acres
Shadscale-grass	35,840 acres
Pinon juniper	190,000 acres
Coniferous timber	5,219,840 acres
Alpine tundra and barren	284,160 acres

244   17. <u>Climatic Conditions</u> - Because of the topography of the subject
tract the climatic conditions affecting the area varied according to elevation.
Overall precipitation averages approximately 17 inches of annual rain and
snow fall. About five times as much snow falls at 14,000 feet as falls
at 5,000 feet. The range of precipitation is from 6 to 60 inches and
it varies in relationship to the mountains. The bulk of the tract
is a great plains area. The average altitude of this plains area
approximates 4,500 to 5,000 feet. It ranges from 3,500 feet on the
easterly borders to about 5,000 to 5,500 feet at the base of the
mountain plateaus. The mountain plateaus range from 6,000 to 8,000
feet in elevation. In the plains area the over-all precipitation was

adequate to support the types of growth which were indigenous, that is range grasses, shrubs, herbs and forage. The growing season varies in proportion to altitude and terrain. The total range of frost free days vary from 30-170 days while the average range of frost free days in the major agricultural area is 120-160 days. The elevation of the whole area creates high, dry summer heat. The low humidity provides warm days and cool nights. Winter temperatures are low, but lack of humidity reduces severity. Most of the tract is classified as semi-arid and has been subject to periodic droughts.

18. _Timber_ - There was virtually no timber on the plains which comprised most of the Cheyenne and Arapaho lands. The timber in the subject lands is chiefly located in the mountain areas. The timber in Colorado had a value only for local consumption. It could not be economically transported by wagon trains, nor even by railroads, to compete with the southern pine or white pine of the lake states, which was still in abundant supply, close to eastern markets, in 1865. The timber in Wyoming had even less value as it was farther away from the settlements near the mining regions. The forest areas of Colorado did contribute to increase the value of mining properties, homes and farms, by furnishing mining timbers, material for fences, houses, etc., which is reflected in the higher value of the mineral lands and the surveyed areas east of the mountains (Def. Ex. 2, pp. 82, 83, 84).

245

19. <u>White Knowledge of Lands</u> -

(a) Prior to the start ,of the 19th century the subject tract was little known to the early Spanish, English, French or American explorers and no permanent settlements were made therein. With the acquisition of sovereignty by the United States of the tract in 1803 through the Louisiana Purchase, American explorers began to penetrate the tract and the characteristics of the area became generally known. Captain Zebulon M. Pike explored the tract, and particularly the upper Arkansas and the headwaters of the South Platte in 1806. Major Stephen H. Long explored the region in 1820 going up the Platte and down the Front Range to the Arkansas. Their reports were widely published. During the fur trade era trading posts were established in the area in the 1830's and 1840's with Forts Bent and Pueblo on the Arkansas, Forts Vasquez and St. Vrain on the Platte and Fort Laramie near the North Platte. In 1835 United States troops under Colonel Dodge followed the South Fork of the Platte up to the mountains; in 1845 Colonel Kearney led more troops over the same route; from 1842 to 1853 all five of the official Fremont expeditions traversed the region. By 1852 the Oregon Trail along the North Platte had been used by 100,000 emigrants passing westward. In 1853 the three explorations searching for transcontinental routes had crossed the tract.

246

(b) The early explorations by officers and agents of the United
States and the publishing of their reports led to the Great Plains area,
stretching eastward from the Rocky Mountains to about the 97th meridian,
being considered as "The Great American Desert." The mistaken idea of
the existence of The Great American Desert prevailed in the minds of
many up to the Civil War and in some quarters until later. The semi-
arid nature of the plains and the scarcity of wood and water detracted
from its desirability and deterred the settlers who were used to a humid
and forest-area background from inhabiting the region. The Oregon Trail
and the thousands who passed over it to the far west, however, did bring
some small settlement to the country it traversed in the way of road
ranches which were the beginning of the cattle business for the area.

20. Population - Beginning with the gold rush of 1858, a number of
towns were established in Colorado near the mining regions, some of which
grew into cities and some of which became abandoned ghost towns.

In the Denver area, the "Lawrence Party" from Lawrence, Kansas,
started Montana City on the South Platte on September 7, 1858, but this
was deserted in a few months. The real beginnings of Denver date from
the organization of the Auraria Town Company on October 31, 1858, which
started a town on the west side of Cherry Creek, near its junction with
the South Platte. General William Larimer arrived on November 16, 1858
and took possession of a site on the east side of Cherry Creek, across
from Auraria, which was named "Denver." Later Auraria and Denver were
combined to form one town.

247

Golden was founded in June, 1859, and became the nominal capital of Colorado Territory from 1862 to 1867.

Colorado City, forerunner of Colorado Springs, was begun in August, 1859.

Pueblo was the site of a trading post with the Indians from 1841 to 1854, when it was destroyed in an Indian attack. In the fall of 1858 the town of Fountain was started east of the mouth of Fountain Creek, and in the winter of 1859-60 a rival town was begun west of Fountain, which became known as Pueblo.

Central City, Black Hawk and other mining towns like Nevadaville sprang up in 1859 as a result of Gilpin County gold mining activities.

Idaho Springs, first known as Idaho, started when George Andrew Jackson discovered gold near the site in January 1859.

248

Leadville, or Oro City, as it was first called, was founded when the gold placer district was discovered on the upper Arkansas in 1860. It was almost deserted in the middle 1860's after the placer gold was exhausted.

The town of Boulder was platted early in 1859 by gold seekers. Cheyenne, Wyoming, was not founded until 1867.

There were numerous mining towns which were once heavily populated but are now either ghost towns or have only a small population, such as Fair Play, Silver Plume, Georgetown, Tarryall, Buckskin Joe, etc., some of which had declined by 1865.

By 1870 the population of Colorado was 39,864 which barely exceeded its 1860 level, a net gain of only 5,587 in ten years. By 1870, many of the Colorado towns or mining camps existing in 1860 were not reported in the census. The Census of 1870 listed only the following towns in Colorado:

Town	Population	Town	Population
Denver	4,759	Central City	2,360
Boulder City	343	Nevada	973
St. Vrain	781	Kit Carson	473
Georgetown	802	Garden City	587
Idaho	229	Trinidad	562
Colorado City	81	Pueblo	666
Canon City	229	Greeley	480
Black Hawk	1,068		
		Total	14,393

This leaves a balance of 25,471 living in small villages or on farms in Colorado in 1870.

The population of the entire Territory of Wyoming in 1870 was only 9,118, practically all of which was concentrated along the route of the Union Pacific Railroad.

Western Kansas, within the boundaries of the subject area was virtually uninhabited in 1865.

The portion of the subject lands within the present State of Nebraska was practically uninhabited in 1865. The population of the Nebraska counties in 1855, 1856, 1860 and 1870 is reported as follows:

In Subject Territory	1855	1856	1860	1870
Lincoln County (part)	--	--	117	206
Cheyenne (w. of 100th meridian)				
Nebraska (e. of 97th meridian, bordering Missouri River	4,494	10,716	23,646	101,204
Nebraska (97th to 100th meridian)	--	--	5,078	21,583
Total Nebraska	4,494	10,716	28,841	122,993
Percent west of 100th meridian	0	0	0.4	0.2

21. Mineral Discoveries and Early Settlement -

(a) Permanent white settlement of the subject tract followed the
discovery of gold in 1858 on Dry Creek south of Denver near the Platte.
The following year saw the great Pikes Peak gold rush into the region
when 100,000 persons reached the mining areas and an estimated 40,000
remained through the winter of 1859-1860. To supply the numerous
mining camps in the hills, supply depots were established near the base
of the Front Range. These developed into the cities of Denver, Boulder,
Colorado City, and Pueblo. Along the streams at the base of the mountains
near the mining camps irrigated agriculture was soon being practiced in
a narrow belt extending north and south of Denver. The produce of these
farms found a market in the mining camps and the new towns. The farms
were located along the South Platte and on Clear Creek, Cherry Creek,
St. Vrain Creek, Boulder Creek, Cache la Poudre Creek, Little Thompson
Creek, Bear Creek, the Fountain qui Bouit and the Arkansas River. About
60,000 acres was the amount of cultivated land in the subject tract as
of October 1865. A belt of land north and south of Denver had been
surveyed by June 1865, which had been divided into sections, containing
a total of 1,207,742 acres.

(b)   A number of events caused the population of Colorado Territory to dwindle from about 34,000 to 28,000 in 1866.   The outbreak of
the Civil War, Indian trouble on the Great Plains in 1864-1865 and the
fact that mining in Colorado had ceased to be especially profitable
were the main factors causing the decrease in population.   By 1870 the
census figures showed the region to again be enjoying population increase
with the inhabitants numbering 39,864.   In the next decade the population
increased to 194,327.

22. Political Subdivisions - Until 1861, the Cheyenne-Arapaho lands
were part of the Territories of Kansas and Nebraska, both created in
1854.   In 1859 the people in the Colorado portion of the territory formed
the extra-legal Territory of Jefferson, elected officials, convened a
legislature and passed laws.   On February 28, 1861, the Territory of
Colorado was created with the present-day boundaries of the State of
Colorado; the portion of Cheyenne-Arapaho lands now in Wyoming continued
to be a part of Nebraska Territory until 1868, and the portions east of
the Colorado boundary were respectively part of Kansas and Nebraska
Territories, as before.   The Territory of Colorado was, in 1861, divided
into seventeen counties, eleven of which were entirely within the Cheyenne-
Arapaho lands, three of which were partly within and partly without, and
three (Summit, Conejos and Costilla) entirely without.

23. Roads and Transportation - (a) The two great historic trails
to the west, the Oregon Trail and the Santa Fe Trail followed respectively

251

the north and south boundaries of the Cheyenne-Arapaho area; the Smoky
Hill Trail traversed the heart of the area. The Santa Fe Trail was in
use as early as 1822 and the Oregon Trail had reached the northwest
boundary of the territory from the east by 1830.

Until the railroads came, the territory was served by animal-drawn
freight and stage lines operating on regular schedules. From 1859 the
Leavenworth and Pike's Peak Express ran stage coaches into Denver from
the east, running a daily schedule after 1861. Starting in 1864 the
Butterfield Overland Dispatch served the country with stagecoaches and
fast freight wagons; in 1865 there were 7,240 wagons, 57,002 oxen,
6,887 horses and mules, and 7,700 men engaged in freighting goods to
Colorado from Plattsmouth (the mouth of the Platte on the Missouri)
alone; the Pony Express provided messenger service to the area in 1860
252 and 1861 and was supplanted by the telegraph company in October of 1861.
Freight amounting to 62,500 tons came into Colorado in 1865.

(b) As of October 1865 there were no railroads in the subject
tract. There was every reason to believe that rail transportation would
be available in the near future. Congress in 1862 had passed an Act providing for the building of the Union Pacific and Kansas Pacific Railroads
across the tract. The Union Pacific began actual construction in 1863
at Omaha but building went slowly at first and by the end of 1865 only
forty miles of tract had been completed west of that point. This railroad reached Cheyenne, Wyoming, in the fall of 1867. As of 1865 the
Kansas Pacific (originally chartered as the Leavenworth, Pawnee, and

Western in 1855) which was to be built through the heart of the subject
tract to Denver, had constructed its line only 40 miles west of Kansas
City. The Kansas Pacific was finally completed to Denver and Cheyenne
in 1870. The Santa Fe Railroad, chartered as the Atchison and Topeka
in 1859, which was to run along the southern border of the subject tract,
had completed its tracks along this border by 1872.

24. Cattle Industry - (a) The cattle business of the region began
as a result of the necessities of the emigrants along the Oregon Trail.
Road ranches were established during the westward movement of thousands
of people to Oregon and California in the two decades before the Civil
War where the emigrants could exchange worn-down work cattle for fresh
stock. The early herds of the northern ranges were the product of such
trade. In the subject tract itself the cattle business may be said to
have had its inception with the discovery of gold and the great rush of
miners and others to the mining districts of Colorado. Train cattle, which
were used to carry the gold seekers to the area, and the stock of the
settlers were used to start the ranches that began to be established
along the South Platte. In 1866, Iliff, who was to become the first
"cattle king" of the northern ranges, was supplying the Colorado mining
camps with beef from a herd that ranged up and down the South Platte
for a distance of 75 miles or more. The Colorado towns were also supplied
by small communities of Mexican settlers engaged in stock growing which
were located close to the southern borders of Colorado Territory along
the upper Rio Grande and its tributaries. By the close of the sixties,

253

there were herds of considerable size in the northern section of the
High Plains of Colorado, Wyoming and Nebraska. Markets were found in
the mining camps, railroad section crews and military posts. Expansion
of the industry so as to fully utilize the enormous pastoral resources
of the region depended upon a supply of cheap cattle that could be used
for stocking the empty ranges and upon a connection with the eastern
market. Texas was to supply the cattle and railroads were the answer
to eastern markets.

    (b) During the Civil War vast herds of cattle had accumulated in
Texas which had been virtually cut off from markets. In 1866 occurred
the first considerable movement of these cattle northward in an attempt
to reach an area of good prices. In time the Indian barrier, the
quarantine laws of Kansas and Missouri passed in 1867, and the western-
moving farming frontier in Kansas had a tendency to bend the cattle
trails farther and farther westward so that the Texas Panhandle came more
and more to be the road to market at the rail connections. and the eastern
third of Colorado the corridor to the northern ranges. As the Texas
cattle drives continued, the pioneer cattlemen of the High Plains saw
the opportunity to benefit by the new markets created by the advent of
the railroads by stocking the plains with Texas cattle. Colorado was the
first to feel the impact of the invasion of Texas cattle. Ranches were
established along the Arkansas and its tributaries. By 1866 the herds
on the South Platte River had increased to 20,000 head.

254

(c) The principle of the "free range" prevailed in the United

States in the Great Plains region for many years after the commencement

of the cattle business in that region. Under this practice the cattle-

man grazed his cattle on the public domain without cost. Access to

water was important in the industry and when the ranges became crowded

it became necessary for the ranchers to buy small amounts of land to

assure themselves of water and pasture. Control of the water meant

control of the adjoining pasture. John W. Iliff, previously mentioned,

was able, as late as 1877, to control 650,000 acres of grazing land by

owning 15,000 acres with access to water in Colorado.

      25. Market Data - (a) There is of record in this case no sale

of a land area comparable in size to the subject tract.

      (b) At or near the time of valuation much interest was being shown

in the Spanish-Mexican land grants located in southern Colorado and New   **255**

Mexico. Several of these grants which were confirmed by Congress con-

sisted of considerable acreage such as the Maxwell Land Grant of

1,714,764 acres and the Sangre de Cristo Grant of 1,000,000 acres.

The activity with respect to the grants in Colorado and New Mexico at

that time centered around the purchase of outstanding interests in the

grants and the attempts to sell or develop the grants. At or about

the time in question the boundaries of many of the grants were not

determined. Whether the consideration stated as having been paid in

certain transactions was based on the belief that the grant could be

proved to include more land than had been confirmed is not now determinable.

The consideration of $162,000.00 named in at least one sale - a nine twenty-fourths interest in the Sangre de Cristo Grant - is described by Herbert O. Brayer in his book "William Blackmore - The Spanish-Mexican Land Grants" (1949), as not being literally true. The fact that there were many undivided interests in most of these grant transactions to be purchased and that the boundaries of many of the grants were still questionable was reflected in the prices paid for such interests. On many of these grants squatters had been settled for a considerable period of time who claimed rights in the lands.

26. Sales transactions involving Spanish-Mexican Land Grants after all, or virtually all, interests had been obtained include the sale of the Costilla Estate of the Sangre de Cristo Grant, the sale of the Maxwell Land Grant, and the sale of the Nolan Grant.

256

(a) Nolan Grant - This tract had been granted by the Mexican government to Gervacio Nolan in 1843. Congress confirmed the grant in 1870 but limited the area to eleven square leagues, the statutory limitation under Mexican law, and provided that the grantees (Nolan's heirs) could select the confirmed tract of some 48,000 acres from within the claimed 300,000 acres of the original boundaries set forth in the grant. Prior to confirmation the Nolan heirs sold the grant for $10,000.00 in 1868 to Annie Blake who in turn, and also before confirmation, sold undivided third interests in the tract to Charles Goodnight, Texas rancher, and Jacob Dotson for $5,000.00 each. These individuals sold the grant to the Central Colorado Improvement Company in 1872 for $130,000.00. The purchasers had "selected the 48,000 acres with the greatest care, leaving out all hills or poor land and taking only the pick of that lying along the South Bank of the river opposite the town of Pueblo." The purchasers also confidently hoped to acquire the 322,000 acres of the grant which had not been confirmed by Congress. The Nolan Grant adjoined the subject tract on the south bank of the Arkansas River and was considered in 1872 to be almost entirely adapted to cultivation by irrigation.

(b) The Maxwell Land Grant - This grant was located some 80 miles south of the subject tract and consisted of 1,714,755 acres with about 265,000 of this acreage being in Colorado and the remainder in New Mexico. This grant originally known as the Beaubien-Miranda Grant was approved by the Mexican government in 1841. The Congress of the United States confirmed the grant in 1860. Lucien B. Maxwell, whose wife was the daughter of Beaubien, purchased the interests, except his wife's, of the heirs of Beaubien and Miranda by 1870 for small sums of money. In May of 1869 the Maxwells entered into an agreement with three persons giving them an option to purchase the grant for $650,000.00. These men elected to exercise their option and a performance bond was delivered to them by the Maxwells. In January 1870 the persons who had held the option sold and assigned their right, title and interest under the bond to the Maxwell Land Grant and Railroad Company. The Maxwells conveyed the grant to the Company on April 30, 1870. The consideration paid by

257

the Company was $1,350,000.00 of which sum the Maxwells under the per-
formance bond received $650,000, the remainder going to the men who
had secured the performance bond from the Maxwells. This land grant
consisted of mostly grazing land but with a fair proportion of agricultural land and gold had been recovered from placer mines and a lode
on the property prior to the sale. The Maxwells in deeding the property reserved certain lands and interests in mining properties.

(c) The Sangre de Cristo Grant - The greater portion of this grant
was located in south central Colorado and the balance in north central
New Mexico. The grant had been approved by Mexico in 1844 and the
Congress of the United States confirmed the grant in 1860. The northern
border of the grant in Colorado was about 55 miles south of the subject
tract. The Sangre de Cristo Grant extended from the east bank of the
Rio Grande River at its western border to the summit of the Sangre de
Cristo Range on the east, and except for the mountain range, lies in
the San Luis valley of Colorado and New Mexico. By 1860 the settlements of Costilla, San Luis de Culebra and Trinchera were in existence.
These were essentially subsistence farming communities. The inhabitants
of the grant had small farm strips which were irrigated but the major
occupation was the raising of sheep and goats. Although the boundaries
of the grant were known in the 1860's the exact acreage, 998,780.46
acres, was not known until it was surveyed. From 1862 to 1865, Colonel
William Gilpin, former territorial governor of Colorado, purchased
five-sixths of the outstanding interests in the grant for the sum of

258

$41,000.00. The purchaser immediately sought to sell all or part of the grant. He sold a nine twenty-fourths interest to one Morton Coates Fisher in 1865 for a recorded consideration of $162,000.00. The authenticity of the stated consideration has been questioned (see Finding 25). Fisher subsequently acquired an additional five twenty-fourths interest in the grant for a reported $90,000.00 which he held in trust for a Colonel Reynolds. A one thirty-second interest in the grant was purchased for $25,000.00.

Since the size of the grant was a drawback to the efforts of the promoters to market it, the owners agreed to divide the grant into its two natural divisions. The north half became the Trinchera Estate and the southern portion the Costilla Estate. Two land companies were to be formed under the plan to purchase the two estates from the owners. In July 1870 the Costilla Estate, consisting of approximately 500,000 acres, was formally deeded to the United States Freehold Land and Emigration Company for a consideration of $500,000.00.

27. <u>Sales of Small Improved Tracts</u> - In Colorado for the period 1860 through 1865 deed records reveal 558 transfers of 160 acres or more in the present day counties of Arapaho, Boulder, Douglas, El Paso, Jefferson, Larimer, Pueblo and Weld. These transactions involved the sale of a total of 107,526 acres for a total consideration of $390,585.00, or an average price of $3.63 per acre. These sales were of small improved agricultural tracts with the bulk of them being in and around the Denver area and the balance in the vicinity of Pueblo. Since these

259

were the earliest farm lands settled they would be select, irrigated
lands located for the most part adjoining the streams in these areas.

28. Railroad Sales - (a) The Union Pacific Railroad which by
1870 had completed its track through Colorado and Wyoming had earned
under the Act granting it alternate sections adjoining its line about
12,000,000 acres of land. It had received about 4,700,000 acres in
Nebraska, 4,600,000 in Wyoming, 700,000 in Colorado and 1,100,000 in
Utah. As of 1873, this railroad had sold no lands west of Grand Island,
Nebraska. By 1883 the railroad had sold none of its grant lands in
Colorado and only 2,520 acres in Wyoming. As of 1883, the Union Pacific
reported that of the 4,762,174 acres in Nebraska there remained
2,580,000 acres unsold, practically all of it west of the hundredth
meridian. Large acreages of these railroad grant lands were within
the subject tract or bordered it.

(b) The Kansas Pacific Railroad received a grant of public lands
to aid in construction of that road of some 6,000,000 acres. These
lands consisted of 2,600,000 in Colorado and 3,600,000 acres in Kansas.
To December 31, 1879, the railroad had sold 1,521,111 acres at an average
price of $3.39 per acre. Forfeited and cancelled contracts for 229,657.16
acres raised the average per acre price to $3.42. These lands, and
those of the Union Pacific, were sold principally on time with interest
at the rate of 6 per cent per annum. The Kansas Pacific lands unsold
as of December 31, 1879, were located chiefly in Western Kansas--about
2,000,000 acres between Manhattan, Riley County and Grinnell, Cove County

and 2,800,000 acres between Grinnell and Denver.

(c) Denver Pacific Railway - By an Act of Congress in 1869 this road obtained its land-grant. It received for its line between Denver and Cheyenne about 821,000 acres. All of these lands were in Colorado and were among the most fertile and valuable portion of the agricultural lands of that state with some of the lands having coal deposits, according to a Department of Interior Report in 1881. Between 1870 and 1880 this railroad sold 199,206.63 acres at an average price per acre of $4.60, and deducting cancelled sales the average price per acre was $4.44 per acre.

29. Mining Production - The total mineral production, mostly gold but with some silver, within the subject tract for the years 1859 through 1865 has been estimated to be as follows:

1859	$ 545,000.00
1860	1,797,000.00
1861	2,067,000.00
1862	2,817,000.00
1863	3,052,000.00
1864	2,869,500.00
1865	2,159,500.00
Total	$15,307,000.00

261

The mineral-bearing area in the subject area consisted of lands in the present day counties of Larimer, Boulder, Gilpin, Park, Lake, Chaffee, Clear Creek, Jefferson, Fremont and Teller. The mines in Gilpin County accounted for approximately one-half of this production with about $7,500,000 being gold lode output. Placer mining, which had been the primary occupation during the early years of the gold rush in the subject tract, was not a business of any importance by the date of valuation in 1865.

30. <u>Mining Methods and Problems</u> - In the early 1860's the mines located on the principal lodes which had been discovered were able to make an economic recovery from the gossan (decomposed) ores found near the surface of the lodes. These ores were treated in stamp mills. As the mine shafts went deeper, however, caps were encountered which increased the cost of mining. When the decomposed ore had been exhausted in a mine, difficulties arose in treating the primary ores which were refractory in character. Only about one-fourth of the gold in these ores was recovered by the best stamp mills. The difficulties met in treating the refractory ore together with the high cost of labor and goods brought on by the Civil War and Indian trouble along the transportation routes in 1864 were the main reasons that mining was dull in 1865. It was reported that not more than 20 or 25 of the 100 stamp mills in Colorado Territory were operating and that mining at that time hardly paid expenses. Some of the lodes were so valuable, however, that they continued to produce. Prospects for improved mining conditions were looked forward to in 1865 with the opening and securing of lines of transportation by the military, the anticipation of a decrease in the expenses in the labor and supply markets, and the hopes that the various processes then being experimented with would permit recovery of more of the precious minerals in the primary ores. The speculative craze in Colorado mining stock in 1864 whereby ownership of many of the mines passed to eastern owners who sent inexperienced operators to run the mines also delayed the development of mining in the region. While some

262

properties continued to be operated profitably in 1865, successful
mining for the area as a whole had to await the coming of the railroad,
the smelting works which saved nearly all of the gold and silver in
the richest ores and improvements in the methods of mining and milling.
The art of smelting was known in 1865 and had been practiced in Wales
for many years. The process was introduced in Colorado in 1867 and
although difficulties were at first encountered the smelting works
progressed and successfully treated the richer ore. The main bulk
of the ores was too poor to be treated except in the stamp mills.
Improvements in these mills in time, however, permitted the saving of
more of the gold contents of the ores.

31. Capital for investment in as huge a property as the subject
tract would undoubtedly have had to been obtained from European investors
in 1865. Frontier conditions then prevailed in the subject tract. Money
in the region was scarce and interest rates in this western area were
high running as much as two percent or more a month. The availability
of eastern capital would have been negligible because of the disastrous
results occasioned by the speculation in Colorado mining stocks in the
years just prior to 1865. At about the time of valuation European investors were seeking new markets in which to invest their money since
the interest rate on European railroad, mining and industrial securities
had gradually declined until a return of four or five percent was highly
thought of by the larger investors. American rail and mining securities
became to be looked upon favorably since they offered not only six to

eight per cent interest but from being sold below their face value the
interest was proportionately higher. The average foreign speculator
also was seeking investments from which a profitable return might be
realized in a short period of time. "This 'short term-high return'
concept was the guiding principle of a large portion of the English,
Scottish and Dutch investors who purchased American securities following
the Civil War" (see Herbert O. Brayer's "William Blackmore," Vol. 1,
p. 335).

      32. As of October 14, 1865, a prospective purchaser of the subject
tract would have had much information available to him with respect to
the mineral bearing lands of the subject tract. He would have been able
to make an approximate estimate of the past mineral production, gold
and silver, within the subject tract. He would know that past production
figures included placer recoveries and that this type of mining as a
business was not then of much importance. The prospective purchaser
would have been informed that while some mining properties were being
profitably worked most of them were either shut down awaiting a decline
in the cost of labor, supplies and transportation and the discovery of
a successful process for treating the product of the mines or were in
the development stage. He would have known that the future of mining
activity, for both gold and silver, in the area depended mostly upon
the development of a process to treat the ores and that while information
with regard to the smelting process was available its adaptability to
the treatment of the ores of this region had not been tested. The fact

264

that railroads would be serving the tract within a reasonable time
would also have been known. The prospective purchaser would consider
the costs of machinery and development work to operate the known discoveries and the costs of prospecting for additional lodes within the
general mineral area. The presence of other deposits such as coal, oil,
salt and clay within the tract was known but there was no immediate
demand outside of small local consumption for them and their value was
but potential. The prospective purchaser would take all of these matters
into consideration and while aware of the speculative nature of mining
in its then state of development for the area as a whole would have
found that the mineral area of the subject tract greatly enhanced its
value.

   33. Townsites - (a) An area of the size of the subject tract with
its other multiple highest and best uses would have and would require
townsites. A minimum of six such townsites, containing 1,280 acres each,
would be a reasonable number to provide economic, financial, cultural and
distribution centers to serve the existing population and to amply provide for possible future permanent growth of the area. As of October 1865
the population of Colorado Territory was less than it had been in 1860.
While the termination of the Civil War and the building of the railroad
many miles to the east were factors that pointed to a foreseeable population increase, the extent of new settlement also depended upon improvement of the economic conditions in Colorado Territory.

265

(b) There is little evidence of record with respect to value of
townsites as such. The valuation report of petitioner's land expert uses,
as one of the indications of value considered as to townsites a reference
to the sale of the townsite of Manitou, Colorado, in 1871 for $30,000.00.
The Mountain Base Investment Fund had been created as an independent land
and town site organization to purchase lands along the right of way of
the Denver and Rio Grande Railway. By 1871, 8,426 acres had been purchased for Mountain Base Company at an average price of $8.81 an acre.
In addition the minerals springs at Manitou and adjoining acreage totaling
about 480 acres had been purchased for $30,000.00. These lands purchased
for the Company included the future sites of Colorado Springs, Manitou,
Palmer Lake, and Monument (see Brayer, "William Blackmore - Early Financing
of the Denver and Rio Grande Railway," pp. 33, 75).

266

34. The Commission finds based on the findings of fact hereinabove
made and the record as a whole that the subject tract, consisting of
51,210,000 acres, had a fair market value of $23,500,000.00 as of
October 14, 1865.

35. Prior to the treaties of cession herein involved there existed
a division of the Cheyenne and Arapaho Indians into two groups. In
October 1859, Indian agent for the Cheyenne and Arapaho Indians W. W.
Bent in speaking of the territory assigned these tribes by the Fort
Laramie treaty in 1851 noted:

> This country is very equally divided into halves by the
> South Platte. A confederated band of Cheyennes and Arapahoes
> who are intermarried, occupy and claim exclusively the half
> included between the South Platte and the North Platte.

A similar confederated band of the same people distinctly
occupy the southern half, included between the South Platte
and Arkansas rivers.

The first group were under the Upper Platte agency and were known and
referred to by government officials as the Northern Cheyenne and Northern
Arapaho Indians while the second group were referred to as the Cheyenne
and Arapaho Indians of the Upper Arkansas agency or the southern Cheyenne
and Arapaho Tribes.

36. Only the Southern Cheyenne and Arapaho Indians were parties
to the Treaties of February 18, 1861, October 14, 1865, and October 28,
1867. Although provision was made in the 1861 treaty for the northern
bands to come in and accept under it, officials of the Government were
unsuccessful in securing a treaty of cession from them until the Treaty
of May 10, 1868. Only the Southern Cheyenne and Arapaho Tribes were
the beneficiaries of the consideration paid by the United States under
the provisions of the 1861, 1865 and 1867 treaties and only the northern
Cheyenne and Arapaho Tribes were the beneficiaries of the consideration
paid under the 1868 treaty by the United States.

37. By the provisions of the 1861 treaty of cession there was
reserved by the Southern Cheyenne and Arapaho Indians a tract for the'
use of the Indians parties to the treaty and for such other separated
members of the Cheyenne and Arapaho Tribes who might be induced to re-
join and reunite with them on the reservation. In 1865 the United States
again negotiated with the Confederated Tribes of Cheyenne and Arapaho
Indians of the Upper Arkansas (Southern tribes) for a cession of the
diminished reservation established by the 1861 treaty. The treaty

267

commissioners who conducted the negotiations in 1865 reported that the
Indians acknowledged no former cession. The 1865 treaty in Article 2
contained a relinquishment of all claims or rights of the Indians in or
to any portion of the United States or Territories, except for a reservation therein agreed to be set apart for the undisturbed use and
occupation of the tribes who were parties to the treaty, and more especially
their claims and rights in subject tract. The United States agreed to
set apart the reservation which was described in Article 2 or such portion
of the same as might thereafter be designated by the President of the
United States. Said Article also provided that the Indians would not be
required to settle upon the described reservation until such time as the
United States extinguished all claims of title thereto on the part of
other Indians. This article was amended by the Senate to add:

268

> Provided, however, That as soon as practicable, with the
> assent of said tribe, the President of the United States
> shall designate for said tribes a reservation, no part of
> which shall be within the State of Kansas, and cause them
> as soon as practicable to remove and settle thereon, but
> no such reservation shall be designated upon any reserve
> belonging to any other Indian tribe or tribes without their
> consent.

Part of the reservation described in said Article 2 was in the State of
Kansas and the balance was land owned by the Cherokee Nation in Indian
Territory. The effect of the Senate amendment was to require the
President as soon as practicable with the assent of the tribe to sub-
stitute a reservation for the lands in Kansas and Cherokee country
described in said Article 2.

    38. On October 18, 1867, the United States entered into a treaty
(15 Stat. 593, II Kapp. 984) with the southern Cheyenne and Arapaho

Indians wherein the United States agreed by Article 2 to set apart for

the absolute and undisturbed use and occupancy of these Indians, and

for such other friendly tribes or individual Indians, as from time to

time they might be willing with the consent of the United States to

admit among them, the following described district of country:

> Commencing at the point where the Arkansas River crosses
> the 37th parallel of north latitude, thence west on said
> parallel--the said line being the southern boundary of the
> State of Kansas--to the Cimarone River, (sometimes called
> the Red Fork of the Arkansas River), thence down said
> Cimarone River, in the middle of the main channel thereof,
> to the place of beginning, * * *.

By Article 11 the Indians relinquished all right to occupy permanently

the territory outside of the above-described reservation but reserved the

right to hunt on any lands south of the Arkansas so long as the buffalo

might range thereon in such numbers as to justify the chase. The United

States by this article agreed that no white settlements would be permitted

on any part of lands contained in the "old reservation" as defined by

the Treaty of October 14, 1865, for three years. Article 10 provided

that "In lieu of all sums of money or other annuities provided to be

paid to the Indians herein named, under the treaty of October fourteenth,

eighteen hundred and sixty-five, and under all treaties made previously

thereto, * * *" the United States would furnish certain clothing annually

for each Indian and expend $20,000.00 annually for 30 years for the

purchase of such articles, as from time to time, the condition and

necessities of the Indians might indicate to be proper. Since by the

Senate amendment to the Treaty of October 14, 1865, the United States

was required to substitute a reservation for the one described in

269

Article 2 of that treaty, the Treaty of October 18, 1867, was supplementary to the 1865 treaty.

39. The Southern Cheyenne and Arapaho tribes did not go upon the
reservation set apart for them by the Treaty of October 28, 1867. They
were dissatisfied with its location and asked for a place upon the north
fork of the Canadian River in Indian Territory. The chiefs of the tribes
in 1868 asserted that they had not rightly understood the real boundaries
of the 1867 treaty reservation. The reason for the misunderstanding was
said to have originated in the different names given to streams by the
whites and Indians respectively. The Superintendent of the Central
Superintendency urged a reservation be set aside for these Indians in
the location desired by them. The Secretary of the Interior and the
Commissioner of Indian Affairs recommended the location of these Indians
on the North Fork of the Canadian. The President of the United States by
executive order of August 10, 1869, approved the establishment of the
reservation recommended by the Commissioner of Indian Affairs. The
reservation so established in lieu of the one designated in the 1867
treaty was bounded as follows:

270

> Commencing at the point where the Washita river crosses
> the ninety-eighth degree of west longitude; thence north
> on a line with said ninety-eighth degree to a point where
> it is crossed by the Red Fork of the Arkansas (sometimes
> called the Cimarron River); thence up said river, in the
> middle of the channel thereof, to the north boundary of
> the country ceded to the United States by the treaty of
> June 14, 1866, with the Creek Nation of Indians; thence
> west on said north boundary and the north boundary of
> the country ceded to the United States by the treaty of
> March 21, 1866, with the Seminole Indians, to the one
> hundredth degree of west longitude; thence south on the
> line of said one hundredth degree to the north boundary

of the country set apart for the Kiowa and Comanche by
the second article of the treaty concluded October 21,
1867, with said tribes; thence east along said boundary
to the point where it strikes the Washita River; thence
down said Washita River, in the middle of the main channel
thereof, to the place of beginning.

The Southern Cheyenne and Arapaho went on and occupied this reservation.

The executive order of the President provided these Indians with a sub-

stitute reservation promised by Article 2 of the 1865 treaty as amended

and the authority of the President to set aside a reservation for the

Indians was also conferred by the Senate amendment to said Article 2.

40. Defendant claims as payments on the claim sums totaling

$7,244,556.85. In support of these payments defendant relies on the

report of the General Accounting Office (Pet. Ex. 113) herein referred

to as the G.A.O. Report. This report shows the disbursement in goods

and services to petitioners directly claimed to have been pursuant to

various treaties in the total amount of $6,740,556.59 and additional

payments jointly to petitioners and other tribes in the sum of

$540,615.33. Defendant agrees that certain items totaling $36,615.07

are not allowable as consideration (Def. Req. Fdg. of Fact 46). The

treaties relied upon to show consideration paid are the Treaty of Fort

Laramie, September 17, 1851 (10 Stat. 749, II Kapp. 594) and the treaties

of February 18, 1861 (12 Stat. 1163), October 14, 1865 (14 Stat. 703),

October 28, 1867 (15 Stat. 593), May 10, 1868 (15 Stat. 665), and the

Agreement of September 26, 1876, ratified by the act of February 28, 1877,

(19 Stat. 254). The Fort Laramie treaty of 1851 and the 1876 agreement

are irrelevant since they do not pertain to any cession of subject tract.

271

41. (a) By the Treaty of February 18, 1861, the United States in consideration of the cession of subject tract agreed in Article 4 to pay the Southern tribes $30,000.00 for 15 years ($15,000.00 to each tribe) beginning when they had settled on their reservation with the Secretary of Interior determining how the sum was to be expended. By Article 5 the Government agreed to expend an amount not to exceed $5,000.00 for five years to provide a mill for sawing timber and grinding grain, mechanic shops with tools, houses for the interpreter, miller, engineer, farmers and mechanics.

(b) By the terms of the Treaty of October 14, 1865, the United States agreed by Article 7 to expend annually for forty years for the benefit of these Indians in such manner and for such purposes as the Secretary of the Interior judged best, an amount equal to $20.00 per capita until they were removed to the reservation provided by this treaty and after removal an amount equal to $40.00 per capita.

42. CONSIDERATION - 1861 and 1865 Treaties - The G.A.O. Report (pp. 65-68 of Pet. Ex. 113) sets forth the following sums as having been disbursed pursuant to the provisions of the Treaties of February 18, 1861 (12 Stat. 1163), October 14, 1865 (14 Stat. 703), and October 17, 1865 (14 Stat. 713):

Upper Arkansas Agency

Direct	$227,163.10
Jointly with other Indians	158,031.46
Cheyenne and Arapaho Reservation	4,427.78
Total	$389,622.34

A. Disbursement Schedule 8 (GAO total - $56,918.32; Pet. Ex. 113, p. 85)

    (a) Of the total $1,100.50 was spent jointly for the Southern

Cheyenne, Southern Arapaho, Comanche, Kiowa, Apache and Caddo. Defendant

agrees that petitioners are chargeable with only two-sixths of the

$1,100.50. The sum of $733.67 is therefore disallowed as consideration.[1]

    (b) The following sums listed as expenditures under Article 4 of the

1861 treaty are items not of the character authorized by said Article 4:

Depredations	$ 150.00
Expenses of Delegations	1,437.50
Misc. Agency Expenses	335.90 [2]
Total	$ 1,923.40

These items are disallowed as consideration.

    (c) The remainder of Disbursement Schedule No. 8, or $54,261.25

is allowed.

B. Disbursement Schedule 9 (GAO total - $272,909.88, Pet. Ex. 113, pp. 90-91)

    (a) While the disbursements are itemized jointly by the GAO under

three treaties (Feb. 18, 1861; Oct. 14, 1865 and October 17, 1865) the

Treaty of October 17, 1865, 14 Stat. 713, II Kapp. 891, did not provide

for payments by the United States and the allowable sums are chargeable

under the remaining two treaties. The schedule shows there was disbursed

"Jointly with Apache Tribe" the sum of $147,034.64. By the October 17, 1865

273

---

[1] There are no population figures of record to show the proportionate
numbers of each tribe to the total of all six groups. Since defendant
agrees to basing it on the number of tribes involved the Commission
has followed that method.

[2] Coeur d'Alene Tribe v. U.S., 6 Ind. Cl. Comm. 1, 36

treaty these Apache Indians were united with the Cheyenne and Arapaho
tribes (Article 1) and became entitled to the benefits of the October 14,
1865 treaty (Article 2). 3/

    (b) Of the items charged directly to petitioners in Disbursement
Schedule No. 9, the following items are not of the character authorized
under the provisions of either the 1861 or 1865 treaties and are therefore
disallowed (GAO Report - pp. 90-91).

Depredations	$51,010.46 4/
Misc. agency expenses	324.12
Expenses of delegations	120.00
Pay of Interpreters	218.25
Total	$51,672.83

    (c) Of the items charged "Jointly with Apache Tribe of Indians"
(GAO Report, p. 90), the following item is not of the character authorized
by the provisions of either the 1861 or 1865 treaties:

Depredations	$ 4,748.00

    (d) Under the heading of sums disbursed "Jointly with other Indians"
there are included items of $391.61 for Expenses of holding Indian

274

3/ Petitioner would have the Commission disallow a third of the total
allowed items so expended "Jointly with Apache Tribe." There is no
evidence of record of the respective populations in 1865 of the
southern Cheyenne, Arapaho and Apache Indians parties to these
treaties. However, an independent search shows the southern Cheyenne
and Arapaho with an estimated population of 3100 in 1865 (Com'r. Ind.
Affairs Rept. 1865, p. 578) and the Apache numbered 288 in 1869
(Com'r. Ind. Affairs Report, 1869, pages 284-5). The Apache Band
was therefore about 10 percent of the total population.

4/ The 1861 or 1865 treaties did not provide for payment of depredations.

councils and $128.16 for Miscellaneous agency expenses. These expenditures are not of the character authorized by the provisions of the 1861 and 1865 treaties and are not allowed.

(e) This schedule includes under the heading "Jointly with Comanche, Kiowa and Apache Tribes of Indians" an item of $464.10 for Transportation, etc., of supplies. Defendant is entitled to have allowed two-fifths of said sum, or $185.64. The sum of $278.46 is disallowed.

(f) Defendant agrees that the items listed under disbursements "Jointly with Apache Tribe" (shown on p. 91 and p. 87 of GAO Report) totaling $24,041.38, may be excluded as consideration.

(g) The remaining items of Disbursement Schedule No. 9, totaling $191,649.44, are allowed.

C. Disbursement Schedule No. 10 (GAO total - $16,453.20; Pet. Ex. 113, p. 93)

The items listed in this schedule were disbursed under an appropriation of June 19, 1860, 12 Stat. 59, providing

> For the purchase and transportation of provisions and presents, and to meet expenses necessary in holding a council with the Arapahoe and Chienne Indians south of the Platte, east of the Rocky Mountains, and north of the Arkansas River, thirty-five thousand dollars.

The appropriation of these funds prior to the treaty of 1861, and the administrative purpose for which they were intended, show they are not allowable as consideration.

D. Disbursement Schedule 11 (GAO total - $7,500.00; Pet. Ex. 113, p. 94)

This sum is identified as "Expenses of negotiating treaty." Pet. Ex. 113, p. 94. The appropriation act (33 Stat. 800) does not identify

it as in fulfillment of treaty promises to the Indians. It is an administrative expense of making the treaty. It is not allowed.

E. Disbursement Schedule 12 (GAO total - $1.34; Pet. Ex. 113, p. 95)

    The appropriation act (24 Stat. 293 (1866), Pet. Ex. 113, p. 468)
which was passed 13 years after the expense was incurred, does not refer
to any treaty, and hence the item cannot be consideration.

F. Disbursement Schedule No. 13 (GAO total - $10,000.00; Pet. Ex. 113,
   p. 96

    The expenditure was made from funds made available by an appropriation
act (12 Stat. 791) in 1863 for the survey and allotment of lands for
Arapaho and Cheyenne Indians. This expenditure is of the character
authorized by Articles 1 and 2 of the 1861 treaty and is allowed.

G. Disbursement Schedule No. 14 (GAO total - $2,203.90; Pet. Ex. 113, p. 97)

276   The appropriation act (16 Stat. 358--July 15, 1870) made available
funds for surveys of exterior boundaries of Indian reservations. The
item is allowed since it was used to survey 31 sections of land for
mixed bloods as provided by Article 5 of the Treaty of October 14, 1865.

H. Disbursement Schedule No. 15 (GAO total - $19,207.92; Pet. Ex. 113,
   p. 100)

    This disbursement schedule charges to Article 5 of the 1861 treaty
the following items:

Miscellaneous agency expenses	$434.30
Pay of misc. agency employees	24.68
Transportation, etc. of supplies	10,538.23

The items of $434.30 for miscellaneous agency expenses and $24.68 for pay
of miscellaneous agency employees are disallowed (Coeur d'Alene Tribe v.

U. S., 6 Ind. Cl. Comm. 1, 36). The item of $10,538.23 for transportation
etc., of supplies is allowed.

(b) The GAO report lists as expenditures "Jointly with Apache
Tribe of Indians" the sum of $118.95 for miscellaneous agency expenses
and the amount of $43.65 for pay of miscellaneous agency employees. These
are disallowed. Of the sum of $5,234.69, one-third or $1,744.90, is
disallowed.

(c) The disbursement schedule shows expenditures "Jointly with
Comanche, Kiowa and Apache Tribes" of $80.50 for miscellaneous agency
expenses which is disallowed. Three-fifths of the $2,146.40 expended
for Transportation etc. of supplies or $1,287.84 is disallowed and
defendant is allowed $858.56.

(d) The GAO report lists an item of $586.52 "Jointly with Comanche,
Kiowa, Apache and Tabequache Tribes of Indians" for Transportation, etc.
of supplies. Of this amount the sum of $195.51 is allowed and $391.01
disallowed.

(e) Of the $19,207.92 GAO total for Disbursement Schedule No. 15
the sum of $4,125.83 is disallowed and the amount of $15,082.09 is allowed.

I. Disbursement Schedule No. 16 (GAO total - $4,427.78; Pet. Ex. 113, p. 101)

The items in this schedule include an expenditure of $1,028.57 for
depredations which is disallowed. The remaining items totaling $3,399.21
are of the character authorized by the Treaties of February 18, 1861, and
October 14, 1865, and are allowed.

J. Summary of Disbursements under the provisions of the Treaties of
February 18, 1861, and October 14, 1865, the 1865 discounted value of

which defendant is entitled to claim as consideration for the cession

of the subject tract:

Schedule No. 8	$ 54,261.25
Schedule No. 9	191,649.44
Schedule No. 13	10,000.00
Schedule No. 14	2,203.90
Schedule No. 15	15,082.09
Schedule No. 16	3,399.21
Total	$276,595.89

43. CONSIDERATION - 1867 Treaty - The report of the General
Accounting Office (Pet. Ex. 113, p. 148) shows the amount of $1,241,371.07
as having been disbursed for the benefit of the Cheyenne and Arapaho
Indians pursuant to the provisions of the Treaty of October 28, 1867,
15 Stat. 593.

A. The 1867 treaty by the terms of Article 1 provided for the payment of depredation damages, in case the tribes failed to deliver up the
wrongdoer, from the annuities or other moneys due or to become due to the
tribes under this or other treaties. A reservation was set aside by
Article 2. By the provisions of Article 4 the United States agreed at its
own proper expense to construct a warehouse; agency building; a residence
for a physician; buildings for a carpenter, farmer, blacksmith, miller
and engineer; a school house or mission building; and a steam circular
saw-mill with grist mill and a shingle machine attached. Article 7
provided that for every thirty children attending school a house was to
be provided and a teacher for a period of at least twenty years. Seeds
and agricultural implements not to exceed the value of $100.00 for the
first year and $25.00 for the next three years were to be provided heads

of families who commenced cultivating the soil under the terms of

Article 8 and this article also provided for a second blacksmith with

such iron, steel and other material as might be needed whenever more

than one hundred persons entered upon the cultivation of the soil.

Article 9 provided that after ten years the United States might withdraw

the physician, farmer, blacksmith, carpenter, engineer and miller but

in the event of such withdrawal an additional sum of $10,000.00 a year

would be devoted to the education of the Indians.

Article 10 of the 1867 treaty provided:

> In lieu of all sums of money or other annuities pro-
> vided to be paid the Indians herein named, under the treaty
> of October fourteenth, eighteen hundred and sixty-five, made
> at the mouth of the Little Arkansas, and under all treaties
> made previous thereto, the United States agrees to deliver
> at the agency house * * *, for thirty years, the following
> articles, to wit:- * * *

279

Under this Article 10 the United States agreed to furnish each Indian

certain clothing and in addition to appropriate annually the sum of

$20,000.00 for thirty years to be used by the Secretary of the Interior

in the purchase of such articles as, from time to time, the condition

and necessities of the Indians might indicate to be proper.

Article 13 provided for the services and pay of the physician,

teachers, carpenter, miller, farmer and blacksmiths contemplated by the

treaty provisions. Article 14 stated that the sum of $500.00 annually

would be expended for three years in presents to the ten persons of the

tribe who in the judgment of the agent grew the most valuable crops

each year.

B. In explanation of the disbursements claimed to have been made
pursuant to the Treaty of October 28, 1867, the General Accounting Office
in Section C of its report states that the amounts appropriated annually
to fulfill the various stipulations of the treaty were set up on the
ledgers of the Indian Office under separate headings, each heading
designating a treaty stipulation, to wit: residence of physician; school-
house; agency buildings; clothing; beneficial objects; pay of employees,
etc. The records indicated that the disbursements were not made entirely
for the purposes for which said amounts were appropriated and the General
Accounting Office used the appropriation headings as carried on the
ledgers of the Indian Office as the basis of allocation by article of
said disbursements.

280

C. The Government claims the amount of $1,241,371.07 as consideration
under the 1867 treaty (Pet. Ex. 113, p. 148). This is the total sum as
shown in Statement No. 14, GAO report. A study of the disbursements
under this treaty discloses that while many of the expenditures are shown
to have been charged under certain articles of the treaty they properly
belong under another article of the same treaty (for example, Article 10 -
beneficial objects stipulation includes pay of teachers, physician,
carpenter and blacksmith which belong under Article 13 disbursements). [5]/
The following sums are shown in Statement No. 14 of the GAO Report
(pp. 140-147) are not allowed since they are not of the character
authorized by the articles of the treaty:

---

[5]/ The allowable sums will be treated as if charged to the proper Article.

Upper Arkansas Agency

    Indian police:
        Pay of police $ 356.68
        Pay of police   243.32
    Misc. agency expenses   230.21
    Pay of misc. agency employees   21,366.87
                and   269.00
    Presents to Indians   448.75
    Pay of misc. school employees   1,410.00
                and   900.00

Cheyenne and Arapaho Reservation, Oklahoma

    Agency buildings and repairs   5,079.12
    Expenses of delegations   3,320.82
    Indian police:
        Pay of police   950.00
    Misc. agency expenses   9,084.58
    Pay of agents   102.75
    Pay of misc. agency employees   12,622.27
    Pay of misc. school employees   1,868.97
    Agency and educational purposes:
        Agricultural aid   32.97
        Agricultural implements and
           equipment   23.40
        Hardware, glass, oils and paints   192.67
        Household equipment   360.42
    Pay of misc. agency employees   24,036.92
    Education:
        Pay of misc. school employees   150.00

Wind River Reservation, Wyoming   73.55

Tongue River Reservation, Montana   412.31

Miscellaneous items
    Livestock (jointly with other
              Indians)   300.00

        Total disallowed $83,835.58

281

D. Defendant is entitled to claim as consideration under the provisions of the Treaty of October 28, 1867, the 1865 discounted value of the allowable items totaling $1,157,535.49.

44. Summary - Treaties 1861, 1865 and 1867

Defendant is entitled to credit as payments on the claim the 1865 discounted value of the allowable items totaling $276,595.89 expended for the Southern Tribes under the Treaties of February 18, 1861, and October 14, 1865, and the 1865 discounted value of the allowable items totaling $1,157,535.49 disbursed for said tribes pursuant to the Treaty of October 28, 1867. In addition defendant may claim as consideration paid to the Southern Tribes the fair market value of the reservation described in Finding 39 which was set aside for the Southern Cheyenne and Arapaho Indians by executive order of the President on August 10, 1869, pursuant to the provisions of the Treaty of October 14, 1865.

45. CONSIDERATION - Treaty of May 10, 1868, 15 Stat. 655,
                   II Kapp. 1012

282   A. The terms of this treaty made with the Northern Cheyenne and Northern Arapaho Indians provided by Article 2 that these Indians would accept as a reservation some portion of the reservation set apart for the Southern Cheyenne and Southern Arapaho Indians by the Treaty of October 28, 1867, or some portion of the reservation set aside for the Brule and other bands of Sioux Indians by the Treaty of April 29, 1868, (15 Stat. 635, II Kapp. 998). The Indians agreed to deliver up Indian wrong-doers to the United States, or if not, the victim was to be re-imbursed from treaty moneys due the tribe (Article 1). The treaty pro-vided for allotment of land to those desiring to commence farming and for a survey of the reservation when ordered by the President of the United States (Article 3).

By the terms of Article 4 the Indians agreed to send their children to school and the United States promised to furnish teachers and schoolhouses for twenty years. Under Article 5, the Government promised to give up to $175.00 worth of seeds and implements over four years to each Indian engaged in farming and the United States agreed to provide a farmer and a second blacksmith when more than 100 Indians had begun farming.

Under Article 6, the United States promised (a) to give each Indian certain clothing each year for thirty years; (b) to give ten dollars for a period of 10 years for each Indian "roaming", and twenty dollars for ten years for each Indian engaged in agriculture, the sums to be used by the Secretary of Interior in purchase of such articles as from time to time the condition and necessities of the Indians might indicate to be proper; (c) to give certain rations for four years to each Indian over four years of age who moved to and settled upon the reservation; (d) to give a cow and team of oxen to each lodge of Indians, or family legally incorporated with them, settled on the reservation. This article also provided that if at any time within the ten years it should appear that the amount of money needed for clothing could be appropriated to better uses for the Indians Congress might by law change the appropriation to other purposes.

283

Under Article 7, the United States agreed to furnish a physician, teachers, carpenter, miller, engineer, farmer and blacksmiths. Article 9 provided $500.00 for three years as agricultural prizes.

B. The G.A.O. Report (Pet. Ex. 113, pp. 216-224) states that Congress, for the fiscal years 1870 to 1899, appropriated a total of
$405,016 to provide for the clothing stipulation of Article 6 of this
treaty, and that the sum of $342,528.98 was disbursed for the benefit of
the Northern Cheyenne and Arapaho Tribes of Indians. The report shows
that Congress in providing for the "roaming" and "farming" stipulations
(beneficial objects) of Article 6 appropriated a total of $223,600.00
from 1870 to 1881. The first nine installments in the various acts of
Congress were designated as being in fulfillment of the "roaming" Indians
provision of Article 6. The first installment of $9,600.00 in 1869 was
computed on the basis of 960 "roaming" Indians and the succeeding eight
installments of $18,000.00 each were on the basis of 1800 "roaming"
Indians. The last $18,000.00 appropriation (in 1877) was labeled "ninth
of ten installments." In 1878, the tenth and last of the ten installments
promised by the treaty should have been, but was not, appropriated;
nothing was appropriated under this provision in 1878. It is noted that
1878 was the first year in which the 1876 Sioux Agreement became subject
to appropriations. However, no appropriation even mentioned the 1876
Agreement until 1881.

In 1879, $35,000 was appropriated as the "first of ten installments"
under the beneficial objects provision of the 1868 Treaty (sic). Congress
appropriated the same amount, with the same identification (except it
was labeled second of ten installments) in 1880. Since in the years
up to 1877 Congress had already appropriated not only the first and

284

second but the first nine of ten installments under the 1868 Treaty and

since appropriations specifically referring to the 1876 Sioux Agreement

commenced with only the third of ten installments, the reference in the

1879 and 1880 Acts to the 1868 Treaty is a slip of the pen, and those

appropriations are really for the 1876 Sioux Agreement.

The first nine appropriations, from 1869 to 1877, totaling $153,600,

are sums which are consideration under the 1868 Treaty, to the extent

actually spent for items contemplated by the "beneficial objects" pro-

vision. To this is added the 1879 appropriation of $35,000, which while

labeled "first of ten" petitioners concede represents the tenth and last

installment. Thus, the total of the relevant appropriations is $188,600.

As already stated the 1880 appropriation of $35,000 labeled "second of

ten", is not relevant to the 1868 Treaty. Of the $188,600.00 a total of

$150,767.72 was actually disbursed in the years 1870 through 1880.

C. According to the G.A.O. report Congress, in addition to the

appropriations of $223,600 set forth in paragraph B above, appropriated

a further total of $255,000.00 applicable in part to the aforesaid stipu-

lation during the fiscal years 1882 to 1889. The report states that each

appropriation act specified that the appropriation was made for the

purpose of fulfilling the stipulations of Article 6 of the May 10, 1868

treaty, as related to Indians engaged in agriculture, and as pursuant

to the agreement of September 26, 1876, as ratified by the act of

February 28, 1877, 19 Stat. 254. Disbursements claimed under these

appropriations are not payments on the claim for the Treaty of May 10,

1868, supra, for the reasons that (1) the Agreement of September 26, 1876,

is in no way supplementary to the Treaty of May 10, 1868 $\underline{6}/$ and (2)
the ten year period for payments for Indians "roaming" and "farming"
in Article 6 of the 1868 treaty had expired.

D. Under the rations provision of Article 6 giving certain rations
to Indians settling upon the reservations provided in the treaty for a
period of four years, Congress during the period 1870 to 1875 appropriated
a total of $244,728.00 for said purpose. Of this amount according to
the G.A.O. the sum of $238,458.48 was disbursed for the Northern Cheyenne
and Arapaho Indians of which $233,662.89 was disbursed for their benefit
directly and $4,795.57 was disbursed for their benefit jointly with the
Gros Ventre and Assiniboine Tribes (G.A.O. Report, p. 228).

E. Under Article 7 of the 1868 treaty, the United States agreed to
furnish a physician, teachers, carpenter, miller, engineer, farmer and
blacksmiths. Pursuant to this provision, Congress appropriated $336,198.23
during the period 1869 through 1911, and $282,694.72 of this total amount
was disbursed according to the G.A.O. Report (pp. 230 and 265). G.A.O.
gives the further sum of $1,931,266.12 as having been disbursed pursuant
to both Article 7 of the 1868 treaty and the 1876 agreement $\underline{7}/$ (see paragraph C above) during the period 1913-1951, from sums made available from
various Congressional appropriations.

286

6/ The 1876 Agreement refers in Article 8 to "The provisions of the
said treaty of 1868" but this applies to the Treaty of April 29,
1868, with the Sioux bands referred to in Article 1 of the Agreement.

7/ Since the disbursements made under the 1876 Agreement are not allowed
as payments on the claim only the provisions of Article 7 of the 1868
treaty are applicable in this case.

F. The G. A. O. Report lists $41,101.34 as spent for "miscellaneous

items", under the 1868 treaty but not under any specified article thereof.

Of this total, $25,374.19 was spent for transportation in 1870 to 1876.

Included in the $41,101.34 is the sum of $1,668.70 (Dis. Schedule 66)

spent for transportation under an appropriation act (24 Stat. 293) which

mentions no treaty and appears to be a general support appropriation.

The remaining $14,058.45 was appropriated in 1882 and 1883 for de-

predations "to be paid from said unexpended balances of treaty funds

belonging to said Northern Cheyenne and Arapahoe Indians." The sum of

$1,668.70 is disallowed. Defendant is allowed $39,432.64.

G. The following items listed in Statement No. 22 (G. A. O. Report,

pp. 242 and 248) as having been disbursed pursuant to the 1868 treaty

at the Wind River Reservation are allowed:

287

Article 6 (Clothing)

Blankets	$ 22,334.10	
Clothing	119,672.85	
Notions	869.90	
Transportation, etc.	16.00	
School Buildings	5,624.83	8/

Article 6 (Beneficial Objects)

Ag. implements & equip.	6,059.45
Clothing	2,317.06
Feed & care of livestock	113.63
Fencing & breaking land	791.70
Fuel, water & light	8.05
Hardware, glass, oils, paints	1,682.61
Household equipment	976.87

8/ Allowed since obligation to furnish same is found in Article 4.

Livestock	700.63
Medical attention.	82.10
Notions	27.93
Provisions	47,281.02
Seeds	379.99
Books, stationery	33.96

Article 7 (Employees Pay)

Blacksmith	15,937.96
Carpenter	16,856.28
Engineer	13,087.39
Farmers	7,543.12
Herders	6,946.90
Mechanics	5,048.00
Miller	895.00
Physician	9,247.69
Teachers	23,135.59

Article 6 of 1868 treaty and
Agreement of September 26, 1876

Pay of herders	352.81

Article 7 of 1868 treaty and
Agreement of Sept. 26, 1876
(Employees Pay)

Blacksmith	157.40
Carpenter	2,153.30
Engineer	178.98
Farmers	587.50
Herder	244.24
Mechanics	1,209.52
Miller	3,233.50
Physician	7,463.47
Teachers	2,563.33

Total	325,814.66

H. The items listed below shown to have been disbursed at the Tongue River Reservation pursuant to the 1868 treaty (G.A.O. Report, pp. 248-254) are allowed:

Article 6 (Clothing)

Blankets	$	16,886.17
Clothing		55,824.10
Notions		11.03

Article 7 (Employees Pay)

Blacksmith	20,071.96
Carpenter	84.00
Engineer	584.58
Engineer-blacksmith	140.45
Farmers	26,771.07
Herders	603.99
Mechanics	3,259.22
Physician	24,535.15

Article 7, 1868 treaty and
Agreement of 1876

Line riders	5,959.40
Blacksmith	24,033.75
Carpenter	22,449.11
Engineer	10,447.73
Farmers	8,833.30
Herders	18,902.33
Mechanics	30,621.85
Miller	19,837.89
Physician	23,444.82
Teachers	26,356.49

	Total	$ 339,658.39

I. The sum of $1,955.43 (G.A.O. Report, p. 254) disbursed pursuant
to the 1868 treaty at Fort Browning, Montana, under the meat and flour
stipulation of Article 6 is allowed.

J. Of the total sum of $14,395.57 disbursed at the Montana Superin-
tendency (Report, p. 254) the amount of $9,600.00 was expended directly
for petitioners and $4,795.57 charged jointly with other Indians. The
following items disbursed under the 1868 treaty and charged to the meat ·
and flour stipulation of Article 6 are allowed:

289

Livestock ($\frac{1}{2}$ of $450.00)	$ 225.00
Provisions and other rations	9,600.00
Provisions and other rations - ($\frac{1}{2}$ of $3,431.82)	1,715.91
Transportation ($\frac{1}{2}$ of $168.10)	84.05
	$11,624.96

K. The items listed below shown to have been disbursed at the Cheyenne and Arapaho Reservation, Oklahoma (G.A.O. Report, p. 255) pursuant to the 1868 treaty are allowed as consideration:

Article 6 - Clothing stipulation

Clothing	$ 3,109.68
Notions	23.75

Article 6 - Beneficial objects

Agric. implements & equip.	21.80
Hardware, glass, etc.	134.60
Household equipment	1.80
Medical attention	77.30
Provisions	1,242.50
Pay of herders	210.00
	$ 4,821.43

L. The following items listed as having been disbursed at the Red Cloud Agency, Wyoming Territory (G.A.O. Report, p. 256) pursuant to the 1868 treaty are allowed: [9]

290

---

[9] The miscellaneous item category has been allowed in paragraph F above.

Article 6 - Clothing stipulation

Blankets	13,854.85
Clothing	15,777.67
Notions	889.02
Transportation, etc.	192.71

Article 6 - Beneficial objects

Agric. implements & equip.	1,101.00
Blankets	781.79
Clothing	4,348.96
Hardware, etc.	1,713.36
Household equipment	713.05
Provisions	21,452.50
Transportation	2,262.35

Meat & Flour Stipulation

Provisions, etc.	125,360.35
	$ 188,447.61

M. The sum of $617.15 disbursed for clothing pursuant to the 1868
treaty at the Red Cloud Agency, Dakota Territory, (G.A.O. Report, p. 257)
is allowable.

291

N. The following items listed as having been disbursed under the
1868 treaty as consideration at the Red Cloud Agency, Nebraska, are
allowed: 10/

Article 6 - Clothing Stipulation

Blankets	$ 24,329.24
Clothing	22,311.98
Notions	675.48
Transportation, etc.	299.22

_____

10/ The item for transportation, etc. of supplies under Miscellaneous item
is covered in paragraph F above.

Article 6 - Beneficial Objects

Blankets	$	5,062.05
Clothing		719.18
Household equipment		18.95
Notions		6.85
Provisions, etc.		41,635.39
Transportation, etc.		9,352.95

Article 6 - Meat & Flour Stipulation

Provisions, etc.	44,801.65
Transportation, etc.	98.35

Article 7 - Employees Pay Stipulation

Herders	2,410.74
Farmers	1,295.12
Mechanics	626.88
Blacksmith	953.87
Carpenter	567.33
Physician	115.38
Total	$155,280.61

292   O. The following items disbursed pursuant to Article 6 of the 1868 treaty at the locations shown are allowed as consideration (G.A.O. Report, pp. 259-264):

Provisions, etc. (Southern Agency)	$	561.53
Provisions, etc. (Milk River Agency)		40,163.06
Provisions, etc. (Upper Arkansas Agency)		14,970.09
Clothing (Cantonment on Tongue River)		57.62
Provisions, etc. (Muscleshell, Montana)		10,857.00
Medical Attention (Ft. Laramie)		154.65
Clothing (Cheyenne Settlement on Tongue and Rosebud Rivers)		2,608.17
Blankets and Clothing (Fort Robinson)		296.14
Blankets, Clothing & Notions (Crow Agency)		3,265.10
Total	$	72,933.36

P. The items listed below which are shown as having been expended
at Fort Fetterman, Wyoming Territory, are allowed as consideration
(G.A.O. Report, p. 261):

> Article 6 - Clothing Stipulation
>
> | | |
> |---|---|
> | Clothing | $ 1,154.55 |
>
> Article 6 - Beneficial Objects
>
> | | |
> |---|---|
> | Blankets | 760.00 |
> | Clothing | 603.00 |
> | Household equipment | 63.00 |
> | Transportation, etc. | 12.55 |
>
> Article 6 - Meat & Flour Stip.
>
> | | |
> |---|---|
> | Provisions, etc. | 726.70 |
> | Total | $ 3,319.80 |

Q. The items listed below which are listed in Statement No. 22 of
the G.A.O. Report as having been expended pursuant to the 1868 treaty
but with "no location shown" on the vouchers are allowed as consideration:

> Article 6 - Clothing Stipulation
>
> | | |
> |---|---|
> | Blankets | $ 3,823.50 |
> | Clothing | 13,157.88 |
> | Notions | 56.75 |
> | Transportation, etc. | 225.26 |
>
> Article 6 - Beneficial Objects
>
> | | |
> |---|---|
> | Agricultural imp. & equip. | 80.00 |
> | Blankets | 441.75 |
> | Hardware, etc. | 48.14 |
> | Household equipment | 30.00 |
> | Transportation, etc. | 147.10 |
>
> Article 6 - Meat & Flour Stipulation
>
> | | |
> |---|---|
> | Transportation, etc. | 100.00 |
> | Total | $ 18,110.38 |

R. Summary - Under the findings of fact in sub-paragraphs F
through R above, the United States is entitled to the 1865 discounted
value of the amount of $1,162,016.42 as consideration for the 1868
treaty.

S. The northern Tribes have agreed among themselves that
the consideration found by the Commission to be chargeable to them
under the 1868 treaty is to be allocated as follows:

Northern Arapaho

Amount Disbursed	Agency Disbursed at	Percent Charged	Consideration Received
$325,814.66	Wind River	100%	$325,814.66
3,800.00	Fort Browning	100%	3,800.00
11,624.96	Montana Supt.	100%	11,624.96
4,446.13	Fort Fetterman	100%	4,446.13
204,753.59	Red Cloud, Wyo.	50%	102,376.79
617.15	Red Cloud, Dakota	50%	308.58
161,338.70	Red Cloud, Neb.	50%	80,669.35
39.22	Whestone, Dak.	50%	19.61
561.53	Southern, Ft. Reno	50%	280.76
40,163.06	Milk River, Mont.	50%	20,081.53
14,970.09	Upper Arkansas	50%	7,485.05
57.62	Cantonment, Tongue R.	50%	28.81
10,857.00	Muscleshell, Mont.	50%	5,428.50
154.65	Ft. Laramie, Wyo.	50%	77.32
18,110.38	No location (Dis. Sch. 65-67)	50%	9,055.19
4,821.43	Chey. & Arapaho Res. Okla.	25%	1,205.36
	Total		$572,702.60

294

Northern Cheyenne

Amount Disbursed	Agency Disbursed at	Percent Charged	Consideration Received
$339,658.39	Tongue River	100%	$339,658.39
296.14	Ft. Robinson, Neb.	100%	296.14
3,265.10	Crow	100%	3,265.10
2,608.17	Cheyenne Settlement	100%	2,608.17
14,058.45	No location (Dis. Sch. 66-67)	100%	14,058.45
204,753.59	Red Cloud, Wyo.	50%	102,376.79
617.15	Red Cloud, Dak.	50%	308.58
161,338.70	Red Cloud, Neb.	50%	80,669.35
39.22	Whetstone, Dak.	50%	19.61
561.53	Southern, Ft. Reno	50%	280.76
40,163.06	Milk River, Mont.	50%	20,081.53
14,970.09	Upper Arkansas	50%	7,485.05
57.62	Cantonment, Tongue R.	50%	28.81
10,857.00	Muscleshell, Mont.	50%	5,428.50
154.65	Ft. Laramie, Wyo.	50%	77.32
18,110.38	No location (Dis. Sch. 65-67)	50%	9,055.19
4,821.43	Chey. & Arapaho Res. Okla.	75%	3,616.07
	Total		$589,313.81

46. The total amount paid by the United States for subject tract as consideration in goods and services under the Treaties of February 18, 1861, October 14, 1865, October 28, 1867, and May 10, 1868, was $2,596,147.80. The Southern Cheyenne and Arapaho Tribes were the beneficiaries of the consideration paid by the 1861, 1865 and 1867 treaties in the amount of $1,434,131.38. The Northern Cheyenne and Arapaho Tribes were the beneficiaries of the consideration paid under the 1868 treaty in the amount of $1,162,016.42. In addition to the monies expended as consideration under the 1861 1865 and 1867 treaties, the Southern Cheyenne and Arapaho Tribes received as consideration for the cession of subject lands the reservation set aside by executive order of the President of August 10, 1869, which are described in Finding 39, the value of which must be determined in subsequent hearings.

47. Although the United States promised to and did pay in goods
and services a total of $2,596,147.80 to petitioners for the cession of
subject tract under the 1861, 1865, 1867, and 1868 treaties, defendant
is only entitled to the discounted value of its promises to pay under the
respective treaties. 11/ The parties will submit the computation of the
"cash value" of the considerations provided for in these treaties as
found by the Commission.

48. The Commission, based upon the findings of fact herein made
and the record as a whole, finds that the consideration which is the
discounted value of the allowable items totaling $1,162,016.42 ultimately
paid to the Northern Cheyenne and Northern Arapaho Tribes for their undivided half interest in subject tract which as of October 14, 1865,
had a fair market value of $23,500,000.00, was unconscionable. The
Northern Cheyenne and Northern Arapaho Tribes are entitled to recover of
defendant one half the value of the subject tract, less the 1865 discounted value of the consideration paid under the Treaty of May 10, 1868,
and less whatever offsets, if any, the defendant may be entitled to under
the provisions of the Indian Claims Commission Act.

49. The Commission further finds that the record does not contain
evidence with respect to the value of the reservation set aside by
executive order of August 10, 1869, pursuant to the Treaty of October 14,

296

11/ Crow Tribe v. United States, Appeal Docket 1-59 (284 F. 2d 361)
    reversing in part as to consideration 6 Ind. Cl. Comm. 98, 124-126.

1865, for the Southern Tribes. Further proceedings will be held to

determine such fair market value in order to ascertain whether the con-

sideration paid the Southern tribes for their respective undivided half

interest in the subject tract was unconscionable.

                    Arthur V. Watkins
                    Chief Commissioner

                    Wm. M. Holt
                    Associate Commissioner

                    T. Harold Scott
                    Associate Commissioner

BEFORE THE INDIAN CLAIMS COMMISSION

CHEYENNE-ARAPAHO TRIBES OF INDIANS OF OKLAHOMA, et al.,
 	
    Petitioners,
 	
    v.
 	
THE UNITED STATES OF AMERICA,
 	
    Defendant.
	)
	)
	)
	)
	)
	) Docket No. 329
	)
	)
	)
	)

THE CHEYENNE AND ARAPAHO TRIBES OF INDIANS, et al.,
 	
    Petitioners,
 	
    v.
 	
THE UNITED STATES OF AMERICA,
 	
    Defendant.
	)
	)
	)
	)
	)
	) Docket No. 348
	)
	)
	)
	)

298

Decided: December 6, 1961

Appearances:

R. G. Wiggenhorn, John W. Cragun, John M. Schiltz, and William Howard Payne, Attorneys for Petitioners.

John D. Sullivan, with whom was Mr. Assistant Attorney General, Perry W. Morton, Attorneys for Defendant.

OPINION OF THE COMMISSION

Holt, Associate Commissioner, delivered the opinion of the Commission.

Petitioners herein are the Cheyenne-Arapaho Tribes of Oklahoma in

Docket No. 329, the Northern Cheyenne Tribe of Indians on the Tongue River

Reservation, Montana, and the Northern Arapaho Tribe of Indians of

the Wind River Reservation, Wyoming, in Docket No. 348. Each of the

three petitioners is a duly organized tribe of American Indians with

a tribal organization recognized by the Secretary of the Interior as

having authority to represent said tribe, and each is authorized to

maintain this action under the Indian Claims Commission Act of August 13,

1946, 60 Stat. 1049, and is an identifiable tribe of American Indians

residing within the territorial limits of the United States.

The petitions in this proceeding were duly filed with the Commission.

Since the petitions in these cases contained claims, among others, per-

taining to the cessions of the same land to the United States they were

consolidated for trial by order of the Commission of May 5, 1952, following

the filing of a stipulation to consolidate by the respective petitioners.

Subsequently, the Commission on November 28, 1958, ordered certain

additional claims set forth in Docket No. 329 to be severed and filed

in a separate petition designated Docket No. 329-A.

Petitioners on August 31, 1955, filed a motion for partial summary

judgment with respect to the proper construction and effect of the Treaty

of Fort Laramie of September 17, 1851, 10 Stat. 749. The Commission,

after considering the contentions of the parties and documentary evidence

with regard to the negotiation and purpose of the said Fort Laramie treaty,

made certain findings of fact on November 1, 1955, which are set forth

in full in the findings of fact herein made. The Commission found that

by the Treaty of Fort Laramie of September 17, 1851, "and the manner

299

of its negotiation and the acts and conduct of the defendant, the
United States of America, immediately before and after the execution
and ratification of said treaty, defendant accepted, acknowledged,
ratified and confirmed petitioners' aboriginal Indian title and right
of occupancy and use of the territory described in Finding 1."

Since the Commission determined the petitioners had recognized
title to the area described in Finding No. 1, it was not necessary to
prove exclusive use and occupancy of the area under Indian title. The
action thereupon proceeded to the valuation stage wherein hearings were
held and evidence received with respect to the value of the lands involved herein.

By a stipulation filed with the Commission on January 31, 1958, the
parties stipulated and agreed that "the date upon which defendant acquired
petitioners' interests, if any, in land described in the Fort Laramie
Treaty for evaluating said land, shall be October 14, 1865."

The lands designated as "the territory of the Cheyennes and
Arrapahoes" in the Fort Laramie Treaty of 1851 consist of an enormous
area which the parties agree contained 51,210,000 acres situated in
what are now the States of Colorado, Wyoming, Kansas and Nebraska.
The lands involved will be referred to herein as the subject tract.
They are located in the heart of the western part of central United
States, bounded on the north by the North Platte River; on the south
by the Arkansas River; on the west by the Continental Divide

300

of the Rocky Mountains; and on the east by a line roughly midway between
the 100th and 101st meridians. Plains lands make up at least eighty-
five percent of the total area; the remaining fifteen percent is composed of mountain peaks, mountain parks and mountain plateaus. The
plains area has an average altitude of 4,500 to 5,000 feet and ranges
from 3,500 feet on the eastern border to 5,000 or 5,500 feet at the base
of the mountain plateaus. The mountain plateaus range from 6,000 to
8,000 feet and some of the mountains exceed 14,000 feet. Three major
watersheds are in the area, the North Platte, South Platte and Arkansas
Rivers.

The bulk of the subject tract is a great plains area which is classified as semi-arid. Along the streams at the base of the mountains are to
be found the agricultural lands of the tract which required irrigation.
Virtually no timber was to be found on the plains. The timber in the
region was found in the mountainous portion. By the date of evaluation
the characteristics of the subject tract were generally well known.
Early explorations of officers and agents of the United States had taken
these men through the tract. The Oregon and Santa Fe trails bordered
the northern and southern boundaries of the area and the Smoky Hill
trail traversed the heart of the tract. The gold rush in 1859 brought
thousands of people into the region.

Prior to the discovery of gold there were few settlers in this vast
region. This was Indian country and on the great plains roamed the
buffalo. Tens of thousands had passed over these plains along the Oregon

301

Trail on the North Platte River by 1850. The plains area was not
attractive to the settlers because of its semi-arid nature and the
scarcity of wood and water. Along the trail, however, some small
settlements in the way of road ranches where the emigrants could exchange their worn down cattle were in early existence. These may be
said to be the beginning of the cattle industry in the plains region.

Although the subject tract was Indian country recognized as the
territory of the Cheyenne and Arapaho Indians by the Fort Laramie Treaty
of 1851, there was little respect for their ownership of the tract by the
whites following the discovery of gold in 1858. In 1859 the great Pikes
Peak gold rush saw some 100,000 persons entering the mining areas and an
estimated 40,000 remained through the 1859-1860 winter season. Supply
depots established at the base of the mountains developed quickly into
the cities or towns of Denver, Boulder, Colorado City and Pueblo. Numerous
mining towns and camps were built in a short time. In 1865 the population
of Colorado Territory was somewhere between 28,000 and 34,000 persons located
for the most part within the subject tract principally in the towns and
mining areas. The early settlers soon discovered that along the stream
at the base of the mountains, near the mining camps in the hills, irrigated agriculture could be profitably undertaken. The farmers found a
ready local market for their produce in the towns and mining camps.

As of 1865 there were no railroads in the subject tract. There was
great expectation that within the reasonably foreseeable future the tract
would benefit from such service. The Union Pacific which had commenced

302

construction at Omaha, Nebraska, in 1863 by the end of 1865 had built

only 40 miles of track west of that point. The Kansas Pacific which was

planned to be built through the heart of the subject tract had constructed

its line only 40 miles west of Kansas City by 1865. The settled portions

of the tract found in a narrow belt along the base of the mountains and

the mining camps were serviced in 1865 by animal-drawn freight and stage

lines. Freight for the most part was transported from Plattsmouth, the

mouth of the Platte on the Missouri, across the plains to these settlements.

Some 62,500 tons of freight were hauled into Colorado in 1865.

The appraisal witnesses for the parties agree that the lands of subject

tract may be classified as having multiple highest and best uses in 1865.

The Commission has found these to be grazing, agricultural, mineral and

town-site lands. There is no dispute between the parties that the bulk

of the area had a highest and best use of grazing lands. This range or

grazing land consisted of 50,252,320 acres. The Commission also found

the balance of subject tract contained 400,000 acres of land suitable for

agriculture, 550,000 acres of land suitable for mineral development or

potentially mineral land, and that 7,680 acres of land would be adequate

in the subject tract for town-site purposes.

Grazing or Range Land

The fact that the plains area was a vast pasture land was evidenced

in the great herds of buffalo which roamed over the region providing

meat and skins for the Indians. Government officials and others in the

subject tract in 1865 and prior thereto recognized the natural advantages

of the country for stock raising. Samuel Bowles in his book "Across
the Continent" published in 1865 noted that what he called the Central
Desert of the Continent was not a desert and worthless by any means.
The soil, he observed, yielded a coarse, thin grass that was green or dry
and that it made the best food for cattle that the continent offered.
Bowles considered it the great pasture of the nation and concluded, "This
is its present use and its future profit." He believed that when railroad
transportation became available the plains would feed the country beef
and mutton and supply large quantities of wool and leather for the nation.

As previously stated the cattle industry in or adjoining subject
tract may be said to have had its beginning with the road ranches established
along the Oregon Trail. The embryonic business gained impetus upon the
discovery of gold with the establishment of towns and mining camps providing a market for beef. The early herds of the northern ranges were
the product of the road ranches, the train-cattle of the freight companies,
and the stock of the settlers. The ranches established to meet the local
demand for cattle were located along the South Platte River. In 1861
Iliff who was to become the first "cattle king" of the northern ranges
was supplying the mining towns with beef from a herd that ranged up and
down the South Platt for 75 miles or more. By 1866 the herds on the
South Platte numbered about 20,000 head. The cattle industry in Colorado,
which was at first a small business with but local markets, came into its
own and expanded greatly with the advent of the railroad and the source
of cheap cattle from Texas after the Civil War which could be fattened for
eastern markets on the vast pastoral resources of Colorado.

Mr. Jeffrey Holbrook, a qualified appraiser, appeared as a witness
for petitioners and his appraisal report was received in evidence as
petitioners' exhibit 112. Mr. Holbrook was of the opinion that subject
tract had a fair market value of $40,968,000, or at the rate of $0.80
per acre on October 14, 1865. In the judgment of petitioners' witness
there was no market data--in the strictest sense of the term--available
to aid in evaluating subject tract; that is, that although there were
sales of land within and around the tract, these fell short of the data
necessary to evaluate it solely on a direct comparison basis. Many of
the sales were remote as to distance and not comparable to any degree.
None were comparable in size. The witness recognized the lack of comparability but was of the opinion they were value indications which could
be used to show (1) that there was a demand for large tracts of land;
(2) that if subject lands were offered at a favorable price they would
sell in one tract; and (3) that a buyer could resell the lands in smaller
tracts at prices equal to the value indicated by the comparable sales.
From his analysis of eight large sales and appraisals in Kansas, New
Mexico and Oklahoma, Mr. Holbrook concluded that these would set the
upper limit of price (exclusive of minerals) for the subject tract which
he stated was about 97 cents an acre. Petitioners' appraiser was of the
opinion that subject land (not considering mineral values) would have
ample demand if priced below what he believed to be the general market
levels. He therefore made an adjustment which he considered would com-
pensate for size and proximity of subject tract to market and concluded

305

that taking into account all general facts a minimum valuation of $0.50
per acre, or $25,605,000 for subject lands exclusive of minerals, was
nominal.

The Commission has considered the selected large land sales or
appraisals in Kansas, New Mexico and Oklahoma which were studied by Mr.
Holbrook. The lack of comparability as to size, location and character
of the land (agricultural) in these transactions, except the Spanish and
Mexican land grants, greatly effects the weight to be given them when considering an enormous acreage, such as subject tract, consisting almost
entirely of grazing or range land, which was remote from markets and
lacked comparable transportation facilities. While the land grant transactions are not comparable in size and are subsequent to the appraisal date,
the sales of the Costilla estate in 1869 and the Maxwell grant in 1870,
306 both of which contained large acreages of grazing land, do indicate that
at or near the date of evaluation there was a market for large tracts of
land.

Two of the most important factors in considering the value of the
grazing lands of subject tract are (1) the open or free range concept and
Public Domain policies existing at the date of valuation and for many years
thereafter, and (2) the great amount of grazing land available to a prospective
purchaser outside of subject tract at the time. The free range practice,
under which an individual, partnership or corporation could run privately
owned cattle on the public domain without cost, was in existence at the
time of valuation. Cattlemen by acquiring possession of land with water

thereon could control large blocs of grazing land on the public domain.
This resulted in curtailing the demand for grazing lands for extensive
ranch operations. Snake or Piute Indians, etc. v. United States, 7 Ind.
Cl. Comm. 526, 559; Pawnee Indian Tribe v. United States, 8 Ind. Cl. Comm.
648, 721, 722. The vast amount of grazing land available for free use
and the public domain policies which made it difficult to assemble large
acreages under the homestead and preemption laws limited the demand for
grazing land.

The railroads by virtue of their land grants earned millions of acres
of land along their routes of alternate sections. The Union Pacific
Railroad which by 1870 had completed its track through Colorado and
Wyoming had received 4,600,000 acres in Wyoming, 700,000 in Colorado,
4,700,000 acres in Nebraska and 1,100,000 acres in Utah. As of 1873 the
railroad had sold no lands west of Grand Island, Nebraska. The line had
sold none of its grant lands in Colorado and only 2,520 acres in Wyoming
by 1883 and of its acreage in Nebraska there remained 2,580,000 acres
unsold, almost all of it west of the hundredth meridian. The Kansas
Pacific Railroad completed to Denver and Cheyenne in 1870 received a
grant of about 6,000,000 acres with 2,600,000 being located in Colorado
and 3,600,000 acres in Kansas. As of 1879 this road had available for
sale about 2,000,000 acres in Western Kansas between Manhattan and Grinnell
and some 2,800,000 acres between Grinnell and Denver. Sales of large
acreages of railroad grazing lands did not take place until long after
the valuation date when the railroads disposed of considerable land to
cattle companies in about the middle 1880's in and adjoining the subject

307

tract at prices of fifty cents to one dollar per acre (see Shoshone
Tribe v. United States, 3 Ind. Cl. Comm. 313, 330-331; and Hoyt Reporter,
Def. Ex. 2, pp. 114-119).

Mr. Homer Hoyt, a qualified appraiser, was an expert witness for
defendant and prepared a valuation report which was received in evidence
as defendant's exhibit 2. This witness divided subject tract into two
areas excepting all mineral rights which were evaluated separately.
Area A, totaling about 49,000,000 acres, contained for the most part
all the grazing or range land. Hoyt's Area B consisted of the balance
of subject tract and is a narrow portion of the tract, extending north
and south of Denver, which included the surveyed lands and areas adjacent
to these surveyed lands. Mr. Hoyt was of the opinion that the lands in
his Area A had a value in 1865 of $980,000, or 2 cents an acre. In
reaching this conclusion defendant's appraiser relied mainly on the sales
of interests in certain Spanish land grants.

308

The transactions involving the sales of fractional interests in the
land grants recite considerations ranging from a few cents an acre to
43 cents and 80 cents an acre. These sales are entitled to little weight
as market data. At the time of the transactions the acreages of many of
the grants had not been determined. The fractional interests in some of
the grants were numerous. The Mora Grant had been made to some 76 persons
in 1835. With respect to the knowledge of the size of the grants, William
A. Keleher in his book "Maxwell Land Grant" states that it is doubtful if
Maxwell had the faintest conception, when he first settled on that grant,

of its potential acreage, "being under the impression probably for many years that it contained between 32,000 acres and 97,424 acres, or twenty-two Spanish leagues. Nevertheless, people of Maxwell's time lived to see the day when the Grant was legally declared to embrace a total of 1,714,764.93 acres. * * *" Keleher also was of the opinion:

> "It is quite probable that at the time the trades /Maxwell's purchase/ were being made for the outstanding interests neither Lucien B. Maxwell nor any of his in-laws or even Guadalupe Miranda knew or understood what the future held for the Grant in the way of acreage."

During the 1860's there were hundreds of Mexican settlers and American squatters on the grants claiming rights in the lands. Even after confirmation of the grants by Congress these people continued to claim such rights and court actions to test the legality of the grants were numerous.

The history of the many transactions regarding the purchase of interests in the grants is involved and obscured with the passage of time. These sales of fractional interests do demonstrate, however, that at or near the valuation date there were men, speculators to be sure, who were willing to gamble by investing a small sum not only on the legality of the grants and their size but also on the risk of being able to dispose of them quickly. The very size of the grants were a detriment to the speculator in finding a ready market for them and the threat of possible taxation of the lands made it imperative that the lands be quickly disposed of.

Sales involving three grants (subsequent to the valuation date in this case) were made after all, or virtually all, interests had been

309

obtained. These included sales of the Nolan Grant, the Maxwell Land

Grant and the Costilla Estate of the Sangre de Cristo Grant. The Nolan

grant lands were selected lands primarily adapted to irrigated agriculture.

The Maxwell grant, located 80 miles south of subject tract, consisted of

1,714,755 acres of land. Comparatively speaking, the Maxwell Land Grant

may be said to be somewhat of a miniature replica of the subject tract.

The majority of its acreage was adaptable to grazing. The percentage of

lands adaptable to agriculture was larger. The grant had settlements

thereon and there was both placer and lode mining activities being carried

on at the time of the transactions resulting in the sale of the grant.

Maxwell, in 1869, entered into an agreement giving an option to certain

persons to purchase the grant for $650,000.00. They elected to exercise

their option and a performance bond was delivered to them by the Maxwells,

310

and they then sold and assigned their right, title and interest under the

bond to the Maxwell Land Grant and Railroad Company. The consideration

paid by the Company was $1,350,000.00 of which sum the Maxwells received

$650,000.00. The Maxwells conveyed the grant to the Company on April 30,

1870, reserving certain lands and interests in mining properties.

Some 55 miles south of the subject tract was the northern boundary

of the Sangre de Cristo Grant which contained about one million acres.

The greater portion of this grant is located in south central Colorado

and the balance in north central New Mexico. Prior to 1865 William

Gilpin, former territorial Governor of Colorado, had purchased a five-

sixth interest in this grant for $41,000.00. In 1865 he sold fractional

interests for considerations averaging about 43 cents and 80 cents an
acre. Herbert O. Brayer in his book "The Spanish American Land Grants"
questions the validity of the recited consideration in one of the sales
averaging about 43 cents an acre. One-half of the grant, called the
Costilla Estate, was sold in 1870 at an average price of $1.00 an acre.
The grant consisted of grazing lands, agricultural lands in the San
Luis Valley and mineral potentials.

The market data with respect to the Spanish-Mexican land grants
disclose that at or near the date of valuation there was a demand for
large tracts of land at a reasonably low price; that the threat of
taxation of a very large parcel of land such as the subject tract would
require its re-sale in much smaller tracts in a relatively short period
of time; and that financial sources were interested in securing tracts
with multiple existing or potential uses which could be developed. The
availability of public and railroad grant lands and the open range policy
would weigh heavily in setting the market value of subject tract at a
reasonably low price. The prospective purchaser, however, would know
that in re-selling in smaller tracts he would have the advantage of being
able to offer to ranchers title to large blocs of land which were difficult
to amass under the public land policies and the alternate sections system
of granting lands to railroads.

311

Agricultural Land

There were 400,000 acres of land on subject tract on which crops
could be raised with irrigation and they were located along the streams.

Crops raised on some 50,000 acres under cultivation included wheat, potatoes and corn.

Petitioners' appraiser, Mr. Holbrook, stated he had examined 8,645 land transfers in Colorado for the period 1860-1865. From these he extracted 558 transfers for size--160 acres or more. The average price per acre paid in these selected sales was $3.63 per acre. The bulk of these sales were in the Denver area and the remainder in and around Pueblo. Mr. Holbrook adjusted this average price per acre by deducting 91 cents to allow for improvements and a further discount for size. Petitioners' appraiser concluded that the crop land had a nominal fair market value of $1,000,000.00 without improvements or at the rate of $2.50 per acre. The adjustment for improvements made by this witness was based on the average improvement cost made in an appraisal of the Cherokee Neutral Lands in Kansas in 1866. No allowance is made for the fact that the Cherokee lands were agricultural and did not need irrigation while the crop lands of subject tract required irrigation which was said to involve much expense and labor. This Commission also noted in The Osage Nation of Indians v. United States, 3 Ind. Cl. Comm. 217, 339, 340, that the value of improvements upon the Cherokee Neutral Lands was considerably in excess of the amount allowed by petitioners' appraiser in the instant case.

Mr. Homer Hoyt, defendant's appraiser, analyzed some 118 sales transactions in Colorado from 1862 to 1866. These were farm sales practically all being in the irrigated area along the streams. He found them to have sold for an average of $2.00 an acre with an average of 160

312

acres for each sale. These sales, he reported, were the prices paid
for the best improved, irrigated farms on streams. He was of the opinion
that not over 50,000 acres along the streams were in cultivation as of
1865 and placed a value of $1.00 an acre on these lands as of the
evaluation date, or $50,000.00. For 370,000 acres of unimproved lands
along the streams which could be irrigated the Government's witness concluded they had a fair market value of $89,000.00, or at the rate of
twenty cents an acre.

In Hoyt's "Area B" there was in addition to the 420,000 acres along
streams an additional 1,008,000 acres of lands in townships which had
been surveyed with section lines defined. These lands, he reasoned,
while having a lower value than lands along streams, had a higher value
for grazing or for possible future townsites than the unsurveyed lands
in the Great Plains, since they were located near the farms, cities and
mining areas. On these 1,008,000 acres he placed a value of ten cents
an acre. For 707,000 acres in "Area B" in which township lines had been
laid down and other adjacent areas that were to be surveyed within the next
few years after 1865 he reached a valuation figure of five cents an acre.

The only sale of record of a large tract of agricultural land similar
to the crop land on the subject tract in the immediate vicinity of the area being
evaluated is the sale of the Nolan Grant in 1872. Congress confirmed this
grant in 1870 but limited the area to eleven square leagues, the statutory
limitation under Mexican law, and provided the grantees could select the
confirmed tract of some 48,000 acres from within the claimed 300,000 acres

313

of the original boundaries set forth in the grant. The Nolan heirs
prior to confirmation sold the grant in 1869 for $10,000.00. Also,
before confirmation, the purchaser from the heirs sold undivided third
interests for $5,000.00 each. The holders of these interests in 1872
sold this "floating grant" for $130,000.00. The purchaser, Central
Colorado Improvement Company, exercised the right conferred by Congress
and selected the 48,000 acres "with the greatest care, leaving out all
hills or poor land and taking only the pick of that lying along the
South Bank of the river opposite the town of Pueblo." The Nolan Grant
adjoined the subject tract on the south bank of the Arkansas River and
was considered in 1872 to be almost entirely adapted to cultivation by
irrigation. After confirmation the heirs and later purchasers of the
estate continued to claim the larger area of 300,000 acres.

314

Townsites

An area the size of subject tract in 1865 required a minimum of six
townsites of 1280 acres each. Mr. Holbrook for petitioners did not
evaluate the towns then existing but instead sought to ascertain the fair
market value of six arbitrary townsites as of October 14, 1865. The value
of these he said was difficult to estimate in view of the assumption that
no towns existed at the time. To arrive at a value he reasoned that
there would be limitations of value consideration, that is, the value
of townsite acreage would be appreciably higher than crop or range land
but lower than speculative lot prices. Mr. Holbrook relied on certain

market data which he stated narrowed value consideration and was in-

dicative of value. He considered as an indication of value the estimate

of $50.00 per acre for townsites placed upon lands in 1871 by a land

company formed by organizers of the Denver and Rio Grande Railroad. He

also considered the purchase of the original townsite of Manitou in 1871

for $30,000.00 and the listing in 1875 of town lots in said town at $25

to $100 each. He further used as a value indication the annual report of

the directors of the National Land and Improvement Company of December 1878

which contained a recapitulation of land bought and sold and which showed,

he states, an average sale price per acre from organization of the company

to that date of $78.70. Mr. Holbrook concluded that a reasonable estimate

of price per townsite acre would approximate $50.00 or $384,000 for the

six townsites.

According to Herbert O. Brayer in his book "Early Financing of the

Denver and Rio Grande Railway" the lands purchased by the land company,

formed by the organizers of the railway, which was estimated by the

land company in 1871 to be worth $50.00 an acre had originally cost the

company $7.88 per acre. Mr. Brayer in a footnote commenting on this

$50.00 per acre estimate of the value of the tillable and townsite land

observed:

> This was land along the right of way from Denver to Colorado
> Springs. The valuation quoted, approximately $50.00 an acre,
> was out of all proportion to the true value of the land. Most
> of the property lay along the railroad, but was unsettled and
> undeveloped. Based upon similar land sold along the right of
> way of the Kansas Pacific, Denver Pacific, and Union Pacific,
> an evaluation of from $10.00 to $15.00 per acre for the entire
> tract would not have been considered an underestimate.* * *

Mr. Brayer's observations clearly show the danger of using estimates
of value per acre as indications of value.

The purchase price of $30,000.00 for Manitou, according to Brayer,
included the purchase of mineral springs and an adjacent tract of 400
acres. The land company that made the purchase had also secured some
additional lands of about 8400 acres at $8.81 per acre which included
the future sites of Colorado Springs, Palmer Lake, and Monument, Brayer's
study reveals.

Defendant's expert Hoyt in his study of the townsite valuation
classified the townsites into (a) developed commercial property, (b)
lots with buildings on them and (c) unimproved lots. He stated it was
necessary to separate the sites from the improvements or buildings on
them and that most sales in 1865 were for improved property for which it
316   was impossible to separate the value of the site from the building. For
commercial property on the subject tract in towns, which he said was
limited in 1865, defendant's land appraiser estimated a total front
footage of 3,000 feet and a value of $30,000.00 at $10.00 a foot. For
improved residential properties with dwelling houses thereon, Hoyt estimated there would be 2,000 lots with a value of $15.00 a lot, or
$30,000.00, and 4,000 unimproved lots on the townsites with a value of
$10.00 a lot for a total of $40,000. Mr. Hoyt was therefore of the
opinion that the townsites on the subject tract had a fair market value
of $100,000.00 as of 1865.

The record is far from satisfactory as to market data concerning
the sales of comparable townsites at or near the valuation date and
with respect to the sales of unimproved lots within the then existing
towns on the subject tract. The parties agree that the existence of
townsites upon the tract should be taken into consideration. The evidence available does show, however, that the townsites would enhance the
value of the tract and that the acreage value for townsites would be
greater than for grazing or agricultural lands.

Mineral Lands

The discovery of gold on a branch of Cherry Creek in 1858 and the ensuing
"Pikes Peak Gold Rush" in 1859 was the fuse that ignited the permanent
settlement of the subject tract. Without this important strike the area
would no doubt have been destined to distant and slow development. Even
after the discovery, settlement for the most part was limited to a narrow
belt along the front range of the mountains and concentrated near the
centers of population, Denver and Pueblo, and in the mining camps for a
number of years.

317

The gold rush in 1859 brought a reported 100,000 persons into the
area in that year and some 40,000 remained the first winter. For the
first few years placer mining was the type of operation engaged in by
the miners. In this method of mining by means of pan, rocker and
sluice recovery was profitable and comparatively simple. By the end of
1863 placer mining had gradually died away because the gulches, most of

them worked over three or four times, had become virtually exhausted.
Lodes had been discovered during the early days of activity. During the
period of recovery from the "gossan" (secondary or oxidized) ore lode
mining was profitable also although a good percentage of the gold from
the ores of the gossan was lost through the inefficiency of the stamp
mill. Extremely rich ore had to be mined to give economic value to the
final product. As the mines grew deeper the decomposed ore was depleted,
miles filled with water and the ore (primary or unoxidized) which was
refractory in character caused serious curtailment of mining in the area.

In the years 1859 through 1865 it is reliably estimated that the
total mineral production on subject tract, mostly gold but with some
silver, was about $15,300,000.00. The mines in Gilpin County accounted
for 80% of lode production during this period and for more than 50% of
the lode and placer recovery. The mineral-bearing area in the subject
tract consisted of lands in the present day counties of Larimer, Boulder,
Gilpin, Park, Lake, Chaffee, Clear Creek, Jefferson, Fremont and Teller.
All mining areas were not successful or worked for very long. Besides
the refractory character of the quartz, other factors intervened to bring
about the depressed condition of mining in Colorado in 1865, following
the sale of many of the mines to eastern mining companies in the speculative
craze which started in 1863. These conditions are succintly set forth by
Ovando J. Hollister in "The Mines of Colorado," published in 1867 (Def.
Ex. 13):

318

> The reasons why capital has been required in Colorado are, that the expense of living and of mining, and the loss in value from the inadequate treatment of the refractory ores, were so great as to exhaust the profits of surface mining, instead of leaving them to be used in furnishing the more costly apparatus required in for deeper mining. The great reason that the companies organized with ample capital in 1864, have made out so poorly, and now, ere they have had any dividends, are called on for more capital, is that the cost of living and work advanced immediately upon the inauguration of their operations one hundred per cent, and nothing until very lately could in the least make it recede.* * *

Hollister, who was editor and owner of the Colorado Mining Journal, blamed

the high cost of living and labor on the shortage of manpower caused by

the Civil War; on transportation costs to Colorado located 500 to 1,000

miles "from civilization in any direction--from any source of supplies;"

the extensive and protracted drought of 1863; the severe winter of 1863-

1864 which hindered transportation; floods in the spring of 1864; and

Indian trouble on the plains in 1864 which interfered with transportation

and communications. This observer also noted that inexperience and ex-

travagance of the operators was a contributing factor to the depressed

condition of mining. Hollister, in 1867, however, was of the opinion that

"a considerable degree of prosperity and improvement may not unreasonably

be looked forward to in the immediate future."

As of 1865 the stamp mills recovered only about one-fourth of the

gold in the primary ores, wasting all the copper and silver. Hollister

stated that the veins in the mines increased in size, richness and uni-

formity as they descended into the earth but a cheap and practicable

process was needed to make the mines as profitable as they were in recovering

319

from the gossan ore. Samuel Bowles who visited the mining area in 1865
noted that not more than 20 or 25 of the 100 stamp mills in the territory
were operating and that mining hardly paid expenses. Hollister reported
40 of the 95 stamp mills in the territory running in 1867. While the art
of smelting was known in 1865 and had been practiced in Wales for many
years, it was not introduced into Colorado until 1867. Although difficulties were at first encountered the smelting process proved to be the
method that saved a very high percent of the richer mineral ore. The
main bulk of the ores, however, were too poor to admit of treatment except
in the quartz mills. Well developed gold mines in Gilpin county sent from
one-tenth to one-fortieth of their ore to the smelter. The success of
mining in Colorado has been said to have come about with the advent of
the railroad to the mining districts, the use of the smelting systems,
320 improved mining and milling and the determination of the miners.

The general land appraisers for the parties engaged mining experts
to make studies of the value of the mineral lands or the minerals on subject tract. Petitioners' mineral expert was Charles C. O'Boyle, a consulting geologist, who made an engineering appraisal of the mining region
and came to an opinion of the intrinsic worth of said region as of
October 14, 1865. Mr. O'Boyle prepared a valuation study (Pet. Ex. 110)
and testified at length before the Commission.

Petitioners' mineral expert evaluated the mining region as a unit
and not as an individual mine or group of mines. His report states that
the time-honored methods in valuing minerals are concerned primarily with

individual mines or comparatively small units of property and that the
precepts underlying the philosophy of such evaluations are only broadly
applicable to large tracts of mineral land containing varied resources
and potential uses. According to O'Boyle, an engineering evaluation of
a mine or an entire mineral region is based on the fact that the minerals
contained therein are a "depleting asset" and the magnitude of value is
controlled by the anticipated income to be derived during the productive
life of the asset and such evaluation determines the "intrinsic" value
of the minerals and does not reflect the additional speculative value
given by the comparable sales method. Mr. O'Boyle relied entirely on
the work of G. W. Henderson, published in 1926, for production figures in
the mining area. These figures indicate, as previously stated, the gross
mineral production for the period 1859 through 1865 was about $15,000,000.00.
Henderson's work did not break down early production on a year to year
basis nor did it indicate whether production came from lode or placer
deposits. It was necessary therefore for petitioners' mineral expert
to make such an allocation. From this study Mr. O'Boyle determined that
these production figures showed that it would be anticipated that the
gross annual product of the mining region could conservatively be placed
at $2,800,000.00.

Having arrived at his yearly anticipated production figure this
witness studied the royalty rates in the west and concluded that a royalty
of 25% of gross proceeds would not be excessive and therefore an anticipated income of $700,000.00 per year would be produced by the 25% royalty

321

on the annual gross income of $2,800,000.00. Mr. O'Boyle then used the
capitalization process known as the Hoskold formula, which was in use
at the valuation date, to determine the basic or intrinsic value of the
mining region as of October 14, 1865. The mathematical formula requires
certain known factors to be used in making the computation. This formula
involves taking into consideration such factors as the gross annual production, the earnings from such production (net profit), the number of
years such earnings will continue, what interest rate an investor would
want on his money and the going discount rate at the time. The interest
rate to the purchaser on his capital investment used by Mr. O'Boyle was
5% and the interest rate on redemption of capital one of 3½%. The expert
determined that 20 years was a reasonable period within which an investor
would want his money returned to him. Applying these factors, Mr. O'Boyle

322

concluded that the basic or intrinsic value of the mining region of subject
tract as of October 14, 1865, was $8,200,750.00.

The actual mathematical solution of the Hoskold Formula is an exact
problem. The calculated valuation figure for a mining property, however,
depends entirely on the validity of the data for the factors considered in
the formula. In the instant case if the "interest rate to purchaser on his
capital investment" was 20% instead of 5% and the "practicable interest
rate on redemption of capital" was 4% instead of 3½% then the intrinsic
value of the mineral lands on subject tract would be computed to be
$2,996,840.00 instead of $8,200,750.00. Assuming the interest rate on
capital investment to be 10% and the redemption of capital interest rate
to be 4% the computation would be $5,240,270.00. Any change in the data

with respect to the "annuity to be purchased" due to the use of a
different yearly production or royalty figures would change the result.
If the annuity were $400,000.00 at ten percent interest rate on capital
investment and 4% interest rate on redemption of capital the intrinsic
value would be $2,994,440.00.

Mr. O'Boyle testified that he used the 5% interest rate figure for
the return on investment because he found that for the period 1865-1885
the average bond yield was 5.39 per cent, and that for 1871 to 1885 the
average stock yield was 5.68 per cent. He concluded 5 per cent to be a
fair equitable value for return of capital because "we had something that
was even better, in my opinion, than a railroad. We had an entire
mineralized region which was an entity in itself, which we controlled,
and it would be a very sound investment, without any risk."

In using the Hoskold formula the interest rate factor is the vehicle
used to express all the hazards of an enterprise. Baxter and Parks in their
work "Examination and Valuation of Mineral Property," 3d edition, 1949,
quote from Hoskold's book "Engineers' Valuing Assistant" (1877) as follows:

> Every purchaser of mining property should have allowance made
> upon his purchase, but the amount of such an allowance, as a
> percentage, must depend upon a point difficult to calculate--
>
> In case of unopened mines it has been my practice in de-
> ducing the present value deferred, to allow 20 per cent to a
> present purchaser, and redeem capital at 5 per cent per annum;
> which I consider in a general way is a safe mode of dealing
> with any mine with average prospects; although in special cases
> where a mine has a more certain character, I have allowed a
> percentage as low as 14, and in some of less certainty, as
> high as 25.

323

A rule cannot be laid down expressing the attendant risk
of mining adventure, as nearly all mines exist under circumstances differing widely from each other. It is a matter
of experiment; each mine must, therefore, stand upon its
own merits, and the amount of percentage to be allowed must
also be varied according to the circumstances of each particular case.

In view of the depressed condition of mining on the subject tract

at the valuation date in 1865, the frontier conditions then existing,

the problem of developing and testing a process to permit profitable

operations of the mines and the fact that we are determining the value

of a mining region rather than a single mine, there is substantial evi-

dence of record pointing to considerable risk involved in the purchase

of such a large mineral area as of the valuation date. As of 1865 it

would also be known that production had fallen off in the Colorado mines.

The collapse of the speculative craze in Colorado resulted in the lack

324 of interest in Colorado mining in eastern financial circles. On or near

the valuation date, however, European investors became interested in

American rail and mining securities. These were looked upon favorably

since they offered not only six to eight percent interest but from their

being sold below face value the interest rate was proportionately higher.

Defendant employed the engineer consulting firm of Barton, Stoddard

and Milhollin of Boise, Idaho, to evaluate the minerals on subject tract.

This firm engaged Mr. Ernest Oberbillig, a mining engineer, who carried

the principal burden of making the valuation study under the supervision

of the partners of the firm. Mr. Sherwin M. Barton and Mr. Oberbillig,

both of whom testified for defendant, are qualified mining engineers.

Defendant's mineral report was received in evidence as defendant's
exhibit one and shall be hereinafter referred to as the BSM report.

Defendant's mineral experts used a valuation method which they
called a direct evaluation method. Based upon mining articles appearing
in the Black Hawk Journal and a review of written materials such as
Hollister's book they sought to reconstruct the conditions existing on
the important mining properties in the mining districts in 1865. These
mineral experts believed that the valuation could be determined by giving
consideration to ten factors for each of the mines located on the lodes
which included past production, blocked ore, grade of ore, costs such as
pumping, mining and transportation and sales recorded for the mine or
parts thereof. As with the use of the Hoskold formula employed by
petitioners' mineral expert, the validity of the approach used by defendant's
mining engineers depended upon the availability and accuracy of the data
obtained for the factors to be considered. For many of the mining properties little data with respect to the ten factors is set forth in the
BSM report. While such an approach might be helpful in determining the
worth of a single mine or a group of mines if all data was available it
is not one suited to an historic evaluation such as in this case. Defendant's
experts concluded that the mineral value, gold and silver, of the subject
tract on October 14, 1865, was $1,215,000.00 and including miscellaneous
minerals such as coal, iron, clay, salt and oil the total mineral value
was $1,420,100.00 as of the evaluation date. Although, for the reasons
previously stated, the approach used has its shortcomings, the BSM study

325

does include many facts with respect to some of the operating mines as
to their state of development, past production, existence of blocked ore,
and profits, if any, taken therefrom which permit one to understand somewhat the state of mining activity in 1865.

Petitioners' general appraiser, Mr. Holbrook, who valued the mineral
lands at 14 million dollars in 1865, did not adopt the valuation amount
for mineral lands arrived at by petitioners' mining expert, Mr. O'Boyle.
Holbrook accepted O'Boyle's acreage and estimated future production but
while using the 5 per cent interest rate for capital investment he made
no allowance for an interest rate for redemption of capital. In addition
to the capitalization approach he considered the cost approach which he
discarded as fallacious and the market data approach based upon a consideration of sales of mining claims in subject tract. Data with respect
to the transfers of mining claims was collected by Mr. O'Boyle. His
statistics show the transfer of some 1800 acres of mining claims in Gilpin
County in 1865 for a total consideration of $5,000,000.00, or at a rate
of $2,500.00 an acre. Mr. O'Boyle in his report notes that if this
figure, or any reasonable fraction thereof, were applied to the entire
mineral-bearing region the value derived thereby would be unrealistic.
In view of the speculative nature of the sale of mining claims and the
sparse supporting data in the record concerning these transactions they
are entitled to little weight except to show that properties were changing
hands in 1865. The speculative character of claims transactions at or
near the valuation date is described in History of Denver, edited for the
Denver Times by Jerome C. Smiley, 1901, as follows:

326

* * *

When one good or fairly good mine was sold to misguided
'parties from the east,' a hundred other claims in the
same locality would be put on the market, and successfully
in the majority of instances.

Collusion between claim-owners who 'inspected' each other's
claims, 'salted' lodes, bogus or misleading certificates,
assays of ore of uncertain origin, were used to tempt and
gratify the insatiable appetite of inexperienced people
for sudden wealth. It was estimated that in about three
years the amount of eastern capital invested in Colorado
mines approximated the total output of all the diggings
from the time of Gregory's discovery to the 1st of July,
1866, when the end of the speculative craze may be said to
have come. Much the larger part of the vast sum became a
hopelessly permanent investment.

* * *

Defendant's general appraiser, Mr. Hoyt, used the capitalization of

royalty on production approach in valuing the mineral deposits. This

witness figured an estimated anticipated yearly production for the mineral

lands of approximately two million dollars. He was of the opinion that a

buyer could be found who would be willing to pay the present value of the

royalty on production. To arrive at this present value Hoyt used a

royalty of 10 per cent of the gross product capitalized at an interest

rate of 25 percent. Defendant's appraiser valued the mineral deposits of

subject tract as of October 14, 1865, at $1,000,000.00.

These different approaches, or variations thereof, and the ultimate

conclusions as to the value of the mineral lands or mineral deposits

reached by the expert witnesses for the parties clearly disclose the

difficult task of reaching a valuation of such a large mineral area at a

remote time. A well informed prospective purchaser of subject tract in 1865

327

would have realized the mineral lands appreciably enhanced the value of
the tract as a whole. This purchaser would have been able to ascertain
that while many of the mines were shut down a small number were still
operating profitably. He could anticipate that in the not too distant
future economic conditions would improve, and better methods of processing and transportation facilities would probably be available. Such
a purchaser, however, would be amply aware of the risk involved in the
purchase of such a large mining area then in a depressed condition,
located in a frontier area and depending for its success upon the development of improved processing and mining methods. The risk involved would
control the interest rate either on the money he borrowed to purchase
the tract or the return which he would expect on his capital. The cost
of development of the existing mines and the prospecting for new lodes
would be high and reflected in his net profit or in the royalty rate which
could be secured if the lands were leased to others. Finally, while the
prospective purchaser would be aware of the optimism for the area expressed by some mining men interested in the region he would be con-
servative in considering the amount of profit he would be able to make
from the transaction.

Fair Market Value

    The Commission based on the findings of fact herein made and taking
into consideration the whole record concludes that the fair market value
of subject tract as of October 14, 1865, was $23,500,000.00.

328

Consideration

As previously set forth the stipulated valuation date of October 14,
1865, in this case is an arbitrary date. In order to ascertain the consideration paid for the subject tract it is necessary to determine by
what treaties or agreements the lands were ceded to the United States by
the Cheyenne and Arapaho Indians. Defendant urges the Commission to
allow the consideration paid to the Indians under the Treaty of Fort
Laramie, September 17, 1851, 10 Stat. 749, II Kapp. 594, the treaties of
February 18, 1861, 12 Stat. 1163, October 14, 1865, 14 Stat. 703,
October 28, 1867, 15 Stat. 593, May 10, 1868, 15 Stat. 655, and the
Agreement of September 26, 1876, ratified by the act of February 28,
1877, 19 Stat. 254. Defendant claims as payments on the claim sums
totaling $7,244,556.85 as shown by a report of the General Accounting
Office (Pet. Ex. 113). Of this total sum, the GAO Report shows disbursements in goods and services pursuant to the treaties directly to petitioners
in the amount of $6,740,556.59 and additional payments jointly to peti-
tioners and other Indians in the sum of $540,615.33. Defendant agrees
that certain items totaling $36,615.07 listed in the GAO Report are not
proper items of consideration. Defendant also contends that certain
lands set aside for the Southern Cheyenne and Arapaho Indians were part
of the consideration for the cession of subject tract.

Petitioners urge that only the proper disbursements made pursuant to
the treaties of February 18, 1861, October 14, 1865 and May 10, 1868 are
items of consideration. It is also the contention of petitioners that no

lands set aside by the various treaties relied on by defendant as reservations for the Cheyenne and Arapaho Indians are part of the consideration for the cession of subject tract and that only the "cash
value" of the items found to have been disbursed pursuant to treaties
ceding the tract should be allowed as consideration. Petitioners further
contend that each of the respective petitioners had their own interests
in subject tract, that is, petitioners the Cheyenne-Arapaho Tribes of
Oklahoma at the time of the 1861 and 1865 treaties, and at all times
prior thereto, owned and occupied an undivided 50.61 percent of the tract
or the equivalent of 25,917,381 acres; the Northern Cheyenne Tribe at
the time of the May 10, 1868 treaty, and at all times prior thereto,
owned and occupied an undivided 25.32 percent thereof or the equivalent
of 12,966,372 acres; and the Northern Arapaho Tribe at the time of the

330

1868 treaty, and at all times prior thereto, an undivided 24.07 percent
thereof or the equivalent of 12,326,247 acres. The percentages used by
petitioners are based on a stipulation made among the parties petitioner
and the figures are based on the respective populations as of November 14,
1958. Petitioners further urge that the Commission should determine the
consideration paid to the separate petitioners under the treaties of
cession (allocating said consideration to the tribes where payments were
not made to one of them directly) and then compare the consideration so
paid to each with their respective interests in the subject tract to ascertain
whether the consideration paid each was unconscionable.

Defendant takes issue with petitioners' contention that the Southern Cheyennes and Arapahos, the Northern Cheyennes, and the Northern Arapahos, as three separate entities, owned three separate interests in the subject area. It is defendant's position that the Fort Laramie treaty of 1851 which this Commission held constituted an acknowledgment or recognition of petitioners' aboriginal title made no distinction as to any separate groups or subdivisions of Cheyenne and Arapaho Indians and that there is no proof of exclusive possession of all or any part of the subject area by separate groups of Cheyenne and Arapaho Indians or of separate and undivided interests in the subject tract by groups within the Cheyenne and Arapaho Indians.

Article 5 of the Fort Laramie treaty of 1851 defines the boundaries of the lands in subject tract as "The territory of the Cheyennes and Arapahoes." The treaty itself did not on its face recognize separate interests in said territory in any separate entities of Cheyenne and Arapaho Indians. In order to be fair and equitable it is necessary therefore to ascertain whether at or near the time of the Fort Laramie treaty and the subsequent cessions of subject tract there did exist any separate entities among these Indians which maintained and asserted separate interests in the tract.

In 1854 the Indian agent for the Upper Platte agency stated the Arapaho were divided into two bands of about equal strength. "One party," he reported, "lives on the Arkansas, the other on the North Platte River, about five or six hundred miles apart, and some years ago the head chief

331

of the Arkansas band was killed by the North Platte Band, and since that
time they have never met." The Cheyenne according to this agent were
divided into three bands in 1854, one residing on the Arkansas River,
one on the South Platte River and the last on the North Platte River
and these had never been together since the treaty (1851?). The Indian
agent was of the opinion that the Arapahos could never be induced to live
together as one nation since they were as hostile to each other as almost
any other tribe on the plains.

In "The Cheyenne Indians" by James Mooney, an article in Memoirs of
the American Anthropological Association, Volume 1, 1905-1907, the author's
historical sketch notes that in 1811 an overland expedition met the
Cheyenne camped about the eastern base of the Black Hills. According to
Mooney, when the Bent brothers established a trading post on the Arkansas
River at the present Pueblo, Colorado, the Cheyenne, decided to move to
that vicinity. The main body of the tribe removed permanently to the
upper Arkansas in 1833 and the remainder of the tribe continued to rove
about the headwaters of the North Platte and Yellowstone. Mooney wrote
"The separation was made permanent by the treaty of Fort Laramie in 1851,
the two sections being now known respectively as Southern and Northern
Cheyenne, but the distinction is purely geographic, although it has served
to hasten the destruction of their former compact tribal organization."
(See Def. Ex. S-68 in Docket 22-A).

The continuing existence of separate groups of Cheyenne and Arapaho
Indians and evidence of separate interests may also be found in the report

332

of Indian agent W. W. Bent in 1859. In writing of the territory assigned
these Indians by the Fort Laramie treaty in 1851 the agent reported the
country to be very equally divided into halves by the South Platte.
According to Bent a confederated band of Cheyennes and Arapahos, who
were intermarried, occupied and claimed exclusively the half of the
territory between the South Platte and the North Platte while a similar
confederated band distinctly occupied the southern half between the
South Platte and Arkansas Rivers.

A study of the reports of the Indian agents discloses that while
there were these divisions among the Cheyenne and Arapaho tribes and the
confederations noted in both the northern and southern groups the respective
tribes each were represented by their own chiefs, that is the southern
Arapaho had their own chief and the southern Cheyenne likewise. There
was a close relationship, however, not only in each respective group but
between the two groups. While one of the confederations may have considered a certain part of the territory as its customary home all Cheyennes
and Arapahos believed they had a right to roam throughout the whole of
subject tract.

333

The division of the Cheyenne and Arapaho Indians into these confederated
bands was noted by government officials and agents when they entered into
treaty negotiations providing for a cession of subject tract to the United
States. In the 1861 treaty made with the southern Cheyenne and Arapaho
tribes provision was made in the treaty for the remaining Cheyenne and
Arapaho to come in and accept under it. The United States, however, was

unable to acquire a treaty of cession from the Northern Cheyenne and Northern Arapaho tribes until 1868. This reluctance on the part of the northern bands or tribes is mentioned in the Commissioner of Indian Affairs Report for 1862 where it is stated "There never having been any boundary between the bands of Cheyenne and Arapaho on the plains, who extended from the Arkansas to the Platt rivers, this treaty of the Upper Arkansas /1861/ is imperfect and indefinite as to the extent of the cession, unless these bands are induced to accept under it. * * * I would urge its immediate settlement by negotiation with the disaffected bands who frequent the Platte river country, that the title to the un-perfected portion of Colorado Territory may be perfected."

Officials of the United States were well aware of the fact that they were dealing with two separate and distinct groups in extinguishing the title to subject tract. This is further demonstrated by the fact that the Commissioners negotiating the 1865 treaty informed the Southern Cheyenne and Arapaho Indians that the treaty then being contemplated related wholly to those bands present and that as others came in under it the annuities would be increased accordingly. Each of these confederated groups owned equal rights in the tract. If the United States had dealt with but one of them for the cession of the subject tract and paid the consideration solely to that group the other certainly would have a just claim today under the Indian Claims Commission Act. It necessarily follows that the consideration paid to each must be taken into account in ascertaining whether the amount received by each was unconscionable for the cession of its undivided half interest in subject tract.

334

As previously stated the petitioners contend that no payments
made under the provisions of the Fort Laramie Treaty of September 17,
1851, the treaty of October 28, 1867 and the Agreement of September 26,
1876 should be allowed as consideration. By Article 2 of the 1851 treaty
the Indian parties to the treaty, recognized the right of the United
States to establish roads, military and other posts within their
respective territories. In consideration of these rights and privileges
acknowledged in Article 2, the United States, in Article 3, agreed to
protect the Indian nations against depredations by people of the United
States. By Article 7 the United States "In consideration of the treaty
stipulations, and for the damages which have or may occur by reason
thereof to the Indian nations, * * *" agreed to furnish certain goods
and services for a period of ten years which at the discretion of the
President could be extended for an additional five years. The Fort
Laramie treaty contains no cession of land to the United States of any
of subject tract but merely acknowledges a right in the United States to
build roads and posts with the government agreeing to pay damages for
such right or privilege.

335

The Treaty of October 14, 1867, however, must be included as one
of the treaties wherein the consideration passing to the southern tribes was
for a cession of their interests in subject tract. Under the provisions
of Article 2 of the 1865 treaty as negotiated a described reservation was
to be set aside for the tribes east of subject tract. When this 1865
treaty came to the United States Senate for ratification, however, the
Senate amended Article 2 to add thereto:

Provided, however, That as soon as practicable, with the
assent of said tribe, the President of the United States
shall designate for said tribes a reservation, no part of
which shall be within the State of Kansas, and cause them
as soon as practicable to remove to and settle thereon,
but no such reservation shall be designated upon any reserve belonging to any other Indian tribe or tribes without
their consent.

The greater part of the lands described in Article 2 as a reservation were

within the State of Kansas and the balance was in the Cherokee Outlet and

belonged to the Cherokee Nation. Another treaty was therefore necessary

with the southern Cheyenne and Arapaho since they were permitted under

the 1865 treaty by Article 3 to reside and range on subject tract until

required by the President to remove to the reservation.

The 1867 treaty provided in Article 2 for a reservation for the

Cheyennes and Arapahos much of which was in the Cherokee Outlet. The

336 United States by the Treaty of July 19, 1866, 14 Stat. 804, with the

Cherokee Nation had in the meantime obtained the right under Article 16

to settle friendly tribes in the Cherokee Outlet but the treaty also pro-

vided that until such lands were occupied by the tribes and payment there-

fore made to the Cherokee Nation the Cherokees were to retain the right

of possession and jurisdiction over the lands. The southern Cheyenne and

Arapahos refused to go on the reservation designated by the 1867 treaty

contending they did not understand the location of the boundaries at the

time of the treaty and desired lands to the south along the North Fork

of the Canadian River.

Upon the recommendation of the Secretary of the Interior and the

Commissioner of Indian Affairs, the President of the United States on

August 10, 1869, by executive order approved the setting aside of a tract
on the North Fork of the Canadian River as a reserve for the Southern
tribes. By the Act of May 29, 1872, 17 Stat. 190, the Secretary of the
Interior was authorized to negotiate with the Southern Cheyennes and
Arapahos for the relinquishment of their claim to the land ceded to them
by the second article of the 1867 treaty said relinquishment to be in consideration of a permanent location for them on lands previously ceded to
the United States by the Creeks and Seminoles. Subsequently, the United
States and the Arapahos on October 24, 1872, entered into an agreement
whereby the Southern Arapaho relinquished all their right to the land
described in Article 2 of the 1867 treaty and in lieu thereof it was
agreed there would be set apart a separate reservation for them between
the North Fork of the Canadian River and the Cimarron River. Later negotiations were entered into with representatives of both the Southern
Cheyenne and Arapaho Tribes and agreements were made with them on
November 18, 1873, whereby they ceded all their rights to the 1867 treaty
reservation and the United States, in lieu thereof, agreed to set apart
separate reservations for these two tribes--for the Cheyennes the country
between the Cimarron River and the Salt Fork of the Arkansas River, and
for the Arapaho the tract of country west of 98° and between the Cimarron
and the Canadian Rivers. None of these agreements were ratified by
Congress and the Southern Cheyenne and Arapaho tribes remained on the
reservation set apart for them by the executive order of the President
issued on August 10, 1869. These tribes were still on said reservation
at the time of the Agreement of October, 1890, ratified by the Act of

337

March 3, 1891 (26 Stat. 989). By this agreement the tribes in Article I
agreed to "cede, convey, transfer, relinquish, and surrender forever
and absolutely, without any reservation whatever, express or implied,
all their claim, title, and interest of every kind and character, in
and to the lands embraced * * *" in Article 2 of the 1867 treaty. The
tribes by Article II of the 1890 agreement also ceded and relinquished
all their claim, title and interest in the tract set aside by the 1869
executive order subject to allotment of land in severalty for the individual
members of the Cheyenne and Arapaho Tribes. The agreement provided that
the allotments were in part consideration for the cession of lands and
that as a "further and only additional consideration for the cession of
territory and relinquishment of title, claim, and interest" in and to
lands the United States would pay the tribes $1,500,000.00.

338

While the 1867 treaty gave to the Southern Cheyenne and Arapaho
Tribes rights to the reservation described in Article 2 thereof the failure
of these tribes to exercise said rights was due to their own reluctance
to accept the lands. The United States by the provisions of the 1865 and
1867 treaties had promised these tribes a reservation. While the Senate
of the United States did amend the 1865 treaty and thereby foreclose the
designation of the lands described in Article 2 of that treaty as a reservation, it did, however, authorize the President of the United States
with the assent of the tribes to select a reservation for these Indians.
A reservation was provided for the tribes by the 1867 treaty but they were
dissatisfied with its location and as a result the President in 1869 by

executive order set aside a tract, desired by the Indians, for their use
and occupation. It is true that this action of the President would not
give the tribes reservation title in the legal sense unless his authority to
select a reservation may be attributed to the 1865 treaty which required
him to designate a tract with the assent of the Indians. While the 1867
treaty attempted to give these Indians a new reservation it was not to
their liking and the action of the President fulfilled the promise of a
reservation originally made in the 1865 treaty. In any event, possessory
rights of the tribes in the tract set aside by executive order were recognized
by the United States by the 1890 agreement which permitted the members of
the tribes to take allotments in severalty and provided for the payment
of a large sum of money for the cession of the lands. For all these
reasons the Commission concludes that the lands described in the Executive
Order of August 10, 1869, were given to the Southern Cheyenne and Arapaho
Tribes in lieu of those lands promised in the 1865 and 1867 treaties as
reservations and as such constituted consideration for the cession of
subject tract. The annuities in goods and services promised in the 1867
treaty were in lieu of those promised in the 1865 and previous treaties
and as such must be regarded as consideration for the cession of subject
tract.

Defendant claims as consideration disbursements made pursuant to the
provisions of the Agreement of September 26, 1876, ratified by the act of
February 28, 1877, 19 Stat. 254. By this treaty with the different bands
of the Sioux Nation of Indians and also the Northern Cheyenne and Arapaho
Indians, the Indians in Article 1 agreed to a reduction of a reservation

which had been set aside by Article 2 of the Treaty of April 29, 1868,
with the Sioux Indians, 15 Stat. 635, II Kapp. 998, and also agreed to
relinquish and cede to the United States all territory outside the
diminished reserve including all privileges of hunting. This treaty
contains no cession of subject tract which had already been ceded by
the Northern Cheyenne and Northern Arapaho Indians by the Treaty of
May 10, 1868, 15 Stat. 665. The "Treaty of 1868" referred to in Articles
3 and 5 of the 1876 agreement refers to the Treaty of April 29, 1868, with
the Sioux and not to the 1868 treaty with the Northern Cheyenne and Northern
Arapaho. The 1876 agreement is in no way supplementary to the Treaty of
May 10, 1868, and the consideration provided for therein was not in lieu
of that promised by the Treaty of May 10, 1868.

340

With respect to the items claimed as consideration under those treaties
which were found to have included cessions of petitioners' interests in
subject tract the Commission has painstakingly analyzed each of the many
disbursements to determine whether they were such as were authorized by
the provisions of the treaty. Detailed findings of fact (40-46) have been
made on the question of allowable items and need not be reiterated herein.
The Commission found that the allowable items under the Treaties of
February 18, 1861 and October 14, 1865, with the Southern Cheyenne and
Arapaho Indians totaled $276,595.89, and under the Treaty of October 28,
1867, with the same tribes they totaled $1,157,535.49. Defendant is en-
titled to credit as payments on the claim the 1865 discounted value of
these allowable items. In addition defendant is entitled to credit against

the southern Cheyenne and Arapaho the fair market value of the reservation
set aside for the southern tribes by the Executive Order of August 10,
1869. As to the Northern Cheyenne and Northern Arapaho Tribes the defendant is entitled to credit as payment on the claim the 1865 discounted
value of the allowable items disbursed pursuant to the Treaty of May 10,
1868, totaling $1,162,016.42.

The payment of a sum which when discounted will be less than
$1,162,016.42 to the Northern Cheyenne and Arapaho Indians for their
half interest in subject tract of 51,210,000 acres which had a fair
market value as of October 14, 1865, of $23,500,000.00, was unconscionable.
Petitioners, the Northern Cheyenne Tribe and the Northern Arapaho Tribe
are entitled to recover of and from the defendant the sum of $11,750,000.00,
less the 1865 discounted value of the allowable items of consideration
totaling $1,162,016.42, and less whatever offsets, if any, defendant may
be entitled to under the provisions of the Indian Claims Commission Act.
The parties in Docket No. 348 will submit a computation of the discounted
value of the allowable items of consideration and the respective tribes
will be charged with such sums as payments on the claim according to the
allocation of the consideration between the Northern Cheyenne and Northern
Arapaho Tribes as agreed upon by said tribes (see Finding 42 S and T).

With respect to the Southern Cheyenne and Arapaho Tribes, petitioners,
in Docket No. 329, the case will proceed to a further hearing to determine
the fair market value of the reservation set aside for said tribes by
Executive Order of August 10, 1869, and the parties will also submit a

341

computation of the 1865 discounted value of the allowable items of consideration under the Treaties of February 18, 1861, October 14, 1865 and
October 28, 1867. In view of the determination of the issues involved
in this proceeding, the Commission will this day enter an order dissolving
the consolidation for trial which was ordered on May 5, 1952.

Wm. M. Holt
Associate Commissioner

We concur:

Arthur V. Watkins
Chief Commissioner

T. Harold Scott
Associate Commissioner